THE READER'S
COMPANION TO
IRELAND

THE READER'S COMPANION TO
IRELAND

EDITED BY **ALAN RYAN**

A Harvest Original

Harcourt Brace & Company

SAN DIEGO   NEW YORK   LONDON

Requests for permission to make copies of any part
of the work should be mailed to: Permissions Department,
Harcourt Brace & Company, 6277 Sea Harbor Drive,
Orlando, Florida 32887-6777.

Library of Congress Cataloging-in-Publication Data
The reader's companion to Ireland/edited by Alan Ryan.—
1st ed.
p.   cm.
"A harvest original."
ISBN 0-15-600559-X (pbk.)
1. Ireland—Description and travel.   2. Ireland—Social life and
customs.   I. Ryan, Alan, 1943–   .
DA969.R42   1999
941.5—dc21   98-23354

Text set in Fairfield Light
Designed by Camilla Filancia
Printed in the United States of America
First edition
E D C B

Permissions acknowledgments appear on pages 291–93,
which constitute a continuation of the copyright page.

THIS BOOK IS DEDICATED TO
DAWN MULVIHILL

WHEN SOME OF THESE IMPRESSIONS OF IRELAND
APPEARED SERIALLY I WAS PRAISED AND ASSAILED IN
EQUAL PROPORTIONS, SOME SAYING THAT I HAD
NEVER SEEN WHAT I DESCRIBED AND OTHERS SAYING
THAT MY DESCRIPTION WAS THE MOST PERFECT EVER
PUT ON PAPER! THAT, I HAVE COME TO THE
CONCLUSION, IS INEVITABLE IF A MAN WRITES
ABOUT IRELAND. IT IS A COUNTRY WHERE THERE ARE
ALWAYS TWO EQUALLY STRONG BUT OPPOSING
POINTS OF VIEW ABOUT EVERYTHING.

—H. V. MORTON

CONTENTS

INCRODUCTION

HERE ARE SOME OF MY OWN PERSONAL SNAPSHOTS OF Ireland.

I am in a club just off Dublin's O'Connell Street where the Wolfe Tones are performing. The club has the appearance but none of the amenities of a Bavarian beer hall: long, narrow tables set too close together and hefty waitresses able to transport heavy trays of beer bottles through the tightly packed crowd.

The Wolfe Tones are terrific, and we all sing along, roaring out the rebel songs with beery gusto. At one point I reach for my cigarettes, which I have left on the table, and find that they are soaked with the runoff from melted ice chips. My neighbor at the table taps me on the arm and offers me one of his. The place is too loud to talk, so I accept it and nod in thanks.

When the Wolfe Tones take a short break, my neighbor and I strike up a conversation. He is a Dubliner himself and he asks what part of the States I'm from.

"New York," I answer.

"What part?" he asks.

I tell him and the name is clearly not strange to him.

"Ah," he says. "What part?"

I narrow my geographic focus and tell him.

He nods again and says, "What street?"

I tell him.

He allows himself a little smile. "What number?"

I tell him my address.

And he tells me the address he once lived at, a block away, and the name of the church on the corner.

He worked in publishing, too, and for good measure his name was also Ryan.

And here's another snapshot:

I'm looking at beautiful Donegal tweed jackets in a shop that's famous for its Irish tweeds, but the selection in my size is sparse. I ask a salesgirl if there are any others in my size and she looks genuinely regretful.

"Ah, no," she says. "It's the end of the season, you see, and they're nearly all gone." Seeing my disappointment, she adds, "They keep telling us we're supposed to be getting more in." But then she lapses into deeper regret and apology. "But I don't think we will, really," she says. "It's very hard to get anything done here. We're a very backward country, you know."

And one more snapshot, this one not my own:

In 1907 Jenny Boshell—twenty-eight years old, blond, pretty—sailed away from Ireland to America to look for work and a better life. I don't doubt that she looked back through tears from the deck of the ship as it sailed away. But I know that once she landed in New York, she never looked back. She lived to be ninety but she never saw Ireland or her parents again, and she never regretted her decision to leave. She didn't marry Irish, either. Instead, she married a tall, handsome young Dane who delivered groceries to the fine Greenwich Village townhouse where she worked as a chambermaid. All her life, the only way to make her truly indignant was to tell her that she still spoke with an Irish accent.

Which she did. Sorry, Nanny.

Jenny Boshell—later Jenny Bjerre—was my grandmother. For her, Ireland held nothing to look back to. She was from Dublin and had no memories of the gloriously green countryside and the beautiful hills seen through pearly mist. She had, in truth, very little to say about Ireland. There were some funny stories, like the one about the time her wicked sister fell off the chair she was standing on as she peeked through a convent fanlight to see if the nuns were really bald. If pressed for information, she would recall that she loved the open spaces of Phoenix Park and the grand shops in Grafton Street, where she would marvel at the clothes and treasures on display in the windows without ever daring to step inside.

Once, when I insisted on knowing what part of Dublin she was from, she finally told me only that it was "the back streets behind the Post Office," and then she would say not one word more. She never spoke about family life, and I've always imagined that it was as stern as it was poverty-ridden. The happiest memory of her childhood was the time she received as a Christmas gift—her only gift—an orange. The happiest memory of her young adulthood was the attention paid her, shortly before she sailed away forever, by a British soldier in his red uniform jacket. But she didn't speak often of these things. For her, the weight of early poverty lasted a lifetime.

So, despite my name, I didn't grow up very Irish and had to discover Ireland for myself.

And now another image comes to mind. One evening in Dublin, I noticed a young woman selling oranges from a broken and sagging pram on a corner near Clery's in O'Connell Street. Hollow-cheeked and defeated, she was the very picture of despair. I was on my way to the Abbey Theatre that evening for the premiere of a new production of *The Playboy of the Western World*. (How many new productions of Synge plays do you suppose the Abbey has staged through all these decades?) Because it was an opening night, all the swells, as Nanny would call them, had turned out in force to see and be seen: the immaculate and ruddy-faced men, the fine-looking women in their lovely dresses, every one of them easily juggling cake plates and cups of tea at the interval like the best of the British on a ballet night at Covent Garden.

Which of those scenes, I wondered, was the real Ireland?

The answer, of course, is easy. Both images are true, just as both would be true if this were Rome or Rio or any city where the needy and the nabobs pass each other every day in the street.

But I'm pretty sure I know where Nanny—or a younger version of her—would have been that rainy night if she'd stayed in Ireland. And she would not have been eating cake.

I tell these stories so that non-Irish readers will have a sense of the complexity of Ireland. Dublin is infinitely more than the sophisticated hotel service at the Gresham or Jurys, or coffee and pastries at Bewley's Café, more than Merrion Square or the Book of Kells or the bullet holes in the General Post Office, more even than Joyce's Bloom ever knew. And so are the country and the people more than the rocky drama of the western coast, the million shades of green in the hills and valleys, the ruined stone cottages, the impossibly beautiful vistas of the lakes, the donkey begging for a handout at the side of the road, and the welcoming landlady of a bed-and-breakfast, like the one who in five minutes produced for me, wet and tired from climbing Croagh Patrick in the rain, a pot of tea and a plate of scones still hot from the oven.

For me, the single most haunting memory of Ireland is the scent of burning peat on the air. It smells like nothing else; it is not like incense or a wood fire. It smells of the earth, which it is; it smells of the land and of hard work, of poverty and of centuries past, of a struggle to survive. It is an ancient and primitive smell, acrid but warm and comforting. It is the smell of living history. Druid priests no longer chant on the clifftops and blue-painted warriors no longer charge down the hills, but I always feel close to them when I smell the scent of burning peat.

You will too.

You'll be driving on a narrow ribbon of road that twists and rises and falls for miles that you can see ahead of you through the soft rain, and there won't be a tree or a house or a human being in sight, and you'll be praying the car doesn't give out in this desolate and godforsaken place, and suddenly you'll smell the burning peat from someplace far away, and you'll think, "Oh, my God!," and all of time will instantly slide away.

These *Reader's Companion* volumes—now covering Mexico, Cuba, Alaska, and South Africa, in addition to Ireland—are meant to provide a wide-screen, time-lapse portrait of the places they focus on. Each author included was there, in the country, on the spot, and this is his or her eyewitness report.

"The whole point of a travel book," Alec Waugh wrote in 1958, "is that it should be dated." The real value of old travel books, he continued, is the way they preserve for us "how certain places struck certain people twenty, fifty, eighty years ago."

I like reliving other people's travels, seeing through their eyes, and then measuring their responses against my own. Perhaps a traveler ten years ago, or a hundred or more, saw something I missed or something that would have meant nothing to me otherwise or something that isn't there anymore.

And, although many of the selections in each of the *Reader's Companion* books describe the very same scenes, the writers do not always agree on what they see. A good example is in *The Reader's Companion to Cuba*. When Richard Henry Dana Jr. visited Havana in 1859, he raved about its beauty. "Have I ever seen a city view so grand?" he exclaimed.

Anthony Trollope visited Havana, too, but his reaction was very different. "There is nothing attractive about the town of Havana," he growled. Trollope also visited in 1859. In fact, the visits of the two writers almost certainly overlapped. They might have passed each other in the street, but they came away with very different impressions.

All of the selections in the *Reader's Companion* books are by visitors to the places they write about, visitors who bring a stranger's questions and curiosity and challenges, not a native's assumptions, to their observations.

And in that, they are just like you and me when we travel.

The writers in this book brought with them to Ireland a wide variety of backgrounds. About half of them are either English or American, and among the others are two Canadians, a Welsh woman, a Chinese man, and a German.

They went to Ireland for quite different reasons. Several—H. V. Morton, Chiang Yee, Jan Morris, and Paul Theroux—went because they made their lives of travel and writing. Novelist and film director Michael Crichton went to Dublin to make a movie. David A. Wilson went for the music. David W. McFadden went to follow in the footsteps of H. V. Morton. Novelist Richard Condon, God help him, went to refurbish a house. Deborah Love and her writer husband, Peter Matthiessen, went on vacation. Elizabeth Shannon went because her husband was appointed the American Ambassador to Ireland. John Coyne went once to bring his elderly father back to the Connemara cottage he'd left long before . . . and again to bring his young son to the land of his origins. British writer Eric Newby, who decided to bicycle through the south and west of Ireland in the dead of winter, went because, it appears, he had temporarily taken leave of his senses. And what a sensitive soul like Arthur Symons was doing banging through the surf in a curragh out to the Aran Islands is anyone's guess.

And there are some surprises. The wildly inventive comic novels of Heinrich Böll are scant preparation for the darkly impressionistic picture he paints here. The great and prolific English travel writer H. V. Morton always wrote vigorously, in documentary fashion, about Spain, Italy, the Holy Land, South Africa, and many other places, but when he comes to Ireland, his prose turns definitely poetic. Maybe it's the place.

Finally, I must tell you this. While I was working on this book, a lady of my acquaintance asked me a question about Ireland. The question doesn't matter, but the assumption underlying it does. She thought Ireland was part of England. When I sputtered a contradiction, she protested, "Of course it's part of England. They have the pound and everything."

I came close to snapping "Typical!" in my carefully honed impression of John Cleese. I resisted the temptation, but that woman's misinformation about Ireland *is* typical. After all the struggle and all the pain and pride, some people still don't know that Ireland is a nation once again.

Or, at least, most of it is. Northern Ireland, a different country, is indeed part of the United Kingdom, just as Scotland and Wales are, and therein lies the source of the continuing troubles and occasional violence. For the purposes of this book, I haven't made a distinction. Most of the selections are about Eire, the Republic of Ireland, but the North is represented here too.

The whole situation is as puzzling as it is painful. In 1997, for example, Britain continued to cling tightly to Northern Ireland even as a Welsh separatist movement—in which writer Jan Morris has been very active, by the way—at last made considerable progress in Wales. And at the same time, in that same year, the tourist boards of both the Republic of Ireland and Northern Ireland managed to mount a joint advertising campaign to promote the wonders and beauties of Ireland—*all* of Ireland—to the world.

In 1998, after long negotiations, the Northern Ireland Peace Accord was signed. Within weeks, there was blood and death in the streets of Belfast.

But—regarding the Republic of Ireland—no, an Irish punt is not a British pound. And no, Ireland is not a part of Britain. Yes, it is an independent country.

And there isn't another like it on all the face of the earth.

My warmest thanks go to Jill Bauman, John Coyne, Linda Funk, Eleanor Garner, Ellen Levine, Dawn Mulvihill, and again to all my pals at the Chariot. Special thanks go to my editor, Christa Malone, who cares about these books as much as I do.

—ALAN RYAN
New York City
October 1998

THE READER'S
COMPANION TO
IRELAND

ARTHUR SYMONS
The Aran Islands: 1896

"SINCE I HAVE SEEN ARAN AND SLIGO, I HAVE NEVER
WONDERED THAT THE IRISH PEASANT STILL SEES
FAIRIES ABOUT HIS PATH, AND THAT THE
BOUNDARIES OF WHAT WE CALL THE REAL, AND OF
WHAT IS FOR US THE UNSEEN, ARE VAGUE TO HIM."

*British poet and critic Arthur Symons (1865–1945) was much taken with the
French symbolist poets. Their work was a powerful influence on his own
writing, already evident in his early volumes of poetry,* Days and Nights *(1889)*
and Silhouettes *(1892). He is perhaps better remembered for his critical studies, which include* The Symbolist Movement in Literature *(1899) and*
Charles Baudelaire *(1920), a biography, as well as books on Robert Browning,
Aubrey Beardsley, William Blake, the Romantic movement, and Elizabethan
drama. His autobiographical* Confessions *was published in 1930.*

*Less well known is the fact that Symons was an avid and thoughtful
traveler. In 1903 he published a collection of observations called* Cities. *A
more focused volume, called* Cities of Italy, *followed in 1907.*

*And in 1918 the London publisher Collins brought out another collection
of travel essays called* Cities and Sea-Coasts and Islands, *which Symons
dedicated to Augustus John. The first part of the book is devoted to the smaller
cities of Spain, digressing occasionally to consider poets, painters, and the
bullfights, and including a rare account in English of early zarzuela. "I am
aficionado, as a Spaniard would say, of music-halls," he writes. The second
part is about London, and the third is an assortment of pieces on places
touched, not always gently, by the sea: Dieppe, Cornwall, Winchelsea, Dover,
and the Aran Islands.*

It was the summer of 1896 when Symons visited the islands. He was thirty-one and already established as a poet. Note that he climbs into the boat with book in hand and can't help but deliver a literary opinion along the way.

For another view of the Aran Islands, see the selection in this volume by Tim Robinson.

FOR TWO HOURS AND A HALF THE FISHING-BOAT HAD been running before the wind, as a greyhound runs, in long leaps; and when I set foot on shore at Ballyvaughan, and found myself in the little, neat hotel, and waited for tea in the room with the worn piano, the album of manuscript verses, and the many photographs of the young girl who had written them, first as she stands holding a violin, and then, after she has taken vows, in the white habit of the Dominican order, I seemed to have stepped out of some strange, half-magical, almost real dream, through which I had been consciously moving on the other side of that grey, disturbed sea, upon those grey and peaceful islands in the Atlantic. And all that evening, as we drove for hours along the Clare coast and inland into Galway, under a sunset of gold fire and white spray, until we reached the battlemented towers of Tillyra Castle, I had the same curious sensation of having been dreaming; and I could but vaguely remember the dream, in which I was still, however, absorbed. We passed, I believe, a fine slope of grey mountains, a ruined abbey, many castle ruins; we talked of Parnell, of the county families, of mysticism, the analogy of that old Biblical distinction of body, soul, and spirit with the symbolical realities of the lamp, the wick, and the flame; and all the time I was obsessed by the vague, persistent remembrance of those vanishing islands, which wavered somewhere in the depths of my consciousness. When I awoke next morning the dream had resolved itself into definite shape, and I remembered every detail of those last three days, during which I had been so far from civilisation, so much further out of the world than I had ever been before.

It was on the morning of Wednesday, August 5, 1896, that a party of four, of whom I alone was not an Irishman, got into Tom Joyce's hooker at Cashla Bay, on the coast of Galway, and set sail for the largest of the three islands of Aran, Inishmore by name, that is, Large Island. The hooker, a half-decked, cutter-rigged fishing-boat of seventeen tons, had come over for us from Aran, and we set out with a light breeze, which presently dropped and left us almost becalmed under a very hot sun for nearly an hour, where we were passed by a white butterfly that was making straight for the open sea. We were nearly four hours in crossing, and we had time to read all that needed reading of *Grania*, Miss Emily Lawless's novel, which is supposed to be the classic of the islands, and to study our maps and to catch one mackerel. But I found most of my mind this passage from Roderic O'Flaherty's *Chorographical Description of West or H-Iar Connaught*, which in its quaint, minute seventeenth-century prose told me more about what I was going to see than everything else that I read then or after on the subject of these islands. "The soile," he tells us, "is almost paved over with stones, soe as, in some places, nothing is to be seen but large stones with wide openings between them, where cattle break their legs. Scarce any other stones there but limestones, and marble fit for tomb-stones, chymney mantle trees, and high crosses. Among these stones is very sweet pasture, so that beefe, veal, mutton are better and earlyer in season here than elsewhere; and of late there is plenty of cheese, and tillage mucking, and corn is the same with the seaside tract. In some places the plow goes. On the shores grows samphire in plenty, ring-root or sea-holy, and sea-cabbage. Here are Cornish choughs, with red legs and bills. Here are ayries of hawkes, and birds which never fly but over the sea, and, therefore, are used to be eaten on fasting days: to catch which people goe down, with ropes tyed about them, into the caves of cliffs by night, and with a candle light kill abundance of them. Here are severall wells and pooles, yet in extraordinary dry weather, people must turn their cattell out of the islands, and the corn failes. They have noe fuell but cow-dung dryed with the sun, unless they bring turf in from the western continent. They have *Cloghans*, a kind of building of stones layd one upon another, which are brought to a roof without any manner of mortar to cement them, some of which cabins will hold forty men on their floor, so antient that nobody knows how long ago any of them was made. Scarcity of wood and store of fit stones, without peradventure found out the first invention." Reading of such things as these, and of how St. Albeus, Bishop of *Imly*, had said, "Great is that island, and it is the land of saints; for no man knows how many saints are buried there, but God alone"; and of an old saying: "Athenry was, Galway is, Aran shall be the best of the three," we grew, after a while, impatient of delay. A good breeze sprang up at last, and as I stood in the bow, leaning against the mast, I felt the one quite perfectly satisfying sensation of movement: to race through steady water before a stiff sail, on which the reefing cords are tapping in rhythm to those nine notes of the sailors' chorus in *Tristan*, which always ring in my ears when I am on the sea, for they have in them all the exultation of all life that moves upon the waters.

The butterfly, I hope, had reached land before us; but only a few sea-birds came out to welcome us as we drew near Inishmore, the Large Island, which is nine miles long and a mile and a half broad. I gazed at the long line of the island, growing more distinct every moment; first, a grey outline, flat at the sea's edge, and rising up beyond in irregular, rocky hills, terrace above terrace; then, against this grey outline, white houses began to detach themselves, the sharp line of the pier cutting into the curve of the harbour; and then, at last, the figures of men and women moving across the land. Nothing is more mysterious, more disquieting, than one's first glimpse of an island, and all I had heard of these islands, of their peace in the heart of the storm, was not a little mysterious and disquieting. I knew that they contained the oldest ruins and that their life of the present was the most primitive life of any part of Ireland; I knew that they were rarely visited by the tourist, almost never by any but the local tourist; that they were difficult to reach, sometimes more difficult to leave, for the uncertainty of weather in that uncertain region of the Atlantic had been known to detain some of the rare travellers there for days, was it not for weeks? Here one was absolutely at the mercy of the elements, which might at any moment become unfriendly, which, indeed, one seemed to have but apprehended in a pause of their eternal enmity. And we seemed also to be venturing among an unknown people, who, even if they spoke our own language, were further away from us, more foreign than people who spoke an unknown language and lived beyond other seas.

As we walked along the pier towards the three whitewashed cottages which form the Atlantic Hotel, at which we were to stay, a strange being sprang towards us, with a curiously beast-like stealthiness and animation; it was a crazy man, bare-footed and blear-eyed, who held out his hand and sang out at us in a high, chanting voice, and in what sounded rather a tone of command than of entreaty, "Give me a penny, sir! Give me a penny, sir!" We dropped something into his hat, and he went away over the rocks, laughing loudly to himself, and repeating some words that he had heard us say. We passed a few fishermen and some bare-footed children, who looked at us curiously, but without moving, and were met at the door of the middle cottage by a little, fat old woman with a round body and a round face, wearing a white cap tied over her ears. The Atlantic Hotel is a very primitive hotel; it had last been slept in by some priests from the mainland, who had come on their holiday with bicycles; and before that by a German philologist who was learning Irish. The kitchen, which is also the old landlady's bedroom, presents a medley of pots and pans and petticoats as you pass its open door and climb the little staircase, diverging oddly on either side after the first five or six steps, and leading on the right to a large dining-room, where the table lounges on an inadequate number of legs and the chairs bow over when you lean back on them. I have slept more luxuriously, but not more soundly, than in the little musty bedroom on the other side of the stairs, with its half-made bed, its bare and unswept floor, its tiny window, of which only the lower half could be opened, and this, when opened, had to be supported by a wooden catch from outside. Going to sleep in that little, uncomfortable room was a delight in itself; for the starry water outside, which one could see through that narrow slit of window, seemed to flow softly about one in waves of delicate sleep.

When we had had a hasty meal and had got a little used to our hotel, and had realised as well as we could where we were, at the lower end of the village of Kilronan, which stretches up the hill to the north-west on either side of the main road, we set out in the opposite direction, finding many guides by the way, who increased in number as we went on through the smaller village of Kileaney up to the south-eastern hill, on which are a holy well, its thorn-tree hung with votive ribbons, and the ruins of several churches, among them the church of St. Enda, the patron saint of the island. At first we were able to walk along a very tolerable road, then we branched off upon a little strip of grey sand, piled in mounds as high as if it had been drifted snow, and from that, turning a little inland, we came upon the road again, which began to get stonier as we neared the village. Our principal guide, an elderly man with long thick curls of flaxen hair and a seaman's beard, shaved away from the chin, talked fairly good English, with a strong accent, and he told us of the poverty of the people, the heavy rents they have to pay for soil on which no grass grows, and the difficult living they make out of their fishing, and their little tillage, and the cattle which they take over in boats to the fairs at Galway, throwing them into the sea when they get near land, and leaving them to swim ashore. He was dressed, as are almost all the peasants of Aran, in clothes woven and made on the island—loose, rough, woollen things, of drab, or dark blue, or grey, sometimes charming in colour; he had a flannel shirt, a kind of waistcoat with sleeves, very loose and shapeless trousers worn without braces, an old and discoloured slouch hat on his head, and on his feet the usual *pampooties*, slippers of undressed hide, drawn together and stitched into shape, with pointed toes, and a cord across the instep. The village to which we had come was a cluster of whitewashed cabins, a little better built than those I had seen in Galway, with the brown thatch fastened down with ropes drawn crosswise over the roof and tied to wooden pegs driven into the wall for protection against the storm blowing in from the Atlantic. They had the usual two doors, facing each other at front and back, the windier of the two being kept closed in rough weather, and the doors were divided in half by the usual hatch. As we passed, a dark head would appear at the upper half of the door, and a dull glow of red would rise out of the shadow. The women of Aran almost all dress in red, the petticoat very heavily woven, the crossed shawl or bodice of a thinner texture of wool. These whom we met on the roads wore thicker shawls over their heads, and they would sometimes draw the shawls closer about them, as women in the East draw their veils closer about their faces. As they came out to their doors to see us pass, I noticed in their manner a certain mingling of curiosity and shyness, an interest which was never quite eager. Some of the men came out and quietly followed us as we were led along a twisting way between the cabins; and the children, boys and girls, in a varying band of from twenty to thirty, ran about our heels, stopping whenever we stopped, and staring at us with calm wonder. They were very inquisitive, but, unlike English villagers in remote places, perfectly polite, and neither resented our coming among them nor jeered at us for being foreign to their fashions.

The people of Aran (they are about 3000 in all), as I then saw them for the first time, and as I saw them during the few days of my visit, seemed to me a simple, dignified, self-sufficient, sturdily primitive people, to whom Browning's phrase of "gentle islanders" might well be applied. They could be fierce on occasion, as I knew; for I remembered the story of their refusal to pay the county cess, and how, when the cess-collector had come over to take his dues by force, they had assembled on the seashore with sticks and stones, and would not allow him even to land. But they had, for the most part, mild faces, of the long Irish type, often regular in feature, but with loose and drooping mouths and discoloured teeth. Most had blue eyes, the men, oftener than the women, having fair hair. They held themselves erect, and walked nimbly, with a peculiar step due to the rocky ways they have generally to walk on; few of them, I noticed, had large hands or feet, and all, without exception, were thin, as indeed the Irish peasant almost invariably is. The women too, for the most part, were thin, and had the same long faces, often regular, with straight eyebrows and steady eyes, not readily changing expression; they hold themselves well, a little like men, whom, indeed, they somewhat resemble in figure. As I saw them, leaning motionless against their doors, walking with their deliberateness of step along the roads, with eyes in which there was no wonder, none of the fever of the senses, placid animals on whom emotion has never worked in any vivid or passionate way, I seemed to see all the pathetic contentment of those narrow lives, in which day follows day with the monotony of wave lapping on wave. I observed one young girl of twelve or thirteen who had something of the ardency of beauty, and a few shy, impressive faces, the hair drawn back smoothly from the middle parting, appearing suddenly behind doors or over walls; almost all, even the very old women, had nobility of gesture and attitude, but in the more personal expression of faces there was for the most part but a certain quietude, seeming to reflect the grey hush, the bleak greyness of this land of endless stone and endless sea.

When we had got through the village and begun to climb the hill, we were still followed, and we were followed for all the rest of the way by about fifteen youngsters, all, except one, bare-footed, and two, though boys, wearing petticoats, as the Irish peasant children not unfrequently do, for economy, when they are young enough not to resent it. Our guide, the elderly man with the flaxen curls, led us first to the fort set up by the soldiers of Cromwell, who, coming over to keep down the Catholic rebels, ended by turning Catholic and marrying and settling among the native people; then to Teglach Enda, a ruined church of very early masonry, made of large blocks set together with but little cement—the church of St. Enda, who came to Aran in about the year 480, and fifty-eight years later laid his bones in the cemetery which was to hold the graves of not less than a hundred and twenty saints. On our way inland to Teampull Benen, the remains of an early oratory, surrounded by cloghans or stone dwellings made of heaped stones which, centuries ago, had been the cells of monks, we came upon the large puffing-hole, a great gap in the earth, going down by steps of rock to the sea, which in stormy weather dashes foam to the height of its sixty feet, reminding me of the sounding hollows on the coast of Cornwall. The road here, as on almost the whole of the island, was through stone-walled fields of stone. Grass, or any soil, was but a rare interval between a broken and distracted outstretch of grey rock, lying in large flat slabs, in boulders of every size and shape, and in innumerable stones, wedged in the ground or lying loose upon it, round, pointed, rough, and polished; an unending greyness, cut into squares by the walls of carefully-heaped stones, which we climbed with great insecurity, for the stones were kept in place by no more than the more or less skilful accident of their adjustment, and would turn under our feet or over in our hands as we climbed them. Occasionally a little space of pasture had been cleared or a little artificial soil laid down, and a cow browsed on the short grass. Ferns, and occasionally maidenhair, grew in the fissures splintered between the rocks; and I saw mallow, stone-crop, the pale blue wind-flower, the white campian, many nettles, ivy, and a few bushes. In this part of the island there were no trees, which were to be found chiefly on the north-western side, in a few small clusters about some of the better houses, and almost wholly of alder and willow. As we came to the sheer edge of the sea and saw the Atlantic, and knew that there was nothing but the Atlantic between this last shivering remnant of Europe and the far-off continent of America, it was with no feeling of surprise that we heard from the old man who led us that no later than two years ago an old woman of those parts had seen, somewhere on this side of the horizon, the blessed island of Tir-nan-Ogue, the island of immortal youth, which is held by the Irish peasants to lie somewhere in that mysterious region of the sea.

We loitered on the cliffs for some time, leaning over them, and looking into the magic mirror that glittered there like a crystal, and with all the soft depth of a crystal in it, hesitating on the veiled threshold of visions. Since I have seen Aran and Sligo, I have never wondered that the Irish peasant still sees fairies about his path, and that the boundaries of what we call the real, and of what is for us the unseen, are vague to him. The sea on those coasts is not like the sea as I know it on any other coast; it has in it more of the twilight. And the sky seems to come down more softly, with more stealthy step, more illusive wings, and the land to come forward with a more hesitating and gradual approach; and land and sea and sky to mingle more absolutely than on any other coast. I have never realised less the slipping of sand through the hour-glass; I have never seemed to see with so remote an impartiality, as in the presence of brief and yet eternal things, the troubling and insignificant accidents of life. I have never believed less in the reality of the visible world, in the importance of all we are most serious about. One seems to wash off the dust of cities, the dust of beliefs, the dust of incredulities.

It was nearly seven o'clock when we got back to Kilronan, and after dinner we sat for a while talking and looking out through the little windows at the night. But I could not stay indoors in this new, marvellous place; and, persuading one of my friends to come with me, I walked up through Kilronan, which I found to be a far more solid and populous village than the one we had seen; and coming out on the high ground beyond the houses, we saw the end of a pale green sunset. Getting back to our hotel, we found the others still talking; but I could not stay indoors, and after a while went out by myself to the end of the pier in the darkness, and lay there looking into the water and into the fishing-boats lying close up against the land, where there were red lights moving, and the shadows of men, and the sound of deep-throated Irish.

I remember no dreams that night, but I was told that I had talked in my sleep, and I was willing to believe it. In the morning, not too early, we set out on an outside car (that rocking and most comfortable vehicle, which I prefer to everything but a gondola) for the Seven Churches and Dun Aengus, along the only beaten road in the island. The weather, as we started, was grey and misty, threatening rain, and we could but just see the base-line of the Clare mountains across the grey and discoloured waters of the bay. At the Seven Churches we were joined by a peasant, who diligently showed us the ruined walls of Teampull Brecan, with its slab inscribed in Gaelic with the words, "Pray for the two canons"; the stone of the "VII. Romani"; St. Brecan's headstone, carved with Gaelic letters; the carved cross and the headstone of St. Brecan's bed. More peasants joined us, and some children, who fixed on us their usual placid and tolerant gaze, in which curiosity contended with an indolent air of contentment. In all these people I noticed the same discreet manners that had already pleased me; and once, as we were sitting on a tombstone in the interior of one of the churches, eating the sandwiches that we had brought for luncheon, a man, who had entered the doorway, drew back instantly, seeing us taking a meal.

The Seven Churches are rooted in long grass, spreading in billowy mounds, intertwisted here and there with brambles; but when we set out for the circular fort of Dun Onaght, which lies on the other side of the road, at no great distance up the hill, we were once more in the land of rocks; and it was through a boreen, or lane, entirely paved with loose and rattling stones, that we made our way up the ascent. At the top of the hill we found ourselves outside such a building as I had never seen before: an ancient fort, 90 feet in diameter, and on the exterior 16 feet high, made of stones placed one upon another, without mortar, in the form of two walls, set together in layers, the inner wall lower than the outer, so as to form a species of gallery, to which stone steps led at intervals. No sooner had we got inside than the rain began to fall in torrents, and it was through a blinding downpour that we hurried back to the car, scarcely stopping to notice a Druid altar that stood not far out of our way. As we drove along, the rain ceased suddenly; the wet cloud that had been steaming over the faint and still sea, as if desolated with winter, vanished in sunshine, caught up into a glory; and the water, transfigured by so instant a magic, was at once changed from a grey wilderness of shivering mist into a warm and flashing and intense blueness, which gathered ardency of colour, until the whole bay burned with blue fire. The clouds had been swept behind us, and on the other side of the water, for the whole length of the horizon, the beautiful, softly curving Connemara mountains stood out against the sky as if lit by some interior illumination, blue and pearl-grey and grey-rose. Along the shore-line a trail of faint cloud drifted from kelp-fire to kelp-fire, like altar-smoke drifting into altar-smoke; and that mysterious mist floated into the lower hollows of the hills, softening their outlines and colours with a vague and fluttering and luminous veil of brightness.

It was about four in the afternoon when we came to the village of Kilmurvey, upon the seashore, and, leaving our car, began to climb the hill leading to Dun Aengus. Passing two outer ramparts, now much broken, one of them seeming to end suddenly in the midst of a *chevaux de frise* of pillar-like stones thrust endways into the earth, we entered the central fort by a lintelled doorway, set in the side of a stone wall of the same Cyclopean architecture as Dun Onaght, 18 feet high on the outside, and with two adhering inner walls, each lower in height, 12 feet 9 inches in thickness. This fort is 150 feet north and south and 140 feet east and west, and on the east side the circular wall ends suddenly on the very edge of a cliff going down 300 feet to the sea. It is supposed that the circle was once complete, and that the wall and the solid ground itself, which is here of bare rock, were slowly eaten away by the gnawing of centuries of waves, which have been at their task since some hundreds of years before the birth of Christ, when we know not what king, ruling over the races called "the servile," entrenched himself on that impregnable height. The Atlantic lies endlessly out towards the sunrise, beating, on the south, upon the brown and towering rock of the cliffs of Moher, rising up nearly a sheer thousand feet. The whole grey and desolate island, flowering into barren stone, stretches out on the other side, where the circle of the water washes from Galway Bay into the Atlantic. Looking out over all that emptiness of sea, one imagines the long-oared galleys of the ravaging kings who had lived there, some hundreds of years before the birth of Christ; and the emptiness of the fortress filled with long-haired warriors, coming back from the galleys with captured slaves, and cattle, and the spoil of citadels. We know from the Bardic writers that a civilisation, similar to that of the Homeric poems, lived on in Ireland almost to the time of the coming of

St. Patrick; and it was something also of the sensation of Homer—the walls of Troy, the heroes, and that "face that launched a thousand ships"—which came to me as we stood upon these unconquerable walls, to which a generation of men had been as a moth's flight and a hundred years as a generation of men.

Coming back from Dun Aengus, one of our party insisted on walking; and we had not been long indoors when he came in with a singular person whom he had picked up on the way, a professional story-teller, who had for three weeks been teaching Irish to the German philologist who had preceded us on the island. He was half blind and of wild appearance; a small and hairy man, all gesture, and as if set on springs, who spoke somewhat broken English in a roar. He lamented that we could understand no Irish, but, even in English, he had many things to tell, most of which he gave as but "talk," making it very clear that we were not to suppose him to vouch for them. His own family, he told us, was said to be descended from the roons, or seals, but that certainly was "talk"; and a witch had, only nine months back, been driven out of the island by the priest; and there were many who said they had seen fairies, but for his part he had never seen them. But with this he began to swear on the name of God and the saints, rising from his chair and lifting up his hands, that what he was going to tell us was the truth; and then he told how a man had once come into his house and admired his young child, who was lying there in his bed, and had not said "God bless you!" (without which to admire is to envy and to bring under the power of the fairies), and that night, and for many following nights, he had wakened and heard a sound of fighting, and one night had lit a candle, but to no avail, and another night had gathered up the blanket and tried to fling it over the head of whoever might be there, but had caught no one; only in the morning, going to a box in which fish were kept, he had found blood in the box; and at this he rose again, and again swore on the name of God and the saints that he was telling us only the truth, and true it was that the child had died; and as for the man who had ill-wished him, "I could point him out any day," he said fiercely. And then, with many other stories of the doings of fairies and priests (for he was very religious), and of the "Dane" who had come to the island to learn Irish ("and he knew all the languages, the Proosy, and the Roosy, and the Span, and the Grig"), he told us how Satan, being led by pride to equal himself with God, looked into the glass in which God only should look, and when Satan looked into the glass, "Hell was made in a minute."

Next morning we were to leave early, and at nine o'clock we were rowed out to the hooker, which lifted sail in a good breeze, and upon a somewhat pitching sea, for the second island, Inishmaan, that is, the Middle Island, which is three miles long and a mile and a half broad. We came within easy distance of the shore, after about half an hour's quick sailing, and a curragh came out to us, rowed by two islanders; but, finding the sea very rough in Gregory Sound, we took them on board, and, towing the boat after us, went about to the Foul Sound on the southern side of the island, where the sea was much calmer. Here we got into the curragh, sitting motionless for fear a slight movement on the part of any of us should upset it. The curragh is simply the coracle of the ancient Britons, made of wooden laths covered with canvas, and tarred on the outside, bent into the shape of a round-bottomed boat with a raised and pointed prow, and so light that, when on shore, two men can carry it reversed on their heads, like an immense hat or umbrella. As the curragh touched the shore, some of the islanders who had assembled at the edge of the sea came into the water to meet us, and took hold of the boat, and lifted the prow of it upon land, and said, "You are welcome, you are welcome!" One of them came with us, a nimble peasant of about forty, who led the way up the terraced side of the hill, on which there was a little grass, near the seashore, and then scarce anything but slabs and boulders of stone, to a little ruined oratory, almost filled with an alder tree, the only tree I saw on the island. All around it were gravestones, half-defaced by the weather, but carved with curious armorial bearings, as it seemed, representing the sun and moon and stars about a cross formed of the Christian monogram. Among the graves were lying huge beams, that had been flung up the hillside from some wrecked vessel in one of the storms that beat upon the island. Going on a little farther we came to the ancient stone fort of Dun Moher, an inclosure slightly larger than Dun Onaght, but smaller than Dun Aengus; and coming down on the other side, by some stone steps, we made our way, along a very rocky boreen, towards the village that twisted upon a brown zigzag around the slope of the hill.

In the village we were joined by some more men and children; and a number of women, wearing the same red clothes that we had seen on the larger island, and looking at us with perhaps scarcely so shy a curiosity (for they were almost too unused to strangers to have adopted a manner of shyness), came out to their doors and looked up at us out of the darkness of many interiors, from where they sat on the ground knitting or carding wool. We passed the chapel, a very modern-looking building, made out of an ancient church, and turned in for a moment to the cottage where the priest sleeps when he comes over from Inishmore on Saturday night to say early mass on Sunday morning before going on to Inisheer for the second mass. We saw his little white room, very quaint and neat; and the woman of the house, speaking only Irish, motioned us to sit down, and could hardly be prevented from laying out plates and glasses for us upon the table. As we got a little through the more populous part of the village, we saw ahead of us, down a broad lane, a very handsome girl, holding the end of a long ribbon, decorated with a green bough, across the road. Other girls and some older women were standing by, and, when we came up, the handsome girl, with the low forehead and the sombre blue eyes, cried out laughingly, in her scanty English, "Cash, cash!" We paid toll, as the custom is, and got her blessing; and went on our way, leaving the path, and climbing many stone walls, until we came to the great fort of Dun Conor on the hill, the largest of the ancient forts of Aran.

Dun Conor is 227 feet north and south and 115 feet east and west, with walls in three sections, 20 feet high on the outside and 18 feet 7 inches thick. We climbed to the top and walked around the wall, where the wind blowing in from the sea beat so hard upon us that we could scarcely keep our footing. From this height we could see all over the island lying out beneath us, grey, and broken into squares by the walled fields; the brown thatch of the village, the smoke coming up from the chimneys, here and there a red shawl or skirt, the grey sand by the sea and the grey sea all round. As we stood on the wall many peasants came slowly about us, climbing up on all sides, and some stood together just inside the entrance, and two or three girls sat down on the other side of the arena, knitting. Presently an old man, scarcely leaning on the stick which he carried in his hand, came towards us, and began slowly to climb the steps. "It is my father," said one of the men; "he is the oldest man on the island; he was born in 1812." The old man climbed slowly up to where we stood; a mild old man, with a pale face, carefully shaved, and a firm mouth, who spoke the best English that we had heard there. "If any gentleman has committed a crime," said the oldest man on the island, "we'll hide him. There was a man killed his father, and he came over here, and we hid him for two months, and he got away safe to America."

As we came down from the fort the old man came with us, and I and another, walking ahead, lingered for some time with the old man by a stone stile. "Have you ever seen the fairies?" said my friend, and a quaint smile flickered over the old man's face, and with many ohs! and grave gestures he told us that he had never seen them, but that he had heard them crying in the fort by night; and one night, as he was going along with his dog, just at the spot where we were then standing, the dog had suddenly rushed at something or some one, and had rushed round and round him, but he could see nothing, though it was bright moonlight, and so light that he could have seen a rat; and he had followed across several fields, and again the dog had rushed at the thing, and had seemed to be beaten off, and had come back covered with sweat, and panting, but he could see nothing. And there was a man once, he knew the man, and could point him out, who had been out in his boat (and he motioned with his stick to a certain spot on the water), and a sea fairy had seized hold of his boat and tried to come into it; but he had gone quickly on shore, and the thing, which looked like a man, had turned back into the sea. And there had been a man once on the island who used to talk with the fairies; and you could hear him going along the roads by night swearing and talking with the fairies. "And have you ever heard," said my friend, "of the seals, the roons, turning into men?" "And indeed," said the oldest man on the island, smiling, "I'm a roon, for I'm one of the family they say comes from the roons." "And have you ever heard," said my friend, "of men going back into the sea and turning roons again?" "I never heard that," said the oldest man on the island reflectively, seeming to ponder over the probability of the occurrence; "no," he repeated after a pause, "I never heard that."

We came back to the village by the road we had come, and passed again the handsome girl who had taken toll; she was sitting by the roadside knitting, and looked at us sidelong as we passed, with an almost imperceptible smile in her eyes. We wandered for some time a little vaguely, the amiability of the islanders leading them to bring us in search of various ruins which we imagined to exist, and which they did not like to tell us were not in existence. I found the people on this island even more charming, because a little simpler, more untouched by civilisation, than those on the larger island. They were of necessity a little lonelier, for if few people come to Inishmore, how many have ever spent a night on Inishmaan? Inishmore has its hotel, but there is no hotel on Inishmaan; there is indeed one public-house, but there is not even a policeman, so sober, so law-abiding are these islanders. It is true that I succeeded, with some difficulty, and under cover of some mystery, in securing, what I had long wished to taste, a bottle of poteen or illicit whisky. But the brewing of poteen is, after all, almost romantic in its way, with that queer, sophistical romance of the contraband. That was not the romance I associated with this most peaceful of islands as we walked along the sand on the seashore, passing the kelp-burners, who were collecting long brown trails of seaweed. More than anything I had ever seen, this seashore gave me the sensation of the mystery and the calm of all the islands one has ever dreamed of, all the fortunate islands that have ever been saved out of the disturbing sea; this delicate pearl-grey sand, the deeper grey of the stones, the more luminous grey of the water, and so consoling an air as of immortal twilight and the peace of its dreams.

I had been in no haste to leave Inishmore, but I was still more loth to leave Inishmaan; and I think that it was with reluctance on the part of all of us that we made our way to the curragh, which was waiting for us in the water. The islanders waved their caps, and called many good blessings after us as we were rowed back to the hooker, which again lifted sail and set out for the third and smallest island, Inisheer, that is, the South Island.

We set out confidently, but when we had got out of shelter of the shore, the hooker began to rise and fall with some violence; and by the time we had come within landing distance of Inisheer the waves were dashing upon us with so great an energy that it was impossible to drop anchor, and our skipper advised us not to try to get to land. A curragh set out from the shore, and came some way towards us, riding the waves. It might have been possible, I doubt not, to drop by good luck from the rolling side of the hooker into the pitching bottom of the curragh, and without capsizing the curragh; but the chances were against it. Tom Joyce, holding on to the ropes of the main-sail, and the most seaman-like of us, in the stern, shouted at each other above the sound of the wind. We were anxious to make for Ballyline, the port nearest to Listoonvarna, on the coast of Clare; but this Joyce declared to be impossible in such a sea, and with such a wind, and advised that we should make for Ballyvaughan, round Black Head Point, where we should find a safe harbour. It was now about a quarter past one, and we set out for Ballyvaughan with the wind fair behind us. The hooker rode well, and the waves but rarely came over the windward side as she lay over towards her sail, taking leap after leap through the white-edged furrows of the grey water. For two hours and a half we skirted the Clare coast, which came to me, and disappeared from me, as the gunwale dipped or rose on the leeward side. The islands were blotted out behind us long before we had turned the sheer corner of Black Head, the ultimate edge of Ireland, and at last we came round the headland

into quieter water, and so, after a short time, into a little harbour of Ballyvaughan, where we set foot on land again, and drove for hours along the
Clare coast and inland into Galway, under that sunset of gold fire and
white spray, back to Tillyra Castle, where I felt the ground once more solid
under my feet.

HAROLD SPEAKMAN

Galway and Dublin, meeting Lady Gregory and W. B. Yeats: 1924

" 'TELL ME, WHY HIS MANNER? WHAT IS THE REASON
FOR SUCH TERRIFIC POSE?' 'IT ISN'T POSE, IT'S THE
MAN.' "

American writer Harold Speakman wrote books about China and the Holy Land, and another about Mississippi, and in 1925 published Here's Ireland, *an account of his travels throughout the country, often in the company of a donkey named Grania. He saw a great deal of the country: Dublin and the lakes of Killarney and the Dingle Peninsula, Galway and the Aran Islands and Croagh Patrick ("swathed like Fujiyama in mist"), Donegal and Belfast and the North. Some of his observations included in the book had previously appeared in the* Bookman, *the* Boston Transcript, *the* Literary Digest, *the* Christian Science Monitor, *and the* New York Times.

Lady Gregory and William Butler Yeats were leaders of the Irish Renaissance, she as a dramatist and stage director and he as both dramatist and poet. Together they founded Dublin's Abbey Theatre in 1904.

Lady Gregory's best-known plays include Spreading the News *(1904),* The Rising of the Moon *(1907), and* The Workhouse Ward *(1908). Coole Park, which was such a powerful inspiration to Yeats, was her estate. Lady Gregory was in her early seventies when Speakman met her.*

Yeats was nearing sixty at the time and, his reputation as a literary treasure of Ireland secure, had recently been awarded the Nobel Prize in Literature. In this period, the mid 1920s, he was also a member of the senate of the newly established Irish Free State. His reputation as a colorful local character, as Speakman discovered too, was also secure.

GALWAY AND LADY GREGORY

1

THE WAY LED ONCE MORE INTO THE HILLS. AS WE jogged slowly up the rising road north of Killaloe where the Shannon widens into the mist-swept waters of Lough Derg, out of the hills came young Lochinvar in the guise of a black Spanish donkey—a dashing young fellow with long hair like Pan, who began to flirt desperately with Herself. She did not care for him, however, and neither did I, so in the character of irate godfather I drove him a little way down the road where he stood staring at me for a few moments in wistful, moody silence. But he was the most persistent young ass in the world and literally followed us for miles, while I stalked along like a crabbed old duenna in back of the cart. And why shouldn't I? Had not O'Leary the tinker said that Herself was only three? She didn't care for him anyway. . . . But at that moment I saw something glistening in the road. She had dropped—shades of Hans Andersen and Madame Du Barry—her shoe!

I picked it up quickly lest Cinderella-wise, she have this prince of the road following us all over the best of the western world.

Along came a man with a herd of cows.

"How are you?" I asked.

"Fine my life!" said he.

"Are you going far down the road?"

"Sure it's the best part of two miles I'm going."

"Well, would you mind driving that donkey down the road with the other animals? He has taken a fancy to my friend here."

"Sure I don't mind at all," he said. "And why should I—for he's me own donkey. Get along wid you, Clematis."

So Clematis, like Charlie Chaplin surrounded by the police, marched homeward in a cluster of rotundly inconsiderate cows. But at the turn in the road, I saw his head, also like Charlie's, swing around in a dazed and astonished good-by.

2

THE SHOE WAS A MATTER FOR IMMEDIATE ATTENTION. I had intended going over the hills to Graney near the Galway border; but the town of Feakle, lying half a mile off the straight road, was nearer.

While the blacksmith at Feakle was replacing the shoe, he noticed that the left wheel of the cart was ailing. He took off the wheel, removed the heavy metal core or "box" from its center, padded the inside of the hub with a gunny sack, pounded the core in again—and broke it.

There were no more "boxes" in the immediate vicinity. With that stroke of the sledge, I became automatically a guest at Feakle for the night.

"You'll have no trouble at all for a room," the blacksmith assured me, as he sent a lad off to forage for another wheel-box. "Just try that house over there."

The young woman who came to the door smiled most agreeably, but she averred that the house was full, and stuck to it. I might find a room across the street at Mrs. O'Flaherty's, she said. . . .

Thus began a strange game in which I was ricochetted from one family to another all the way down the long village street, having no idea whether I was being popped from friend to friend or enemy to enemy. In either case, the result was the same.

All but one gave excuses, and good excuses, with a friendly smile. Mrs. Keane had a sick sister she was tending; Mrs. Carrigan had a friend and her baby visiting her; Miss Mulcahy had one room but it was rented to a doctor and he might return at any hour of the night. It was only Mrs. Jones who did not have the kindness of a courteous refusal about her, and when I smiled pleasantly at her later on in passing by, she launched a look at me which would have shriveled the most case-hardened tinker in Connemara or even in Mayo.

So I went gloomily into a tiny public house, took out my map, and sat down at a table between a saucer-eyed old man and an old man with a bent back and a pendulous nose which he rested on his crossed hands— which in turn were resting on the top of a blackthorn stick.

"Biddie Erly . . ." the saucer-eyed old man was saying. "Her name and fame went through all the land. She lived in a mud-wall cabin in the parish of Glenee and she could tell you the doings of the spirit world. She was genuine, oh I suppose the most genuine of her class that ever lived. When you'd go there after breakin' your leg, she'd tell you where you came from and how you did it."

"That's right, now," said the other. "There was a sea captain, and his arm swelled up from the hand to the shoulder. The local clergy were opposed to Biddie Erly because she was wrong with the church (but she was right just the same!). So the sea captain went out a round-about way and came to her, and she said, "Go home, man, and go to bed earlier. And he got over it all right. . . ."

"She could prophesee too," said the saucer-eyed old man. "She could prophesee into the future."

"Excuse me," objected the nose, "I don't believe in propheseein'. I only believe in *the lines.*"

"Pardon me," said the saucer-eyed, "I believe in *propheseein'.*"

Evidently this was an old argument, for they began excusing each other and begging each other's pardon until I thought there would be a fight, to avoid which, I asked:

"What do you mean, may I ask, by 'the lines'?"

"I mean, *what is written.* Sure, anybody can prophesee, now! I can look out the window and prophesee we'll have rain. But what is in the lines is true. You have a map there (beggin' your pardon) with the roads and all marked on it. It is true. It is in the lines. . . . Excuse me. We are ignorant men."

"As for me," said the other, "*I believe in propheseein'.*"

"If that is the case," I said smiling, "I wish you would tell me where I am going to stay tonight."

They bestirred themselves at that and called a few more men about the table.

"Have you tried O'Flaherty's and Burke's and Sullivan's and Cassidy's. Think of that, now! *What* a village without a bed for a stranger!"

At last a large, kindly fellow said that if nothing else turned up, he had a house that he was building. The loft was finished and there was hay in it I could use for bedding; and of course the donkey would be welcome in his shed.

So, between a layer of hay and a layer of potato bags, and barricaded against the breezes of the loft by rows of gasolene cans, I spent the night quite comfortably. But there must have been some complexes or suppressions at work, for several times during the night, I found myself announcing aloud that Mrs. Jones could take her house, and her bed, and her warm blankets, and her black looks, and go right to the devil.

Not that I really wished her any bad luck . . .

3

THE CART WHICH HAD BEEN REPAIRED LATE IN THE EVE-ning was waiting for me, but the blacksmith was nowhere to be seen. His shop was closed. His house was closed too, and the window curtains drawn. If I had been the man that Mrs. Jones thought me, it would have been easy enough to slip away through the early morning without settling the considerable bill which I would no doubt have to pay. While waiting for the blacksmith to appear, I recalled what he had done in the way of repairs.

The donkey's shoe had been heated, reshaped, and replaced. The cast metal wheel-box had been removed at considerable labor, padded, and refitted—during which process it had broken, this, however, at no fault of the blacksmith's. Another wheel-box had been furnished and refitted to the wheel, after which proceeding, both axles had been greased and the wheels replaced. The bill, I feared,—particularly for the second wheel-box—might run into a matter of pounds.

A head appeared at the blacksmith's window.

"Good morning. How much do I owe you for repairs?" I asked.

"Let me see, now. . . . Altogether, that will be . . ."

On my word of honor, he mentioned a sum of money, which, in American, comes to something less than thirty-three cents!

4

IT WAS ON THE AFTERNOON OF THIS DAY THAT WE crossed the high frontiers of the County Clare into Galway of the West—the playground and workground of John Millington Synge of *The Well of the Saints* and the Playboy and *Riders to the Sea*; of Lady Augusta Gregory of *Grania* and the Irish Folk History Plays, and *The Workhouse Ward* and *The Rising of the Moon*; of William Butler Yeats of *The Wild Swans at Coole*; of Callinan, and of the wandering Raftery; and more recently, of Liam O'Flaherty. Here too, had come George Moore, and Chesterton, and "A. E."

And of painters, such men as Walter Osborne of the early nineties, who was the first painter to be chased out of the fishermen's quarter or Claddagh in Galway by women in red petticoats; and Augustus John, who was the second; and Sir William Orpen, whose study of an Irish buckeen hangs in the Metropolitan Museum in New York City; and Jack Yeats, the brother of the poet; and Paul Henry with a painting in the Luxembourg; and Lamb and Wilcox and Keatinge.

Then as I went on, with my thoughts upon Synge and Yeats and the rest of that goodly company, Herself, who was ambling along beside me, suddenly gave a snort of astonishment and stopped in her tracks. We had passed many a locomotive and motor car and rock breaker and fiery steam roller, but this was the first time on the journey that Herself had shown the slightest sign of surprise. I followed her gaze with considerable interest to the side of the road. There stood—a cow with her leg in a splint. And there stood Herself, staring out from between her blinkers like an ancient village gossip peering through her spectacles.

"Ocht, the poor thing!" I could almost hear her say, "she'll *niver* look the same after that! Be me faith, won't all the neighbors be listenin' now, whin I tell thim about it!"

"Oh, get up!" I said. Whereupon she turned on me an outraged eye, squealed a small squeal, lifted her hind legs three inches off the ground, and stalked off up the road.

"If that is the way you are at the age of three," I thought, "Heaven help the one you are traveling with when you come into your full wickedness!"

Then as we went up into the fresh wind of the highlands beyond Kilclaran, along came a little boy with his hair in a black bang over his eyes and a bag of books over his shoulder. We talked together about such important matters as school and hurling, and he gave me a page out of his copybook to read which told about taking care of burns. "Apply strips of lent soked in anny kind of oil (carron oil is bes) to the burned surface." I asked him if he could use a penny, that is, if he were very sure he could use a penny, because I wouldn't like to give one to him unless he felt sure he could use it.

"Aye," he said, "aye," and walked away gazing into his hand with a look as though he had met King Midas himself coming down the road.

Now the country, which had been a waste of small gray bowlders, ran down hill and turned into woodland. And from a wooded park beside the road, one could hear the sound of axes against trees, which in our age is usually a sad sound; and on the road were dozens of donkey carts and horse carts and a stream of little boys carrying off green, trailing branches considerably larger than themselves. And here, a short way beyond the wooded park, was the village of Gort.

A valuable and entertaining book might be written about the personality of Irish villages—a volume, which as far as I know, has not yet been written. Why, for example, is one village physically neat and mentally active while another in similar surroundings is untidy and stupid? Why are villages sullen or merry or brutal or benevolent? What is it that makes this village tolerant of a man's donkey cart because of his face, while that village is intolerant of his face because of his donkey cart?

Gort is a friendly village. Immediately I came down its main street, I was aware of a kindliness, which, in spite of certain kindly souls in Feakle, had not been in the air. Here was a pleasant hotel with a paddock where a donkey might roll on her back. Here was a proprietor so affable that he led her to the paddock himself. And here was his daughter, Mollie Glynn, not long home from school; and an introduction, then her small, powerful motor car, and my host inquiring if I would like to go for a ride.

When we were perhaps a mile out of the village, Mollie Glynn asked, "Would you like to see Lady Gregory's house at Coole Park? It is only a mile or two away. Perhaps she is home herself. We shall see."

5

SHE CAME ACROSS THE GREAT STUDY TO MEET US— small, white-haired, vivacious—with simple, charming dignity. She wore a black dress and there was a veil about her hair. Mollie Glynn presented me.

"It was good of you to come, Moira. How is your mother? . . . I'm glad of that. . . . And you are writing a book about Ireland, Mr. Speakman? That is a very large subject. What line are you following in it?"

I told Lady Gregory where my interest lay.

"And is Ireland as you expected it to be?"

"It is more than I expected it to be. I half expected to find that the qualities which we have been taught to look upon from childhood as Irish, were gone."

"Ireland has had her troubles," she said. And though she did not speak sadly nor wish us to know of what she was thinking, I knew that she was remembering, as every mother must, beyond other memories, the death of her son, who had died in the Great War.

Then Mollie Glynn, also seeing that there were other things to be talked about, spoke of the people who that afternoon had been taking away wood which the woodcutters had cut on Lord M's demesne. The taking had been entirely unauthorized. The Civic Guard had arrested twenty of them and there would be fines to pay.

"How sad it is too," Lady Gregory said, "to see all the wood disappearing. When I came through town on Friday I saw a number of carts filled with logs. Formerly it was peat they used. Even the trees here at Coole Park are being cut, but that is on property which has been sold, so one can't complain."

I remarked upon the splendid trees which surrounded the house.

"Yes, Coole has been well spoken of at different times. Yeats, you know, has written many of his poems here. He called one of his books *The*

Wild Swans at Coole. 'A. E.' and Synge liked it here too, and George Moore."

It surprised me that she should speak so pleasantly of George Moore, who had made criticisms of her work which, from across the Atlantic, had seemed to be the not altogether fair-minded criticism of one who in this particular case would put beauty of expression through a stiff course of literary philology.*

"Oh, I forgive him lots," she said lightly, "for the nice things he said about Coole."

"And was it here at Coole that you met Synge?"

"No, I met him many years ago on the Aran Islands. I saw a man in civilian clothes out there with a guide, wandering about. I was a little annoyed at that, for I thought I had found the islands from a literary point of view myself, and he looked as though he were thinking about the sort of thing that I was thinking about. . . . Here is one of his books."

From a wide, double-partitioned bookcase, she took down a first edition of *The Playboy of the Western World* with its inscription in the crabbed hand of the great dramatist. "And here is a book by one of your own countrymen," she said, reaching for another volume.

"To Lady Gregory," I read, "whose inspirational work has helped raise the ideals of her country . . ." or at least, it was something like that, for my eye had jumped to the signature: "from her friend, Theodore Roosevelt."

Now that we had risen we might look around the spacious study with its great Empire desk, its many memoirs of literary friendships, its portraits and sketches by Sargent and Jack Yeats and by Lady Gregory's son, who had been a painter.

Here on the opposite wall was a portrait of her grandson by Augustus John. "Is it a good likeness?"

"Well, his eyebrows aren't pulled up that way, and his ears don't stick out—but it has his character. When I sit at my desk I can almost imagine that he is in the room. I wish he were. He'd love to see your donkey. Have you had the same animal all the way from Cork?"

"I have; and I'm hoping to have her for the whole trip, although there were some in Cork who said it was not possible."

"And what do you call her?"

---

*Mr. Moore's chief criticism of Lady Gregory's work seems to rest in the point that in his opinion, the dialect of many of her plays is not the spoken dialect, ancient or modern. One prefers Mr. Gilbert Seldes, who says that it is perfectly possible to write dialect without imitation of sound, and to do it effectively and honestly.

"I call her 'Herself'—but that isn't very satisfactory. Would you suggest a name?"

Lady Gregory smiled. "What is she like?"

"Well, she's an ordinary, gray Irish donkey, very wise, but not as young, I think, as the tinker I bought her from told me. She has considerable character of her own, and a bit of pepper in her disposition, but she has never lain down in harness or refused on any occasion to go ahead."

"What would you think of Grania? Would that be too romantic? Grania 'walked all Ireland' with Diarmuid in the old Irish legend; and your Grania's name may live in story as the other's has."

Thus my companion of the road—probably at that moment enjoying her customary baptism of mud in the paddock—received the benediction of a mighty name.

But here was another room, a room lined from floor to ceiling with books—among them a magnificent ancient black-letter Froissart, a Clarenden's *History of Revolution* from 1702, and the prison Bible of an old Irish patriot whose name I have forgotten. As we looked at the classics which had belonged to her husband and at the art books which had belonged to her son, we talked about all manner of things from the objectivity of Greek art to the subjectivity of the Abbey Theatre in Dublin where most of her plays were first produced. And now, as we were about to take our leave, she returned from the table where she had been writing for a moment, with one of her own books in her hand, saying, "I wouldn't like you to go away without having something to remember Coole by." And in the book was written:

If I reproduce this inscription, please believe that it is not one of those ridiculous attempts to gain reflected merit through association, but only to complete the picture of a gracious Irish lady. And if other pages of this book bear the imprint and the impression of other people who may be celebrated for a few hundred years more or less, it is not because I have forgotten even for a minute the man who works with a spade along the side of the road.

It is he—not the rest of us—who will extend unchanging beyond all our little horizons to the far edge of such an eternity as the world shall have. And when that eternity flickers out into the vastness of a richer, more widely-dimensioned space, it is he who will be there, leaning on his spade or its equivalent, and giving some queer comment of humor or philosophy or sorrow which will make that passing a finer and dearer and more human thing than it otherwise could possibly have been.

And there is no one who understands this better than Lady Augusta Gregory.

MR. YEATS AND OTHERS

1

AT THE DUBLIN STATION, A MAN WAS WAITING FOR me—a producer of plays whom I had met at "A. E.'s."

"Do you know 'Mac' who makes caricatures for the Dublin papers?" he asked.

"No, but I've seen and like his work."

"*Her* work," corrected the producer. "He's a woman. I've been ordered to deliver you, dead or alive, to Lower Baggot Street to have your picture made."

So, nothing interfering, we took a tram to Lower Baggot Street, and came into a house and into a studio, the walls of which were hidden by pen portraits of the famous and infamous, drawn naïvely with sudden lines and an intuitive knowledge of character which approached genius. Then "Mac" came in, a tall woman with dark, keenly-observant eyes who carried about her, even in moments of great seriousness, the capacity for laughter. And (though this does not happen frequently) it was only a few moments later that we found ourselves standing alone—in spite of the presence of the show man—at the beginning of a friendship which was to last beyond the farthest shores of Ireland.

As we prepared to go to the Arts Club for luncheon, I saw upon the walls of the studio the drawing called *Chin Angles*.

"Do you like it?" asked the lady, knowing perfectly well that I liked it, and enjoying my mirth.

"*Like* it! It's one of the best things of the kind I've ever set eyes on! I've met 'A. E.,' but have only seen William Butler Yeats distantly in a top hat at the Tailteann Games. I'll have to take your word about his looking like that."

"No you won't."

"Why not?"

"Because he and Mrs. Yeats are coming with us to luncheon at the Arts Club."

2

"WHICH," INQUIRED MR. YEATS ADDRESSING THE CEIL-ing, "is the gentleman who is traveling with a donkey?"

But no answer came from on high; so "Mac," after an appropriate moment of waiting, designated the individual in question. "Ah," said Mr. Yeats. Another moment of waiting followed, temporally no longer than the other, but psychologically quite long enough. "Let us go in," said "Mac" brightly.

At first there was talk of the Tailteann Games, their scope and their success. The producer told of one of the contestants, a young chap who had reduced his pole vaulting to a mathematical formula. He vaulted by the numbers. It was astonishing and interesting. We were interested and astonished. Some one else spoke about the distinguished visitors at the Games, or perhaps about the absence of some of them. Mr. Yeats remarked that he had written the invitations but that many had never been answered. D'Annunzio, for one, had not answered his. It was likely, of course, that D'Annunzio received hundreds of letters a day.

"And probably the recent temple services in his villa garden keep him busy."

"Incidentally, that is very good press agent material," said the producer.

"The papers say that he never opens his mail anyway," remarked some one else.

Mr. Yeats smiled understandingly. "I have reached a point where I do not answer letters either," he said. "It becomes more and more difficult to find time in which to work. When I went down to London recently to write, Mrs. Yeats opened all my letters here, and sent on only three important ones. Three."

"But a hundred unanswered letters would prey on my mind," said "Mac." "They would do things to the subconscious."

Yes, perhaps so. That was a great subject, the subconscious.

"Our subconscious mind will eventually be proved to be of a mathematically precise nature. It is possible for the subconscious mind to do that, which, to the conscious mind would be an impossibility. For example, the hand under its influence can draw freehand, a mathematically exact circle duplicating another circle. But if you were to force it, it would lose its authority. If you were *asked* to draw the circle you couldn't do it." Often the subconscious had the power of prophecy about it, too. A man in London had been telling Mr. Yeats about his financial troubles. Quite offhand the poet had replied, "Don't worry about it. Some one will come from America in six weeks and make it all right." And that was exactly what took place. Some one *had* come from America and made things all right!

A phenomenon like that was either explained by memory or by preview. A man going into the Underground in London, presumably for the first time, might feel that he had been there before. He might really have been there before and have forgotten, or he might have come there in a dream . . .

"But which side do you take, Mr. Speakman, in the recent trouble in China?"

(O good Lord, Mr. Yeats, which side do *I* take? That's so, I *did* write a book about China once. Wu Pei-fu, Tao Kun, Sun Yat-sen . . . Just hold off a moment and let me see which side I do take.)

Fortunately we turned quite quickly to the matter of opium. He was rather curious as to the effect of opium, and I explained my own reactions to it. He had never smoked opium, he said, but had tried mescal and hasheesh. With hasheesh, after he had looked into the shadow of a curtain, he could see colors *taking form* there. He had wondered how colors could take form, but on analysis, he found that they really had form. When he pressed his finger tips together getting physical sensation, the color would change.

So, with anecdotes and problems and speculations on the occult, the luncheon continued pleasantly to the coffee and Benedictine. Now Mr. Yeats must get back to his work. Today had been an exception. He almost never went anywhere to luncheon. We said good-by to him, and to the charming lady who is Mrs. Yeats. We returned to the studio. It was then, of course, that a second luncheon began.

3

FOR THE SAKE OF SANCTUARY, WE WILL DESIGNATE THE speakers as Voices. Thus the second repast also becomes occult.

Voices:

"Do you think he enjoyed his lunch?"

"I certainly do."

"I wonder whether he and Mrs. Yeats heard me when we came into the club."

"Why, what did you say?"

"We were late, you know, but they weren't in sight so I said, 'Not here yet, *thank goodness*.' Then I lifted the curtain—and there they were just inside!"

"Tell me, why his manner? What is the reason for such terrific pose?"

"It isn't pose, it's the man."

"He believes in pose. He tells young poets to acquire pose."

"Was he bored, or what?"

"No, he is different if he is bored. Besides, I can tell by Mrs. Yeats whether he is bored or not."

"I'd hate to have him for an enemy!"

"I don't agree with you at all. I think it would be an asset to have him for an enemy. When a man of his strength shows enmity, it immediately draws sympathy for the other side."

"I am sensitive to that man."

"So am I, and I admit it."

"That is more than I am. I absolutely refuse to be awed by people."

"I can't talk naturally before him. Never could. Don't know why at all. Can't tell you . . ."

"What remains in my mind is the beauty of his English—the English of a great poet and a true intellectual modified to fit the intellectual requirements of his listeners."

"Thanks!"

"Thanks!"

"Never mind, I am including myself too!"

"His eyes are strange, aren't they?"

"Yes; but I'm a coward. I always draw him with glasses. One ought to do his eyes only one way—like this:

⊗ ⊗

"Speaking technically, there is a flat plane above the bridge of his nose near his forehead. Only the right lens of his glasses is bifocal and—"

"Enough, enough, lay off MacDuff!"

"He is very susceptible to his audience, isn't he?"

"Right-o! 'I am Sir Oracle; when I speak, let no dog bark.'"

"By the way, H. S.—when you sit by a distinguished guest, *don't* put up your elbow on the table for protection between!"

"It wasn't for protection. I was trying to make a lever of my arm to get as near as possible, for he spoke in a rather low voice."

"It looked to me like protection."

"On my word of honor, it was not!"

"He doesn't say good-by when he leaves, does he?"

"No. Just as in a play, you never say, 'He went out.' It is simply, 'Exit, William Butler Yeats.'"

"He makes a jolly good exit too."

"That exit today could have very well been the end of a play."

"It was. A very pleasant comedy."

H. V. MORTON

Galway, Claddagh, Connemara, and climbing Croagh Patrick: 1929

"THAT TOWN IS HALF IN THE WORLD AND HALF OUT OF IT. IT IS A FRONTIER POST, AND THE WINDS FROM THE END OF THE WORLD BLOW INTO IT DAY AND NIGHT."

The English travel writer H. V. Morton wrote fifty or so books, published between the 1920s and the 1960s and often reprinted, that made him, very likely, the most widely read travel writer of the twentieth century. While many other writers of travel books have certainly attained greater literary celebrity, it was through Morton's eyes and sensibility that countless readers learned to see the world. He wrote extensively about the different countries of the British Isles; about the nations of Europe, where he was especially interested in Italy and Spain; and about the Holy Land and the Near East. His books, often titled In Search of . . . , A Traveller in . . . , *or* A Stranger in . . . , *were much praised in their time. Reviewing one of them in the* New York Times, *Orville Prescott called Morton "English, urbane, immensely cultivated, a man with a lively curiosity and an indefatigable interest in people, places and the historical past." That is certainly true. For his 1936* In the Steps of St. Paul, *Morton used as his guidebook* The Acts of the Apostles.

A selection from Morton's In Search of South Africa *appears in* The Reader's Companion to South Africa.

The selection that follows is from In Search of Ireland, *published in 1930. Morton's 1929 visit, his first, came only seven years after "the Treaty of 1922 . . . gave to the Irish Free State . . . the same constitutional status in the British Empire as the Dominions of Canada and New Zealand, the Commonwealth of Australia and the Union of South Africa," ending centuries of* discord that Morton frankly calls "the most unhappy and regrettable chapter in the history of Great Britain." The Irish constitution of 1937 and the 1949 birth of the Republic of Ireland were still to come. And still to come, too, seventy years after Morton's visit, are the "friendship and sympathy between two . . . warm-hearted and kindly people" that he wished for.

In another selection in this Reader's Companion, David W. McFadden follows in Morton's footsteps through the west of Ireland.

Of Morton and his book, McFadden writes, "We had In Search of Ireland in our house when I was a kid and I read it several times. Morton was a nice man, people responded well to him, and, if they hadn't, he wouldn't have noticed. He was a well-wisher, an optimist, a Pollyanna, a rank sentimentalist, a gladhander, a promoter of peace and goodwill, a schmoozer, and he always seemed to be on the lookout for a free meal. He was funnier than he realized. He was a certifiable Everyman."

I CAME OVER THE MOUNTAINS OF CLARE INTO THE grey town of Galway as men were lighting lamps in the harbour. An unearthly afterglow lingered in the sky, a dull red haze hung over the hills like the dust flung from chariot wheels, and the edges of the Atlantic were washed in a colour so strange and so vivid, almost a pale green, that melted marvellously into the blue of the dusk. And as the light was drawn out of the sky a few stars hung over the grape-blue heights of Connemara.

Such a velvet softness pervaded Galway, and in those first moments I felt, as one feels sometimes on meeting a stranger, that a new loyalty had come into life. Galway did not seem to belong to any part of Ireland that I have seen; it seemed to belong only to itself.

I know now that the strange beauty that flies like dust through Galway is the spirit of Gaelic Ireland, something that is a defiance to time, something that is like a declaration of faith. Galway must be almost too beautiful to an Irishman. He must feel about it as an Englishman would feel if, in an England conquered for centuries, and speaking a foreign tongue, he came one night to a little town in Somerset and heard men talking English.

When the hotel porter was unloading my luggage he drove away a determined old woman shrouded in a black shawl who was trying to tell me something. I went after her and asked her what she wanted. Her husband was out of work and her sons were out of work. She was a gentle old creature, and when I placed a shilling in her hand she said:

"May the Virgin bless you and bring you safe home."

I encountered her twice during my first walk round Galway, and each time she repeated her blessing with a gratitude out of all proportion to the miserable gift, so that I felt that my first steps in the West were taken in sanctity. . . .

I went through many a narrow street, past a ruined Spanish house, for Galway reflects Spain in the eyes of its people, and, here and there, in a square house with a central courtyard and a gate flush with the street. The drapers' shops of Galway introduce you to the gorgeous colour of the West. Outside are stacked piles of scarlet flannel, which the fisher-women—though the fashion is dying—make into wide brilliant skirts.

But what a town of yesterday! The curse of Cromwell lies heavier on Galway than on any other Irish town. It is a town of dead factories and great houses brought to decay. In the Middle Ages Galway was the Bristol of Ireland. Its very name has the ring of a great city in it—London, York, Bristol, Dublin, Galway; there is something high and authoritative about such names.

The fourteen Anglo-Norman families of Galway, who gained for their town the title of "Galway of the Tribes," were the most exclusive families in Ireland. I believe that they intermarried for so long that special dispensation had more than once to be obtained to establish canonical legality. They founded the fortunes of the town. The quays were stacked with the wine casks of Spain. The galleons of Galway were as accustomed to the ports of Spain as they were to Irish waters. During the Civil War, Galway remained loyal to Charles, but Cromwell had his way with it in the end, and Galway has never recovered.

Its inhabitants a hundred years ago numbered 40,000; to-day the population of this once mighty seaport is reduced to that of a small English country town. Only 14,000 people live here among the ruins of past endeavour.

I met an Irishman in the hotel who told me this story: "During the war a German submarine appeared in the bay and the captain gave orders to bombard Galway. A young officer who was making a reconnaissance sent down the message: 'Galway *has* been bombarded, sir.'"

My friend thought this was a screamingly funny story; but I could not laugh at it.

I was lucky enough to meet a little pink-faced, middle-aged Irishman known to every one as Michael John. If you have ever fished in Galway you will know him well!

We went round the town together, to the Church of St. Nicholas, patron saint of children, sailors (and thieves!), where a bell hangs taken (no one knows how or why) from an abbey in France; we went to gaze at an old Spanish house in which the term "lynching" and "lynch law" originated; and Michael John told me the grim story.

In 1493 John Lynch FitzStephen, Mayor of Galway, went over to Spain to improve trade relations between that country and Galway. He was entertained by a rich merchant named Gomez, whose son, a handsome young Spaniard, returned to Ireland as his guest. Lynch had a son named Walter, and the two young men became friends. Walter Lynch was in love with a girl named Agnes, whose father, a merchant of Galway, spoke Spanish perfectly, and was delighted to welcome the young Spaniard to his house. Walter Lynch became madly jealous, and one day, in the height of his passion, he stabbed the Spaniard and threw his body in the sea.

Walter Lynch was arrested and confessed his guilt. His father, as mayor, pronounced the death sentence. But no man in Galway would execute the boy! The mob attempted a rescue, but before this could be made, and in sight of the crowd, Lynch hanged his own son.

"I suppose he felt he had to do it," said Michael John, "for the honour of Galway. His son had not only committed murder, he had violated the laws of hospitality. After the hanging Lynch went to his home, and was never seen again by living man. . . ."

It is by the strangest perversion of meaning that "lynch law" means to-day the vengeance by a mob on a criminal.

We went to the salmon weir on Galway River, which Michael John knows as a man knows his own land.

"A little later in the year," he said, "this is the most surprising sight in Ireland. You can look down from the bridge and see great salmon, thirty-and forty-pounders, packed as tight as sardines in a tin! You wouldn't believe it unless you saw it! Back to back they are, waiting like a great crowd at a ticket office to get up to the lakes from the sea. . . ."

This narrow river is the only entrance from the sea to 1,200 miles of lakes.

I suppose the river by Galway Weir is the angler's paradise. They tell a story of a fisherman who died from excitement here, but they do not end the story with the funniest part of it. The local paper after reporting the event said: "Our readers will be glad to learn that the rod which Mr. ——

dropped was immediately taken up by our esteemed townsman, Mr. ——,
who found the fish still on, and after ten minutes' play succeeded in landing
it—a fine, clean-run salmon of fifteen pounds."

That, I am sure, is the perfect epitaph!

We went over the dangerous wooden weir above the rushing water,
and were just in time to see a man with a boathook murder an amazing
salmon which turned the scale at forty-two pounds! He was as big as a
shark and thick. Two nets are out for salmon, but a clear passage must be
left by law. A fish gets caught by sheer bad luck or natural foolishness.
Every week-end the nets are lifted, also by law, so that a sensible salmon
should come up from the sea on a Sunday.

"What do you do with salmon?" I said to the man who was weighing
the monster.

"London," he replied briefly.

&

THE CLADDAGH AT GALWAY IS ONE OF THE MOST
remarkable sights in Europe. I find it almost inconceivable to realize that
a man can breakfast in London and lunch the next day within sight of this
Gaelic village.

Nothing is more picturesque in the British Isles than this astonishing
fishing village of neat, whitewashed, thatched cottages planted at haphazard
angles with no regular roads running to them. If you took three hundred
little toy cottages and jumbled them up on a nursery floor you would have
something like the Claddagh. It is a triumph of unconscious beauty. The
houses have been planted at all kinds of odd angles, one man's back door
opening on to the front door of his neighbour.

"How on earth did this happen?"

"When Galway was the City of the Tribes," said Michael John, "the
native Irish had to live outside the walls. They formed this little town. They
were as proud as the Tribes."

Outside every Anglo-Norman town there grew up one of these "Irish
towns." The Claddagh is the only one that survives. Michael John can
remember the last "king" of the Claddagh; for this community has for
centuries observed an unwritten law, administered, until recently, by a
chief, a fisherman like the rest, whose verdicts were never questioned.

When the Halls wrote their book on Ireland nearly a century ago the
king was still a power in the Claddagh:

"This singular community are still governed by a king, elected annually, and a number of by-laws of their own; at one time this king was absolute—as powerful as a veritable despot; but his power yielded, like all despotic powers, to the times, and now he is, as one of his subjects informed us, 'nothing more than the Lord Mayor of Dublin or any other city.' He has still, however, much influence, and sacrifices himself, literally without fee or reward, for 'the good of the people'; he is constantly occupied hearing and deciding causes and quarrels, for his people never by any chance appeal to a higher tribunal. Even when a Galway person offends, who is not a Claddagh man, he is punished by their law; for instance, a gentleman complained of the price of a cod he had bought from one of the singular community; it was in his estimation too dear by 'a tester,' and he refused to pay at all; he told the fisherman to summon him, which would have been contrary to Claddagh law, and so was not done; he thought he had conquered. Requiring some fish for a dinner-party a day or two after, he went to order some of another fisherman in a different part of the Claddagh. 'No, sir,' was the reply. 'I can't serve you until you have paid So-and-So for the cod.' 'And what is that to you?' was the inquiry. 'I will pay *you*.' 'Not until you have paid him. We Claddagh men stand by each other.' "

The Halls then go on to describe a visit paid by them to the king's cabin:

"His majesty, however, was at sea; but we were introduced to his royal family—a group of children and grandchildren who for ruddy health might have been coveted by any monarch in Christendom."

Mr. Stephen Gwynn has some interesting things to say about the Claddagh folk in A Holiday in Connemara, now out of print, which was published in 1909. He was once a Parliamentary candidate in this district:

"My own opinion is," he writes, "that we have here the descendants not of Spain but of that older Irish race who built the great dun of Aran— the Firbolgs, 'men of the leathern wallet,' whom the taller, stronger Milesian breed drove back into the outlying mountains and islands. When one sees fair hair in this community it is such as one finds—in the south. . . .

"Election times show up curiously the separateness of this community. The borough area of Galway comprises two outlying parishes, with a crowded population of small labouring farmers—Irish speakers to a man. These people come in cheerfully to support the Nationalist party with voice and vote (and not with voice and vote only) because they are part of Ireland and the issues which interest Ireland generally interest them also. But to the Claddagh man you can only talk about the Claddagh; Ireland has no appeal to him. The land question does not touch him, for he has no land; the revival of fisheries along the coast has done him no good, for he was catching fish before, and had his own sufficient market. . . .

"Of one thing I am convinced—that to argue with the Claddagh you must speak in Irish. I went down there to make acquaintance with the men at a time when I was not looking for votes, and was directed to get into talk with an oldish fisherman who stood apart from the rather voluble group surrounding me. He would not answer a word until I tried him in Irish, and then he discoursed freely and fairly. We fell into talk of technical matters relating to boats, and soon I was out of my depth, and told him so; whereupon he continued in excellent English. When he had finished, 'Why would you not speak English to me at first?' I asked. 'Ah,' he said, relapsing into Irish, 'if we talked English you would be a wiser man than I; in Irish it is not that way the story is.'"

Mr. Gwynn goes on to give a fascinating glimpse of the Claddagh. I would give anything to have been with him at this time:

"A few days later," he writes, "I had to go through the whole village, house by house, and it was odd enough at three or four in the afternoon to find strong young men rising up between the blankets in a corner of the dark little house. That, of course, is natural in any fishing community, whose work is mostly done by night. But a thing struck me which I have never seen elsewhere in Ireland, where generally men have a prejudice against handling babies or doing anything else that is taken to be women's work. But here, in at least a dozen houses, I found the women bustling about while the man stood or sat with an infant on his arm—and holding it as a woman does, the arm making the same soft line where it supported the infant as a hammock holds a sleeper. It was curious to see, and very pretty—natural enough, too, when one considered; for the women must be out most of the day hawking their fish at the street corners. Yet more than anything it stamped on my mind that feeling of distinctness and aloofness in the Claddagh and its people. I have never found any other community in Ireland so alien, so shy, and so hard to know."

I walked through the Claddagh late one afternoon. The fishers were out, for I saw only very old men standing at the corners smoking their pipes. There was one who might have stepped from a Spanish galleon. There was nothing of the Firbolg about him; he was pure Spanish: tall, thin, sallow, long-headed, with fierce dark eyes, a pointed beard, and in either ear a thin gold ring.

It is a pity that the Claddagh has attracted the attention of sanitary authorities. Many of the lovely white houses have been pulled down and in their place have come the most hideous little modern houses I have seen—worse and more hateful to the eye even than the atrocious bungalows of Sussex.

I saw a sight typical of the modern Claddagh. From a primitive thatched house came a smart young girl in a fashionable felt hat, blue tailor-made costume, and flesh-coloured silk stockings. Her mother accompanied her to the door. The older woman belonged to a different generation—almost, so it seemed, to a different world. She wore the wide red skirt of a fisherwoman; her feet were bare, and with one hand she held a grey shawl over her shoulders.

"That's it, you see," said Michael John. "The girls change from their working clothes and put on their finery to go out at night. Some of the smartest girls you'll see in Galway go home to a Claddagh cabin. . . ."

There came towards us a girl who walked like a queen—in men's boots! She bore on her head a big round wickerwork basket in which the Galway women sell fish. She was a beauty of the dark kind. She was going home to put on stockings, high-heeled shoes, and a tight little black felt hat! It was, I felt, somehow unfortunate that after resisting the world for so long the Claddagh should have capitulated to Mr. Selfridge.

"In the old days the Claddagh never married outside itself," said Michael John. "But now that's over. A Claddagh girl will marry a Galway boy."

&

AT NIGHT THE CLADDAGH IS MOST BEAUTIFUL. There are no street lamps. You find your way through the maze of houses by the light that falls through windows and open doors. The path of earth has been beaten hard by the feet of generations going back to the Norman conquest of Ireland. The limewashed houses with the peat reek coming from their chimneys shine in the half light. The children who in daylight play on the squares of beaten earth and before the cabin doors have been put to bed. It is quiet and watchful and full of the chirping of crickets. Figures of men stand in little groups in the dusk talking in the Gaelic. Sometimes they pause and cry out softly:

"Goot night."

Lights shine in the small windows. Through open doors you see little rooms with low ceilings. They are warm, clean, and comfortable; but so small. You wonder how certain of these long-limbed Gaels can live in them and move about. It seems strange that the Gael, who hates the feeling of walls, has not developed a more roomy domestic architecture. It is odd, here and also in the Highlands of Scotland, to see giants with their heads bent in case they might hit the ceiling. Perhaps the Gael has never bothered to build himself real rooms, because he would be just as miserable within big walls as small ones.

Beyond every little open door you see, sharp as an interior by Peter de Hooch, a woman bent above some task, sometimes with the fine colour of scarlet on her; now and again an infant cries and a woman's tender voice soothes it, singing an Irish lullaby like little waves falling on a shore; and in these rooms, warm with the peat fires and loud with crickets piping in the ashes, a red light is burning before the Sacred Heart.

☿

THE PARAPET OF GALWAY BRIDGE IS WORN SMOOTH as glass by the arms of those who lean over it when the salmon come up from salt water. This is one of the sights of Ireland.

At first when I looked down into Galway River I could see nothing. Then something which I took to be weed moved strangely; and I realized that I was looking down on the backs of hundreds of salmon. I have never seen anything like this great crowd of fresh-run fish with the sea-lice still on them lying still, fanning themselves with their noses towards the sweet lakes. Could I have dropped a brick into the river I must have hit at least ten eighteen-pounders; for they lay side by side, apparently touching, edged together in one incredible queue.

Now and then some monster would seem to become impatient, and he would, with a muscular movement, urge himself forward; but so tight were his companions pressed about him that he would make no progress and be forced to fall back into his place.

There were three earnest salmon fishermen on the bank below me. I watched them casting for at least an hour and—not a rise did they get! One man constantly hit the water immediately above at least thirty mighty fish, but not one of them took the slightest interest in the fly!

Yet men must catch fish in this place or they would not pay two pounds a day for it, and on the condition that they keep only one in three.

Stephen Gwynn, a great fisherman, has said that one man killed a ton of salmon in about three months' fishing. So thick are the salmon in

Galway River that I find it difficult to understand how it is that if you do not hook a fish in the orthodox manner you do not hook him in a fin or in his tail!

In the early morning you will lean over the bridge and see that the salmon have moved up in the night. There are only two or perhaps three left. One morning I saw for the first time that fish which killed an English king—the lamprey. He was a curious fellow, half fish and half eel, lying low down against the stones of the river-bed and swaying with the stream.

I KNOW NOW WHERE THE WORLD ENDS. It is a grey land, and the gold clouds ride up over the edge of it, shouldering one another, slow as a herd of steers. The land is as grey and speckled as a piece of homespun tweed. It is grey with hundreds and thousands of little stone walls. They run up to the edge of the sky, and they fall into dips and hollows, criss-crossing like the lines of your hand. These grey walls guard the smallest "fields" in the world. They are not real fields: they are just bits of rocks sprinkled with soil. Some of them are no larger than a dining-table, some of them are oblong, some square, some almost circular, some triangular; and to every one is its own little breast-high wall, so that the land, silver-grey wherever you look, is, as I say, just like a big piece of the tweed that they weave in the hills.

The white road twists like a snake between the grey walls, and over it walk strong, barelegged girls, wearing scarlet skirts and Titian-blue aprons. They swing from the hips as they walk with the grace of those who have never known shoe leather, and they carry on their backs great loads of brown seaweed in wicker baskets. Or they ride, sitting sideways with their bare legs to the road, above the tails of placid donkeys, over whose backs are slung baskets piled with peat.

If you speak to them they shake their tangled heads, and say something, which sounds pretty, in Irish. They are shy as fawns with a stranger; but when you have gone on they burst into peals of laughter.. . . .

Behind the grey land, moving round in a solemn dance as you go over the twisting road, are blue hills—hills blue as the sea at Capri—with the biggest and the most golden clouds on earth like haloes over their heads. Among the blue hills and the grey fields, and beside the blue waters of little roughs and on the edges of sudden peat bogs, stand small cabins, incredibly poor and marvellously white, with hens round the door pecking round fat black pots.

And the sound of this land is the click of a donkey's hoofs on the road and the ring of a spade like a crowbar which men drive into the rocky soil. When the sun goes out this place is as grey as a ghost.

Connemara . . .

How can it exist in the modern world! In years of travel I have seen nothing like it. It begins suddenly as soon as you leave Galway due west by the coast road through Spiddal to Clifden. It is a part of the earth in which Progress—whatever we mean by it—has broken in vain against grey walls; it has been arrested by high hills and deep lakes to the east and by the sea on the west. These people have been locked away for centuries by geography and poverty. I have been into the tomb of Tutankhamen in Egypt, but entering Connemara gave me a finer feeling of discovery and a greater sense of remoteness from modern life!

They are so poor that no one has ever tried to exploit them; their land is so poor that no one has ever tried to steal it. There are no railways, no shops, no motor-cars, no telegraph poles. There are three things only: the Catholic Faith, Nature, and work.

Connemara could not be more astonishing than the discovery in England of a forgotten country in which men spoke the language of Bede or Alfred the Great, wore Saxon clothes, and prayed to Saxon saints. Connemara is the most surprising thing in the British Isles. It is nearer to St. Patrick than it is to Dublin.

As I went on in a kind of stunned astonishment I realized that I was an impertinence. Connemara is not used to motor-cars! Cows lowered their heads before me, backed away with glazed eyes and distended nostrils, exposed a flank to an imaginary death, and retreated up the road with every sign of terror. Dogs ran barking furiously after me. Girls riding donkeys leapt off with a flash of bare legs and a flurry of scarlet skirts and held the noses of their steeds away from me; long-haired sheep fought madly together for the gap in the stone wall; geese lengthened their necks towards me like serpents and made vague oathful noises as I went by; hens, who all the world over are an excitable, suicidal people, flung themselves into an ecstasy of panic and performed mysteries of self-preservation beneath my careful wheels.

In fact, the whole Gaelic countryside said, in a variety of mooings, bleatings, brayings, gabblings, yelpings, and cluckings: "Look out! Here is something quite horrible and deadly from the outside world!"

Near the coast I saw, drawn up outside cabins or leaning against grey walls, the queer canoes, called curraghs, in which the fishermen of Connemara dare the perils of the ocean; and dare must be the right and only word! They are light as feathers, and made of skins or canvas stretched over a wooden frame. They are exactly the same as the coracles used by the Ancient Britons in the time of Caesar.

I stopped before one cabin and asked if I might examine the curragh drawn up near their manure heap. A young girl and an old woman were inside, both wearing those beautiful scarlet skirts, the girl washing potatoes and the woman tending a black pot which hung above a turf fire burning in an open hearth. The cabin was bare except for a chair and table and a wooden bench standing on the hard earth floor. On the wall hung two bright pictures of the Holy Family.

"Can I look at your boat?" I asked with a broad grin. There is no country in which a broad grin is more useful!

"You can," said the girl.

The old woman, who was deaf, asked the girl in Irish what I wanted; she replied in Irish, then the old woman smiled and nodded.

While I was examining the flimsy boat a sturdy young man lounged over to me. There was nothing of a peasant's boorishness about him. He smiled, said the boat was not much good now because it was old. He employed it to get seaweed to manure the potato patch. From the pocket of his homespun sleeved waistcoat peeped a copy of a New York morning paper! Somehow that brought me to earth! It was rather like meeting Brian Boru with a cigar in his mouth!

His three brothers, he said, were in America! He would like to go too, but he was the eldest son and had to look after the "land." I looked towards the "land," and my heart sank for this firstborn. New York must be a great place, he said. It was, I felt, nearer to him than Galway.

A few miles farther on I saw a man making a "field"! The mystery of the stone walls was solved! They are not so much a sign of ownership as a necessary preliminary to a "field." The whole of Connemara in ancient times must have been subjected to a fall of stones the size of a man's head. A "field" is made by gathering up these stones and making a wall of them round the rock from which they have been removed! (Do any people on earth scratch a living from more villainous soil?)

While I watched him a big, dark girl sprang over a stone wall and walked over the sharp rocks in her bare feet with a basket of earth on her back. This she poured on the cleared rock, laughed a moment with the man, and, taking up her basket, leapt over the wall again like a deer.

I went on down the road. Grey walls; white cabins; little chapels, so small, many of them, that when the people tramp in for miles on Sunday morning the priests celebrate Mass in the open. But always grey walls and little poor fields spread with sea-weed. I saw a lovely thing on a hill. Children poured out of a small corrugated iron school. The hill rang with laughter. They danced round in a circle, their little bare legs flashing in the sunlight, and in the centre of them, wind-blown, tall, slim, was a young girl, the teacher.

So I came at length to a kind of hotel; and in it was a fisherman from the city. He knew Connemara.

"Happy?" he said. "I wish I was as happy as these people. They are, of course, always discontented, their land is bad, they are poor, the young people have their minds on America—the real capital of Connemara is New York—but they do not know real unhappiness! They are outside the world!"

"How do they live?"

"Hundreds of the white cabins you see are kept on dollars. The sons and daughters in America send home money every week, or when they can. You notice how good-looking the people are. There is nothing mean about them. They are real men and women. They are the real Irish. They have been driven into this wild land, some say by Cromwell, but that's all nonsense! It must have begun centuries ago, before the Normans came, perhaps. They are the real Milesians. You could not evolve a type like that in a few generations. They are as old as the hills; and as strong. . . ."

I watched the sun sink into the sea at evening, and I saw night fall over the grey land at the world's end. And I knew then the strangeness that blows through the town of Galway like dust.

That town is half in the world and half out of it. It is a frontier post, and the winds from the end of the world blow into it day and night.

☩

"THERE IS NO 'LAND' IN CONNEMARA," WROTE PA-trick Kelly in *The Dublin Magazine* of March 1925. "Mountains there are, and beautiful lakes, and swiftly flowing streams, and deep, narrow creeping streams and swamps and stones, and little patches of more or less sheltered ground where the meagre crops are grown—but there is no 'land'; that is to say, Connemara—or at least the greater part of Connemara—has no farms. And it follows from this that all the theory of all the theorists concerning agriculture and so-called 'improved methods of cultivation' might as well be preached to the Man in the Moon as to the inhabitants of Connemara. Why, the poor tiller in that great lone country, working on tradition, is able to get a better return from his miserable nine or ten acres of indescribable soil than would the best Professor of Agriculture in Europe, were he to condescend, spade in hand, to try his luck and test his skill beyond the hills of Maam. . . .

" 'Under what possible conditions will the people of Ireland in Connemara be thoroughly satisfied?" a fly-fishing tourist once asked. He was what is called a 'practical man' and 'practical men' have never accomplished anything worthy of note in the world. However, the question is a good one and very easily answered.

"The people of Connemara will be thoroughly satisfied when the climate of Ireland accepts responsibility as its guiding principle, when America is the America of the Irishman's dream, when immigration, so far as Ireland is concerned, is no longer restricted by the authorities at Washington, and when poteen is manufactured from barley and rye (three parts barley and one part rye) and not from chemicals, as it is.

"Connemara is over populated, and that's the truth, sad or otherwise. It has been said that an attempt will be made by the Government to remove some of the people to the rich lands of Leinster. The people of Connemara will not leave their beloved home, with all its strange charms and strong traditions, for Leinster, or any other part of Ireland, if they can possibly help it. Either Connemara or America. There is no third place within the range of their vision.

"It has been said by ardent admirers of the people of Connemara that they have no faults. This is wrong: they have more than one fault. They are inclined to depend too much upon the supposed omnipotence of the Government. They might of themselves, and at very small cost, improve their homes and make them more comfortable. They might with profit pay a little more attention to drainage. They might, also with profit, study the great virtue of that simple combination called soap-and-water. They might show a little more love for the poetry of flowers. . . . But what can you expect? The young have their eyes fixed on America and the old upon heaven.

"America! In that single word lies the solution of the dislike now openly expressed in Connemara of the Irish language, or, rather, of the teaching of Irish in the schools. They say—and who can answer them to their satisfaction? 'Why are our children taught so much Irish at school?— what wonder if I *was* Irish! It is English they want. They must go to America to earn their living, and English is of use to them in America and Irish is not.' And then with a shake of the head they will tell you the story of the girl who was sent back from the office of the American Consul in Dublin because she failed the English test. She returned to Connemara in tears. America, the land of her waking dreams, and perhaps of the dreams of her sleep, was lost to her for ever. . . ."

A true and tragic thing is said in this same article:

"Connemara is a strange country, a country of contradictions. Its nominal capital is Clifden, but its real capital is Boston in the United States of America."

&

I AM WALKING ALONG A ROAD IN CONNEMARA. IT IS a narrow white road that runs between sloping fields cut across by breast-high boundary walls. A thin rain ceases and the sun shines. Now and then to my left I get a glimpse of the sea coming into a creek that is edged with saffron-coloured weed, but as I go on the shoulders of the hills cut off this view and I am again surrounded by small hills, by sudden miniature bogs where stacks of peat are drying; and over the crests of these hills and on their inhospitable flanks are set small limewashed cabins, rudely thatched and surrounded by a queer assembly of things: an old barrel at the door; felled tree trunks, a stack of turf, an odd little hayrick bound by rope and propped up by poles. A fishing-net is nailed to dry against the side of a cabin. Sometimes a hen, making busy ruminating noises, will walk out of a cabin and stand a moment in the sunlight on the threshold, looking round with one foot lifted rather like a man-about-town putting on his gloves on the steps of his club.

In the centre of a "field" a piece of ground higher than the rest has never been levelled. A thorn bush grows on its summit. The farmer who owns this useless and heart-breaking land has cultivated all round the tiny hill, leaving the hillock to sprout weeds and thorns. The reason why he has done this is simple and well known. The high ground is a fort or rath. The people say that such forts were built by the Danes. Some people think that this word is a corrupted form of De Danann, the mysterious people called Tuatha de Danann—"the tribes of the Goddess Danu." They are said to have conquered Ireland by virtue of great magic. But the druids of the people of Mil were too strong for them; and magic meeting magic, Tuatha de Danann were forced to fly and take refuge in the fairy mounds.

Every countryman in the West of Ireland knows that these places are haunted. It is on record that a labourer gave up the land which he had secured under the Labourers Act and upon which a well-disposed district council was willing to build him a house because, as he wrote to the council, "on no account would he interfere with the fairies' home."

That is why in the West you see so many raths with their trees waving above them, the standards of an invisible world; and all round the meagre crops are growing but never intruding on the territory that belongs to fairyland.

"What are the fairies?" Padraic Colum asked a blind man whom he met on a West of Ireland road.

His face filled with an intensity of conviction.

"The fairies," he said. "I will tell you who the fairies are. God moved from His seat, and when He turned round Lucifer was in it. Then Hell was made in a minute. God moved His hand and swept away thousands of angels. And it was in His mind to sweep away thousands more. 'O God Almighty, stop!' said Angel Gabriel. 'Heaven will be swept clean out.' 'I'll stop,' said God Almighty; 'them that are in Heaven, let them remain in Heaven; them that are in Hell, let them remain in Hell; and them that are between Heaven and Hell, let them remain in the air. And the Angels that remained between Heaven and Hell are the Fairies.' "

What he said was as true to the man as one of the Gospels.

Saxon fairies are naughty children like Puck, who loved to turn the milk sour and knock fat women from their milking stools. In Scotland the fairies are sinister and terrible. I have talked to men who have seen Highland fairies. I know a young man who drives the village hearse in a lochside village in the far north. He sees fairies and "ghost lights" before anyone dies, and, being a practical youth, he at once cleans up the hearse! But these Scottish fairies are mostly terrible. A Scotsman would kill a fairy as he would kill a stoat.

Mr. Yeats has commented on this. He attributes it to the stern the-ological character of the Scot, which has made "even the devil religious." But in Ireland the people have settled down in kindly tolerance side by side with their old gods, which is, of course, what all fairies are.

"Our Irish fairy terrors have about them something of make-believe," writes W. B. Yeats. "When a peasant strays into an enchanted hovel, and is made to turn a corpse all night on a spit before the fire, we do not feel anxious; we know he will wake in the midst of a green field, the dew on his old coat."

This graciousness to fairies is, I think, all part of the aristocratic hospitality of Ireland. Only mean and low-born people are ungracious to a guest. In the old days when heroes walked the world disguised as common men—just as Ulysses came home from his wanderings—you never knew for whom you poured wine or broke bread. Your common harper might rise up and, casting off his rags, become a god.

And on the roads of Connemara I feel as though I am in Ancient Greece, and that men know that a stranger with all the mystery and potentialities of a stranger is abroad upon the roads. They look at me with a gentle yet searching interest, as though I might be an old god playing a trick in a tweed coat.

If this were so, and a wandering god from the old times came to them and proved himself, they would not, I think, betray him to the priest. They would take him in, sorry for him and vaguely proud of him also; and they would give him milk and kill a fowl for him and go short of potatoes in order to feed him. Not until he was far off down the road beyond the wrath of men would they, I am sure, go to confession!

☙

AS I GO ALONG THE ROAD I MEET AN OLD WOMAN driving a black calf. She wears a wide scarlet petticoat. Her feet are bare. The calf is small and long-legged, lean and dung-spattered. To the left the hungry land lifts itself in a lacework of stone walls; to the right the sea runs in to a fretwork of estuaries, the black rock slippery with seaweed.

The scene is one ready made for a painter, and one that has been painted again and again by the younger school of Irish artists. When I have seen these canvases hanging on the walls of a Bond Street gallery during some annual show of Irish art I have admired the composition, the sincerity, but I have doubted the colouring.

In Connemara, on fine summer days, the hills are an intense blue and the sky behind them is sometimes almost a fine pale green. Just behind the outline of a hill the sky is often a lighter colour, a pale incandescent greenish-blue, that flings the hill out in a heroic manner; the light almost trembles behind it.

There is something heroic about Connemara. I do not mean the heroism of the men and women who till stony ground or the heroism of women who bring up big families on a few shillings a year: there is something deeper than this, something that goes back beyond written history; something that will not be caught in a net of words.

And against the grape-blue hills and the green sky an old barefoot woman in a red skirt drives a black calf.

I sit down on a stone and think about her for a long time. Why did she seem important?

☒

I TALKED TO A YOUNG FISHERMAN WHO HAD brought ashore a pot full of blue lobsters.

"Will you sell one to me?" I asked.

I had an idea that I might take the lobster to my next hotel and ask them to cook it, not as a test of Irish manners, but because I can seldom resist lobster.

The young man replied that he would like to sell me a lobster, but he was not at liberty to do so. He worked for a man who sold all the lobsters caught in the neighbourhood so that they did not belong to him but to his master.

"To whom does he sell them?"

He said that French trawlers called for them at regular intervals.

I stood there on a slippery rock wondering how many times I have sat in a Paris hotel, a string orchestra playing and a *maître d'hôtel* leaning forward with a religious expression and a poised pencil, saying:

"The lobsters are—magnificent!"

I could not help laughing.

The young man looked hurt and embarrassed, so that I hastened to explain.

"I think it rather funny that I should have to go to Paris to eat one of your lobsters."

He did not think it at all funny, because it meant nothing at all to him; but he flung back his head and laughed as a compliment to my sense of humour.

But it is rather odd. I shall never eat lobster in Paris again but I shall see the Atlantic sweeping into the fretted coast of Connemara, a little cloud sitting on the head of a blue hill, and I shall hear in imagination the young fisherman's voice and the sound of yellow sea-weed popping in the warm sun.

Connemara to Paris . . .

It is hardly possible to believe that two such places could have any traffic one with the other, or even that they can exist in the same world.

&

I HEAR MEN AND WOMEN OF CONNEMARA SINGING in the fields. Sounds go a long way in this still country. I hear the click of spade against stones and a voice lifted in some old Gaelic song. I would give anything to understand it. I have never wished to understand a foreign tongue so much. I remember hearing Arabs sing in the desert at night, but I was quite content to be told what they were singing. I have heard the Moorish Spaniards of the Balearic Islands making up long, loud songs on the mountains; but I was quite happy to be told that the man was singing "I am a man and I love you, look at my fine brown arms and the muscle on me," while the woman replied, "I am young and beautiful but not for the like of you."

But in Connemara, although these songs are just as foreign in sound, I feel drawn to them in a way impossible to explain so that it is almost pain to be for ever in ignorance of them. I would love to fling back a verse over a stone wall as I go on.

The manner in which these Irish peasants have kept alive the traditional literature of the Gael is one of the wonders of the world. They are not yokels in the English meaning of the word. I never meet a good specimen of a Connemara man without wondering what fine blood runs in his veins; for among these people are the O's and the Mac's of the ancient nobility.

"It has been said," writes Padraic Colum in *The Road Round Ireland*, "that in England the country people have a vocabulary of from 300 to 500 words. Doctor Pedersen took down 2,500 words of the vocabulary of Irish speakers in the Aran Islands. Doctor Douglas Hyde wrote down a vocabulary of 3,000 words from people in Roscommon who could neither read nor write, and he thinks he fell short of 1,000 words of the vocabulary in actual use. He suggests that in Munster—especially in Kerry—the average vocabulary in use amongst Irish speakers is probably between 5,000 and 6,000 words."

Stephen Gwynn has finely sketched this hidden side of the Irish peasant's life in *Irish Books and Irish People*:

"There is nothing better known about Ireland," he writes, "than this fact; that illiteracy is more frequent among the Irish Catholic peasantry than in any other class of the British population; and that especially upon the Irish-speaking peasant does the stigma lie. Yet it is perhaps as well to inquire a little more precisely what is meant by an illiterate. If to be literate is to possess a knowledge of the language, literature, and historical traditions of a man's own country—and this is no very unreasonable application of the word—then this Irish-speaking peasantry has a better claim to the title than can be shown by most bodies of men. I have heard the existence of an Irish literature denied by a roomful of prosperous educated gentlemen; and, within a week, I have heard, in the same county, the classics of that literature recited by an Irish peasant who could neither write nor read. On which part should the stigma of illiteracy set the uglier brand?

"The Gaelic revival sends many of us to school in Irish-speaking districts, and, if it did nothing else, at least would have sent us to school in pleasant places among the most lovable preceptors. It was a blessed change from London to a valley among the hills that look over the Atlantic, with its brown streams tearing down among boulders, and its healthy banks, where the keen fragrance of bog-myrtle rose as you brushed through in the morning on your way to the head of a pool. Here was indeed a desirable academy, and my preceptor matched it. A big, loose-jointed old man, rough, brownish-grey all over, clothes, hair, and face; his cheeks were half hidden by the traditional close-cropped whisker, and the rest was an ill-shorn stubble. Traditional, too, was the small, deep-set blue eye, the large, kindly mouth, uttering English with a soft brogue, which, as is always the case among those whose real tongue is Irish, had no trace of vulgarity. Indeed, it would have been strange that vulgarity of any sort should show in one who had perfect manners, and the instinct of a scholar, for this preceptor was not even technically illiterate. He could read and write English, and Irish too, which is by no means so common; and I have not often seen a man happier than he was over Douglas Hyde's collection of Connacht love-songs, which I had fortunately brought with me. But his main interest was in history—that history which had been rigorously excluded from his school training, the history of Ireland. I would go on ahead to fish a pool, and leave him poring over Hyde's book; but when he picked me up, conversation went on where it broke off—somewhere among the fortunes of

Desmonds and Burkes, O'Neills and O'Donnells. And when one had hooked a large sea-trout, on a singularly bad day, in a place where no sea-trout was expected, it was a little disappointing to find that Charlie's only remark, as he swept the net under my capture, was: 'The Clancartys was great men too. Is there any of them living?' The scholar in him had completely got the better of the sportsman.

"Beyond his historic lore (which was really considerable, and by no means inaccurate) he had many songs by heart, some of them made by Carolan, some by nameless poets, written in the Irish which is spoken today. I wrote down a couple of Charlie's lyrics which had evidently a local origin; but what I sought was one of the Shanachies who had carried in his memory the classic literature of Ireland, the epics or ballads of an older day. Charlie was familiar, of course, with the matter of this 'Ossianic' literature, as we are all, for example, with the story of Ulysses. He knew how Oisin dared to go with a fairy woman to her own land; how he returned in defiance of her warning; how he found himself lonely and broken in a changed land; and how, in the end, he gave in to the teaching of St. Patrick ('Sure, how would he stand up against it?' said Charlie), and was converted to Christ. But all the mass of rhymed verse which relates the dialogues between Oisin and Patrick, the tales of Finn and his heroes which Oisin told to the Saint, the fierce answers with which the old warrior met the Gospel arguments—all this was only vaguely familiar to him. I was looking for the man who had it by heart. . . ."

Mr. Gwynn then describes how he journeys on, coming at length to a man called James Kelly, who knew many songs written "in very hard Irish, full of 'ould strong words.'"

"I should like to send a literary Irishman of my acquaintance," he continues, "one by one to converse with James Kelly as a salutary discipline. He was perfectly courteous, but through his courtesy there pierced a kind of toleration that carried home to one's mind a profound conviction of ignorance. People talk about the servility of the Irish peasant. Here was a man who professed his inability to read or write, but stood perfectly secure in his sense of superior education. His respect for me grew evidently when he found me familiar with the details of more stories than he expected. I was raised to the level of a hopeful pupil. They had been put into English, I told him. 'Oh, aye, they would be, in a sort of a way,' said James, with a fine scorn. Soon we broke new ground, for James had by heart not only the Fenian or Ossianic cycle, but also the older sagas of Cuchulain. He confused the cycles, it is true, taking the Red Branch heroes for contemporaries of the Fianna, which is as much as if one should make Heracles meet Odysseus or Achilles in battle; but he had these legends by heart, a rare acquirement among the Shanachies of to-day. Here then was a type of the Irish illiterate. . . . When I find an English workman who can stand up and repeat the works of Chaucer by heart, then, and not till then, I shall see an equivalent for James Kelly."

When darkness falls over Connemara I cannot look at the glow from turf fires shining high on the hillside in cabin windows without wondering how many old stories from the fresh youth of the world are remembered over the white ash.

&

SHE WAS PERHAPS EIGHTEEN YEARS OF AGE, SLIM, tall, and her fine legs were bare. A scratch near her right knee had dried in a thin line to her ankle. It matched her skirt, which was blood-red. Her feet were black with sea-slime, and she stood on an overhanging ledge of rock grasping a long, primitive rake with which she lifted great bunches of dripping sea-weed from the edge of the lagoon. There was a soggy pile of it, waist-high, beside her.

She was in that part of the Connemara coast where the Atlantic, running in between tall hills, spreads out, contracts, and pushes itself towards the land in wide, blue lagoons, in thin creeks and rivulets, which, heavy with a brown fringe of sea-weed, lap gently against the rocks. The men in this part of the world scratch the hard soil with spades like crowbars, while the young girls go down to the edge of the sea and bear up on their broad shoulders baskets of sea-weed with which to encourage the reluctant earth. . . .

When I sat on a rock near her and lit a pipe she took no notice of me. Curlews were crying, gulls were sweeping in low, wild circles, and the sun was almost warm.

I would not call her pretty, but she was sensational in her complete unconsciousness of sex. Here, within twenty-four hours of London, was a primitive woman. She was more primitive than Eve, who was obviously a completely sophisticated person. This girl did not know that she was a woman. She had no idea that she was cast in the same mould as Helen of Troy. It had never occurred to her that she might be beautiful, because the traditions of her tribe, which go back to remote ages, tell her that the man she will marry demands not beauty but strength of hip and shoulder and arm, and the ability to carry baskets of sea-weed from the shore to the potato-patch.

I looked at her and wondered at what period in history women became vain.

Artists invariably paint primitive women gazing at their beauty in pools of water, combing long and lovely hair, and exhibiting an aesthetic pleasure in their own persons. But is this true? Did woman believe that she was beautiful until man had time to tear himself away from the potato-patch and make up a few poems? Surely that began all the trouble. Before that time woman was, it occurred to me as I watched her, just a convenient fetcher and carrier, uncombed, unwashed, devoid of vanity, unconscious that she was anything to brag about, because no man had told her! Perhaps the beauty of woman is a comparatively recent discovery!

The girl grubbed up great gobs of sea-weed and splashed them on the salty pile. Now and then her tangled hair fell into her eyes, and she shook it upward with a bare arm. She had never wanted any of the things for which her sisters (separated from her physically by a few hills, but actually by exciting centuries) sacrifice their digestions and their peace of mind.

Those fine legs had never known, or wished to know, the feel of silk. From the look of her head she had never owned a comb. Possibly she had never seen herself, except such portions of her that became reflected by chance in a still pool beside the sea. She had never experienced a complete bath.

Yet in spite of it all, she was attractive. She pleased the eyes. I longed to be able to paint her or to cut her in marble as she stood, strong and poised, above the sea, her feet gripping the slippery rock, her toes curved and muscular, like the toes of a savage. Then she, perhaps sensing my interest, turned to me a pair of enormous empty dark eyes.

She was not pretty, but—she might so easily have been beautiful.

I pondered a number of problematical things as I admired the magnificent, efficient movement of her arms regularly forking up the weed and splashing it on the pile. She would never know romance as other women know it. Men do not marry for love in agricultural tribes. They marry land or cows or sheep or the potato-patch that runs next to theirs, whichever seems to them the best dowry. There is a proverb in rural Ireland that it is unlucky to marry for love. Scots have a proverb: "As loveless as an Irishman."

But, suppose some man from the outside world fell in love with her, a man in flight from the artificiality of sophisticated women, a man who loved her simplicity and her primitiveness, and her magnificent ignorance, what would happen to her? Suppose he took her to a city and tried to fit her into his way of life? From Connemara to Curzon Street?

There was a fineness about her, characteristic of all the Connemara peasants, and a queer smothered nobility. That also is typical of men and women here. She looked in fact better bred than most of the women in a fashionable hotel in London or Paris. What would a bath and a Paris gown do to her?

And such girls do enter the modern world. They go in their blood-red skirts to the emigrant ships, weeping and sobbing, to step out with an astounding adaptability into the life of America. . . .

She filled the basket to the brim with sea-weed, and, bending one shoulder slightly, swung it up with one quick movement of her arm to her back. Then, stepping like a goat over the jagged rocks, she went towards the land.

I saw her later outside a white cabin talking to an elderly woman over the half-door.

"May I take your photograph?" I asked.

She looked at me with her great Spanish eyes, then she placed her chin on her shoulder and blushed with a kind of hoydenish coyness. I was confused and ashamed for her. She lost her vague queenliness and became a stupid country wench. I asked her name, and she became silly again and shook herself like a little girl of six.

" 'Grania,' she's called," said the woman.

"You have lived in cities?" I said to the woman.

"Yes, I was a servant to Lord X——"

"Has Grania ever been to a city?"

"She has not."

"She has never wanted silk stockings, cinemas, lip-sticks, face-powder, and cigarettes?"

The woman bent herself double with laughter over the half-door.

"Did ye hear that, Grania?" she said.

"I did," said Grania, and laughed, too.

She then lost her shyness and became solemn, never taking her big, smoky eyes from me.

"Grania," I said, "you have a name like a queen. What would you do with a shilling?"

She thought a minute, dropped her eyes, and lifted them again, whispering something in Irish:

"She says," said the woman, "that she would buy an apron."

"A blue one like the sky?" I asked.

"Yes," said Grania, in English. (O Grania! and I thought you had no small vanities!)

I held out a shilling in the palm of my hand, and she came slowly like a child and took it with fingers ice-cold with sea-water. . . .

There was an important silence.

"There's no use in telling lies, sir," said the woman earnestly. "It's not an apron she'll buy with a shilling. But," and she paused, looking at me solemnly, "she'd be buying one if it was one and sixpence she had!"

Grania came blushingly and took another sixpence. Then we all burst out laughing.

"I shall come back some day, Grania, and look for you standing by the sea in your red skirt and with our blue apron, looking like a queen in a story. . . ."

"Yes," said the woman, "and if you're a good girl the gentleman will take you away with him, Grania. . . ."

Then we all burst out laughing again and said good-bye. . . .

I turned at the bend of the road and saw Grania, standing on a wall with the wind in her matted hair, looking after me and lifting one long arm in farewell.

☘

THE ONE-ROOM CABIN LIES A MILE OR SO FROM THE road over a hill; and inside live a man, a woman, and eight children. The next cabin, which is rare in this district, is three miles away, and the nearest shop, such as it is, ten. They are in the backwoods of Connemara. This family is linked to the world of men only by a belief in God, otherwise they would be as lost as mountain sheep without a shepherd.

As it is, they are a lonely outpost of Christian culture—if that is not too strong a word—rather like a wild flower springing in the footprint of a saint. They live in the Shadow of God. They talk about Him as though He helped them that morning to bake the soda-bread in the peat-embers, and was with them last night to drive the pig in from the perils of the peat-bog.

St. Columba, who left Ireland 1,365 years ago to convert the North of England, is a greater reality to them than any living man. They talk about him with the circumstantial detail of eye-witnesses, so that at first you think they are describing some one they encountered last week in the hills. They tell you how he cured his mother's toothache and how he rebuked his son that day when they were driving back cows from the fair at Bal-lyhean—simple stories made up by them and their fathers on the hillside or round the fire at night, and repeated so often that they have become true.

They live in a cruel beauty, for the wildness around them was never meant to give food or shelter to man or beast. Their consumptive-looking cows roam the rock sadly in search of herbage, a poor scapegoat creature, lean as a rake, and their three potato-patches, none larger than a small carpet, are dotted about the landscape, ten minutes' walk one from the other, because only in these patches does some geological crack or seam permit the presence of a thin soil.

They are so used to insufficient food that hunger is fortunately something they do not notice. . . .

But if you offered to remove them to better land in another county they would fight you with pitchforks to the death!

The man is a mystery. He is not aware that I know he "did" six months recently, for making poteen. They caught him red-handed one misty day in the hills—fell right on him, in fact—as he was brewing "the stuff" over peat in a cave. Prison has left no mark on him. I suppose he just sat in his cell thinking about St. Columba—or Columcille as he calls him in Irish.

I have never seen a more ragged man. His trousers are unbelievable. He must have owned and inherited perhaps twenty pairs during his life, every one of which is represented in the present astonishing garment. If he fell asleep in the hills, I am sure the leprechauns would come out and play chess on him!

Like all his tribe, he is gentle, well-mannered, with thoughtful, dark eyes, and a thin, high nose. There is a stray touch of decayed aristocracy about him. The first time you see him you think: "Hullo, what an old tramp!" and you address him gruffly, anticipating roughness, but when he replies courteously with a smile and a well-turned sentence you feel abashed and apologetic!

How he keeps his large family I do not know. (Perhaps they keep themselves.) He appears to sit about all day on a big stone, smoking his pipe, looking round the hills, waiting apparently for something that never happens. . . .

I wonder if the peat-bog could tell a different story . . . but, let us change the subject, and meet his wife!

The cabin is dark because the windows, which are set high up, are no larger than sheets of foolscap, and everything in it smells of peat. A peat-fire, that has not gone out probably for centuries, burns with a clear vermilion flame and powders into white ash as fine as talc. Above this fire hangs a big black pot. On the wall are pictures of the Holy Family and the Flight into Egypt.

The woman kneels on the earth floor, rocking a cradle in which peeps the monkey face of a five-months-old infant; round her crawl and climb, bubble and dribble, three babies between the ages of one, two, and four years. Two bigger boys are at school. Two strapping girls, one twelve and the other fourteen, are vaguely useful about the place, slapping an infant out of the fire, stirring the black pot, or taking a turn at the cradle.

The mother of this hearty tribe is about thirty-six, but she looks quite fifty. Beauty seems to fly in a night in Connemara. It is distressing to see lovely young girls aged by hard work in the twenties, and by lack of care and insufficient food. This woman has been romantically beautiful, and even now, with care, kindness, flattery, a visit to a dentist, a hairdresser, a dressmaker, and a bathroom she would still be attractive. She belongs to that thin, whipcord Latin type, and her big eyes, dark, gentle, and warm, with long centuries in the depth of them, look straight into you.

The most earnest social reformer could not patronize these people. There is no class barrier to negotiate. There is grim poverty, but not the squalid poverty of a slum; it is not pitiful poverty, because these people feel no self-pity.

They would be very puzzling to a parson's wife, or to a busy, bent-on-improvement district visitor!

So we sit and talk intimately about babies, teething, coughs, the difficulty of bringing up babies. In other words, we discuss her life.

She rocks the cradle, a hen walks in, takes a look at the assembled multitude, makes a querulous comment, pecks something from the floor, and wanders out.

"And it's only two I'm after losing," says the mother, with a touch of pride. So there were two more children! I ask her how on earth a doctor manages to get to such cabins in the hills, and she says that she has never seen a doctor a her life.

It's hard work to get enough food, she says, with big girls growing up. They live on potatoes and eggs, when there are eggs, and milk. They never have meat. But, glory be to God! they are all safe and hearty, and Brigid going to America soon. . . .

The two big daughters nudge one another and giggle at this. They are red-skirted, bare-legged, and ragged as their father, and their faces almost as red as their skirts. How on earth do these wild children settle down in America?

It will be better for everybody when Brigid goes to America because the first thing she will do will be to send a shilling or two home every week to keep the white cabin in Connemara. This is to me a marvellous thing about these people; there is more than filial piety in it; possibly it is another angle of that passionate attachment to the land which can have no parallel in any other country.

The two boys tramp three miles to school, and the whole tribe tramps three miles to Mass, wet or fine, on Sunday morning.

The woman looks curiously at my cigarette-case! Yes, she would like a cigarette! When I hold the match towards her, she grasps the cigarette and holds the end of it to the match as if it is a firework! She laughs, and confesses that she has never had a cigarette in her hand before. I have to show her how to light and hold it. The girls roar with laughter at their mother and make jokes in Irish.

Outside on a stone the head of the family sits smoking and watching the clouds roll up over the hills. We talk of the difficulty of growing food in such a spot. He says that he is, thanks to God, better off than many a man. Over there, now—he points with his pipe across the hills to the sea—men live on the edge of the rocks and carry the sea-weed all day and even the earth in wicker baskets. . . .

"But they love their rocks?"

"They do," he says, "and it's not leaving them they'd be, if you gave them all the Plain o' Meath! But 'tis starvation!"

"Yet they are happy?"

"Aye, it's happy they are, sure enough, but—'tis just starvation!"

That seems to me to sum up Connemara! But, for the life of me, I cannot pity them!

THERE IS A VERSE SPOKEN BY PEASANTS IN THE WEST as they rake the embers of their turf fires before going to bed. It has been Englished as follows:

> *I save the seed of the fire to-night,*
> *And so may Christ save me;*
> *On the top of the house let Mary,*
> *In the middle let Brighid be.*

> *Let eight of the mightiest angels*
> *Round the throne of the Trinity,*
> *Protect this house and its people*
> *Till the dawn of the day shall be.*

One night at the end of a long evening spent in a Connemara cabin I watched the farmer rake his fire. He tidied the little pile of glowing turf, and then he damped it down with ashes in order that the fire might live until the morning.

This act, which is performed in thousands of white cabins when night comes over the hills, is symbolic of Ireland. The burning peat, one may fancy, is the Gael; the ashes are the centuries of suppression under a foreign power; the darkness needs no comment, and the morning is the Ireland of the future. When these ashes are raked off in the morning there is a faint pinkish heart of fire in the turf, and the peasants blow upon it until a flame bursts out and new fuel is added on the hearth.

The makers of modern Ireland who believe that the future of the nation is bound up with a revival of all Gaelic things have gone to the Gaelic west for their inspiration. Here, it seems to me, is a strange locked-up force. These strong, proud men, technically illiterate yet with the manners and instincts of scholars and gentle-folk, have a racial strength which must influence the future of Ireland. They are the same breed as the Highland crofters. How many famous generals, surgeons, lawyers, and literary men born in small Highland crofts owe their success in life to the fact that the whole family slaved to send the clever one to college?

The same thirst for scholarships, the same almost fanatical faith in a University education is not yet visible in the West of Ireland. But it may come. It seems to me that when these young Gaelic-Irish dream not of

Chicago and New York but of academic honours, and an Ireland that can offer them distinguished careers, something new and powerful will have come into the life of this nation. The Gaelic Revival so far has been due to the work of University men and others who have gone from the cities into the Gaeltacht; the second, and more vital, stage will be when these young Gaels of the west come to the cities determined to use not their hands but their brains.

⊗

CLIFDEN, THE CAPITAL OF CONNEMARA, LIES IN the shadow of the Twelve Pins. These mountains are among the most fascinating that I have ever seen. They dominate the landscape in Connemara, now to your left and again to your right as you move through this country; sometimes the clouds swing low and decapitate them; often, especially at evening, they stand up in a sky blue as the Bay of Naples.

Clifden is a small, clean, stone-built town with one wide main street. The hill on which it is built slopes to an estuary that points straight out over the Atlantic to America.

In the post office I waited while a young Connemara girl, fresh as a peach, painfully addressed a letter to New York; and then I drew twenty pounds in much-travelled one-pound notes—money that had been wired to me—and not one person in the post office showed any surprise, although this sum must have seemed to them real wealth.

It was strange to make contact with the outside world in the hotel. Here were fishermen with the accents of Dublin and England. The most interesting person, however, was a chauffeur whom I met at the bar; rather, his story was interesting. He asked me if I had noticed an elderly American at luncheon. I had. A thin, sallow man who wore horn spectacles.

"That's himself," said the chauffeur; and there was something sympathetic and kindly in his attitude.

He told me in that dramatic narrative manner which most Irishmen possess that as soon as a certain liner had docked at Cobh this American rushed to the garage where the young chauffeur worked, and chartered a car to take him to a little town in County Mayo. He explained that he wanted to "run up" to see his brother and then rush back and catch the next boat to America.

On the journey north from Cork to Mayo there was plenty of time for my companion's honeyed tongue. And the American, proving not so sallow and uncommunicative as he looked, told the Irishman a lot about himself and his mission. He had emigrated from Mayo thirty years previously. For years his conscience had pricked him because, in spite of success, he had never been home to see his elder brother, whose tragedy it was to stay in Ireland to inherit an uneconomic farm. He had returned at last and was about to pay a surprise visit to his brother.

Unlike every American previously encountered by this chauffeur he was a "terrible teetotaller entirely." He even kept a keen eye on his driver, and when once, at Limerick, the young man had been discovered with his face in a pint of porter the American had lectured him sternly, ordering him to abstain from all liquor while in his service.

They arrived in the town in Mayo and the American was appropriately affected. He made his way to the old home, opened the door, but a strange face greeted him:

"Will it be old Pat Murphy ye want—him that keeps the saloon?"

"The saloon?" cried the American, horrified and indignant.

"Aye; that's himself. . . ."

They went to Pat Murphy's saloon in the little street. There, sure enough, was the favourite brother sitting up behind the counter fast asleep. The American's heart melted at the sight so that he forgot the smell of stale drink that haunts all Irish saloons.

"Pat!" he said, going round and shaking him gently. "Pat, do ye know who's here?"

For answer Pat gave a grunt and slid gently to the floor, dead drunk.

"And he stood there and looked at him a while," said the chauffeur; "then he turned on his heel and he said, 'Take me back to Cork. It's the next boat I'll be catching. . . .'"

The young man drank up and put his cap straight.

"An' niver a word has he given me from that time to this," he said. "And to think a man would come all the way from America for that. He's a hard man entirely, I'm thinking. Still, it's sorry for him I am, taking it to heart the way he does. . . ."

I watched the American get into the motor-car and sit there with the set face of a Puritan elder.

☙

BEHIND THE TWELVE PINS LIES THE LOVELY MOUN-tain country of the Joyces. This was a family of Welsh descent which settled in this part of the West by permission of the dominant O'Flahertys in the last year of the thirteenth century.

Connemara lives on the sea and the fruits of the sea, but the people of the Joyce Country live upon the mountain. Their active little sheep graze on the splendid uplands, and the wool is taken from them, washed, and spun in the cottages on the hillsides and made into Irish tweed on hand-looms. It would be easy to confound the Joyce Country with Connemara; they exist side by side on the map, but a difference not only of clan separates them: the vast difference in all the ways of life that separates fishermen from mountaineers.

The journey from Clifden through Letterfrack to Leenane is, I think, one of the most perfect scenes in the West of Ireland. I went along this road on a bright day with the sea intensely blue and huge golden clouds sailing above the crests of the hills. Ahead of me, dominating the scene, was the highest mountain of the north-west—Muilrea—and next to him was Ben Bury and Benlugmore, three monsters that rise up into the sky from an arm of the sea.

Leenane lies among the mountains on the edge of a great fiord called Killary Harbour. Connemara is now a dream. The country has changed. The great hills slope up to barren summits, and the sound is not that of a spade hitting the rock but the bleating of sheep and the clack of a shuttle. Near the post office is a wooden shed where all day long a hand-loom bumps and bangs as the wool from the Joyce Country sheep is turned into homespun. It is a finer, closer tweed than that of Kerry; in fact, rather like Donegal, but lacking the sudden specks of colour: excellent hard stuff with the colour of the Joyce Country in it.

As I went on round the eastern limit of Killary Harbour I saw five young men pulling in a salmon net. They formed a group that might have come from the very dawn of the world. They wore homespun tweed. Their sleeves were rolled above their muscular elbows. Their necks were baked red with wind and sun. As they pulled they shouted to one another in Gaelic; and slowly the great net was hauled in to shore.

It was an exciting moment. I nearly broke my neck scrambling down to the water's edge to be in time to see it. As the net was pulled slowly towards the bank, the water, perhaps fifteen yards out, suddenly boiled with furious life, the sun shone on four feet of living silver as the great fish leapt and lashed in the net. The men sang out in their excitement and pulled, one directing them in Gaelic. The salmon leapt up into the sunlight.

I saw the whole of him: a silver monster, an eighteen-pounder with great shoulders on him and a tail with the kick of a mule in it.

It was a moment I shall never forget: the sun on the opposite hills; the scent of wild thyme; the splashing at the water's edge; the Gaelic shouts that sounded like war-cries; the bright, leaping body in the net: over it all the simple splendour of a lost world.

☯

IN CONNEMARA AND IN THE MOUNTAINS OF THE Joyce Country women age swiftly, but while the bloom of youth is on them they are like queens.

Padraic Colum has beautifully described the women of Connaught:

"The hard conditions of Connacht life have helped the Connacht woman to development and personality. The size of the holding of land does not permit the man to develop his constructive and organizing faculty. The woman becomes the personality amongst the Connacht peasantry. The civilization is of her creating. It is a civilization of the hearth. One cannot fail to note the number of words for 'child' that is in constant use; there is a word for the child in the cradle, the child creeping on the floor, the child going to school, the child well-grown—naoidheah, lanabh, malrach, piaste—words as soft and intimate as a caress. The tragedies of Connacht life come closest to the woman: as a child she sees the elder sister who has reared her leave home for America; as a wife she lives alone while her husband works abroad, and often her child is born while its father is labouring in the fields of England or Scotland; as a mother she sees her rearing go from her as they grow into boyhood or girlhood. . . ."

I realize in Connaught one feature of the English landscape which is seldom or never seen in Ireland: a courting couple. In England boys and girls, arm in arm, are met with on every country road, or you see groups of country lads and lassies walking out together. In Ireland, as I noted in Kerry, the separateness of the sexes is remarkable. Love is perhaps in Ireland not a sentimental obsession as it is in England. In Connaught, and the West generally, men seldom marry for love: they marry, to some extent, for land.

Match-making, which in England would horrify us by its deliberate, cold-blooded unsentimentalism, goes on in the country districts of the West. Stephen Gwynn gives a remarkable account of this formality in his *Holiday in Connemara:*

"The son of the house gave me the fullest description of an Irish match-making that I have ever heard, and I set it down as an inspiration for some novelist.

"He went with the suitor's party, some eight or ten of them. Their coming was expected, for the match had been fixed, so to say, in principle; and accordingly the house was made ready. They were shown into a room with three long tables, furnished with uncut loaves and butter (I heard of no other food), but there was a glass and tumbler to every place, bottles of whisky on the board, and a barrel of porter somewhere handy. The bride's friends were there in equal numbers, and the parties ranged themselves on opposite sides of the tables. The host sat at the head of the centre table; on his right was the suitor's spokesman, on his left the bride's spokesman. Any student of Ossianic lays will remember that when Finn came to marry Grania, the Fianna were on one side of the board, and King Cormac's chiefs and princes over against them on the other.

"When, after the Homeric fashion, they had 'put off the desire for eating and drinking," the host opened the proceedings. 'Creud ta sibh ag iarraidh?' he asked—'What are you come for?' But the phrase ag iarraidh is ambiguous and means either 'What are you asking?' or 'What are you seeking?' (an ambiguity that reflects itself in the Anglo-Irish use of 'looking.' 'He'll be looking ten pounds for that heifer'). And, singularly enough, the boy's spokesman did not know his manners. 'Ceud punt' (a hundred pounds), he answered brusquely. This was a shocking solecism, but his neighbour saved the situation. 'And a woman with it,' he put in. 'That is a better story,' said the bride's spokesman. But the proper answer should have been, 'Seeking a wife for this boy we are'—and so on by courteous approaches to the real issue. However, battle was joined. The boy's spokesman, backed by the others, began praising the suitor: how he had a well-stocked farm; was sober as well as rich; had no brothers to divide his inheritance. To this the bride's party answered by praising the girl, as industrious and (again Homerically) skilled in the arts of needlework. In the upshot the hundred pounds was agreed to. Then a new discussion arose as to whether it should be in stock or in cash, and the award was made at sixty pounds in cash, and cattle to the value of forty. Then the stock had to be discussed and specified. Lastly, the father dealt with the question of the ceremonial heifer, which is always given with the bride by any father who wishes to hold up his head in the country. He must buy one, he said, having no heifer beast that he would think good enough to send with his daughter.

"Then when the business was settled down to the last detail, the father said: 'We don't know yet if the woman you are looking for is in the house at all?' A message was sent, the girl came in and her health was drunk; and after this ceremony was over, the mother emerged from her retreat in a wall cupboard behind curtains where she had been unofficially present. It is not lucky for a woman to assist at a cleamhnas, or match-making. Then the tables were ranged aside to clear the floor for a dance; but one table was set in a corner where the old men drank till morning. Tea was provided for the young people.

"'Was it a love match?' I asked. The boy's mother arranged it all: the girl was older than he.

"And in truth there is no society where marriage is more a matter of arrangement than among the Irish Catholic tillers of the soil—and none where the marriage-tie is more binding."

☙

WHEN LENT CAME IN THE YEAR A.D. 449 ST. PATRICK retired to a great mountain in Connaught to commune with God. He fasted there for forty days and forty nights, weeping, so it is said, until his chasuble was wet with tears.

The medieval monks possessed detailed accounts of St. Patrick's fast. They said that to the angel, who returned to him every night with promises from God, the saint said:

"Is there aught else that will be granted to me?"

"Is there aught else thou wouldst demand?" asked the angel.

"There is," replied St. Patrick, "that the Saxons shall not abide in Ireland by consent or perforce so long as I abide in heaven."

"Now get thee gone," commanded the angel.

"I will not get me gone," said St. Patrick, "since I have been tormented until I am blessed."

"Is there aught else thou wouldst demand?" asked the angel once more.

St. Patrick requested that on the Day of Judgment he should be judge over the men of Ireland.

"Assuredly," said the angel, "that is not got from the Lord."

"Unless it is got from Him," replied the determined saint, "departure from this Rick shall not be got from me from to-day until Doom; and, what is more, I shall leave a guardian there."

The angel returned with a message from heaven:

"The Lord said, 'There hath not come, and there will not come from the Apostles, a man more admirable, were it not for thy hardness. What thou hast prayed for thou shalt have . . . and there will be a consecration of the men of the folk of Ireland, both living and dead.'"

St. Patrick said:

"A blessing on the bountiful King who hath given; and the Rick shall now be departed therefrom."

As he arose and prepared to descend from the mountain mighty birds flew about him so that the air was dark and full of the beating of wings. So St. Patrick stood, like Moses on Sinai, and round him all the Saints of Ireland, past, present, and to come.

In this we can see the Irish belief in the inflexible determination of their saint: "a steady and imperturbable man." And it was said that while upon this mountain in Connaught St. Patrick banished all snakes from Ireland.

This mountain, Croagh Patrick—or Patrick's Hill—lifts its magnificent cone 2,510 feet above the blue waters of Clew Bay. It is Ireland's Holy Mountain. Once a year in July a pilgrimage is made to the little chapel on the crest. Atlantic liners drop anchor in Galway Bay, bringing Irish-Americans who wish to ascend the mountain for the good of their souls. As many as 40,000 pilgrims have climbed the mountain in one day; and many of the more devout remove their shoes and socks and take the hard path barefoot.

The morning broke dangerously clear and fine. I took a stout stick and prepared to climb the mighty flank of Ireland's Sinai. As I approached it, admiring the high pattern of wheeling clouds over its head, I could see far off the little Mass chapel like a cairn of stones on the crest.

I plodded on over a rough mountain path worn by the feet of the faithful century after century. A wind blew in from the Atlantic bringing rain with it, and in a few moments the earth was hidden in a thin grey mist. I was disappointed, but went on in the hope that the sky would clear in time and give me what must surely be the grandest view in Ireland.

There are few experiences more uncanny than climbing a mountain in mist and rain. As I went on and up, the mist grew thicker, and the drizzle fell in that peculiar persistent Irish way that wets you to the skin before you are aware of it. Above me was this grey wet pall, below me the same mystery; only the rocks under my feet were real, and there was no sound but the falling of water and the click of a dislodged stone rolling behind me down the path.

There is something terrifying, at least to me, in the mists that cover mountains—mists that hide you know not what; mists that cut a man off from the world and deny him the sight of the sky. To be lost on a mountain in mist is to experience all the horror of panic, for it seems to you that you might lose the path and go wandering vainly in circles answered only by a mocking laugh which seems to hide in all mountain mists. But I consoled myself by the thought that Croagh Patrick is a holy mountain from whose ravines and gullies all demons have been banished. Suddenly, right before me rose a white figure, and I looked up to a statue of St. Patrick.

The saint, I discovered, stands there to hearten pilgrims, for the real climb begins behind him. The path ends. The climber ascends, picking his way over a steep gully, the loose stones sliding beneath his feet; and as I went on the joy of climbing in rain came to me, so that I loved the wetness of my cheeks and hair and the movement of the mist which told me that I was in a great cloud that hid Croagh Patrick from the eyes of men.

I came to a cairn of stones: one of the Stations of the Cross. And as I stood there asking my Catholic ancestors what to do about it I heard a voice, and out of the mist came an unlikely and preposterous sight. A middle-aged woman was painfully descending the path. She looked exactly as though some one had taken her up in the very moment of buying six yards of *crêpe de Chine* at a Grafton Street draper's and had blown her on top of Croagh Patrick. No sooner had she become startlingly clear in the narrow circle of my vision than another figure materialized from the mist: her husband. He also was incredible. He wore a bowlar hat. It seemed so odd to encounter a bowlar hat on a holy mountain. We said what a bad day it was. They asked if there were any more people coming up behind me. They told me it was their first pilgrimage. The woman was worried. She had lost a rosary among the stones. If I found it would I post it to her in Limerick? I thought how strange it was to English eyes: two solid, middle-aged people of the comfortable kind going off together to pray on the summit of a holy mountain.

"God be with you and bless you," they said gravely; and I went on into the damp cloud.

Onward in the mist I went, hot and weary and happy; once I thought I had found the lost rosary, but it was only a piece of torn shoe-lace that had fallen into a hollow of the rocks. I passed another Station of the Cross and soon found myself on the peak of Croagh Patrick, 2,510 feet above Connaught, with the mountains of Mayo north of me, the blue Atlantic west of me, and south the mountains of the Joyce Country and the Twelve splendid Pins of Connemara. But, alas, not one glimmer of it shone through the wet cloud that hung over the holy mountain. . . .

On the summit of this height is a little Mass chapel. I was told in Connemara how this building was made. Cement in seven-pound bags was carted to the foot of the mountain and every pilgrim regarded it as an act of devotion to carry one of these to the top. Many a man, I was told, made the ascent more than once for the honour of carrying up material for the construction of this tiny oratory.

I went inside and knelt down. The place was very small and ice-cold. A young priest knelt in prayer. The wind howled round the little building in soft gusts, and I wondered what it felt like to be there in the great storms that swept in from the Atlantic. Even though the walls of the little chapel cut off the sight of moving mists there was something in the air of the chapel that told of a chilly solitude far from the comfortable earth. I was conscious that, outside, the mountain mists were sweeping past; the cold air told of a remote solitude; the rudeness of the little sanctuary was that of a shrine built on an outpost of the world. The kneeling priest never moved. He might have been carved in stone. He reminded me of some knight keeping vigil before the altar.

I tiptoed out and sitting on a wet stone ate the sandwiches and the cheese that I had brought with me. I sat there wet through, longing and hoping against hope that the clouds would rise and show me the distant earth. The wind that sweeps over the head of Croagh Patrick is the cruel whistle that comes to all great mountains; and in the sound of it, even though you cannot see two yards before you, is a message of height, of dizzy drops, of jagged gullies and awful chasms.

It was on this height, as told by the medieval monks, that St. Patrick flung his bell from him only to have it returned to his hand; and at each sound of the bell the toads and the adders fled from Ireland. . . .

I went down over the wet stones. I came gratefully to the white statue of the saint. I had left the clouds above me, but the rain was falling, blotting out the sea and the hills.

ROBERT GIBBINGS

Galway, Connemara, birds, and bogs: 1940s

"I CALLED AT THE MUNSTER AND LEINSTER BANK TO
INTRODUCE MYSELF. NO, THEY HADN'T HAD ANY
ADVICE NOTE ABOUT ME AS YET, BUT IF IT WAS
ONLY A MATTER OF MONEY, THERE'D BE NO
TROUBLE ABOUT THAT."

In the 1990s there has been some interest in biographies of rivers and bodies of water. Half a century ago, in the 1940s, English writer and naturalist Robert Gibbings was having great success with his Sweet Thames Run Softly *and* Coming Down the Wye, *handsomely decorated with the author's own sensitive and detailed wood engravings. His books were so popular, in fact, that his American publisher, E. P. Dutton, packaged three of them "in cellophane" for Christmas giving in 1945.*

When Gibbings crossed over to Ireland to wander in the west and write Lovely Is the Lee, *he found himself at least as interested in the human population as he was in the birds and beasts and waterways. In the following selection, he does write about both birds and bogs, but this genial traveler doesn't miss any of the human quirks he encounters.*

Gibbings's story about the bus he waited for—and then waited in while it tarried outside a cottage for a tardy passenger—should not strike a stranger to Ireland as outrageous. One morning, at a country bed-and-breakfast where I was staying in the west of Ireland, the guests were exchanging sightseeing tips over a hearty breakfast when the landlady asked one of us his plans for the day. He was an Irishman himself and clearly had been staying at the house for some little while. He said he thought he might have another try at going into Galway for the day. "I think I'll just walk up the road," said he, "and see if the bus comes."

The operative word was "if," and the uncertainty of his project didn't seem to trouble him a bit.

GALWAY IS A PLEASANT PLACE IN WHICH TO DO BUSI-ness. Soon after my arrival I called at the Munster and Leinster Bank to introduce myself. No, they hadn't had any advice note about me as yet, but if it was only a matter of money, there'd be no trouble about that. They had plenty of it. They'd be only too glad to accommodate me. They added that if I wanted a day's shooting or the loan of a car or a bicycle it would be equally simple. I went into the chemist's across the road from there and heard so much about trout that I forgot what I had gone in to buy. I collected my watch from a jeweller who had made some minor repairs to it. "How much is that?" I asked. "Yerra nothing at all." I went into a stationer's to buy a few postcards. "Can we send them for you?" I was asked.

I said to a man from over the border: "It reminds me of Tir na n-Og, the land of the ever young." He said: "It *is* Tir na n-Og. They *have* the secret of perpetual youth. Did you ever see such clear eyes except in children? Did you ever see such ready smiles except in children, or such fun and pranks, such irresponsibility, and, at times, such naughtiness? They talk of a land that is far to the west, a land where they never grow old, where there is no consciousness of time. That land is here."

In Galway, too, you find yourself talking to every one as if you had known them all your life. It is impossible to stand still in any one place in the town for two minutes without getting into conversation. When I was buying a few stamps in the post office a man, about to send a telegram, said to me: "Did you hear about the bishop who came over from England to fish in Lough Corrib? He hadn't a bit of luck for days and days. Then, at last, he landed a trout. 'D'you know,' said he to the boatman, 'that fish has cost me twenty pounds?' 'Thin I hope to God ye don't catch another,' said the boatman." Probably an old story, probably told of many other lakes, but nowhere on shorter acquaintance than in Galway post office.

I was standing outside a hardware shop noting the different local patterns of spades, some with a single step, some "eared" on both sides, some with straight sides, some tapering, when a woman said to me: "Have you ever read De Quincey? Hasn't he the wonderful English? My husband is inside buying rat traps."

Towards that same evening I asked a man if he could tell me the way to the college. "Know the way to the college?" he said. "If I was to take off me two boots and put them on the pavement before me, they'd find their own way there." He lived less than half a mile further up the road, but he'd never been inside. He was "no good at the books." He would like to have travelled. Once he did have a mind to go to Ameriky, but when the time came he was "wanting the courage." So he had a drop of drink and when he woke up in the train 'twas in Dublin he was instead of Queenstown. "Hadn't they a right to control me," he asked, "the same as an ox or a horse?" But they gave him a ticket back to Galway and he never left the town since. Then we got to talking about the weather. He said that "Friday goes against all the rest of the week. If 'tis fine six days to Thursday it will be wet on Friday. If it is wet to Thursday it will be fine Friday." But he didn't know what to think of the weather we'd been having. He'd never seen anything like it. "The moment it's settled it changes." I told him that it had been clear enough to see the Aran Isles that morning. "If you can see the Arans," he said, "it's a sign of rain, and if you can't see them it's raining."

Eventually we reached Maggie Ann Ashe's select bar where, within half an hour, I had accepted an invitation to go trawling with some of her fishermen clients. So, at five o'clock next morning, I found myself on the deck of their hooker, and we were sailing down the silver stream of the setting moon. And because there was a three hours' sail to the fishing grounds I lay down on the hatch, and, because it was January, the captain covered me with a sail. And I didn't wake till half-past seven when the dawn was breaking and the crew were preparing to shoot the trawl. And at eight o'clock they shot it, and then we had tea, and then we had the whole day before us to watch the gannets diving and the razor-bills skimming the waves and the gulls swooping and soaring. And at twelve o'clock we had more tea, and a potato or two, roasted on the stove in the cabin, and at half-past three they put the nose of the boat into the wind and hauled the trawl. And then the deck was alive with flapping fish, whiting, plaice, pollack, soles, and skate. And by the time they were packed, nine boxes in all, we were half-way up the bay, on the way home, and an hour later I was walking back to the hotel with a dozen plaice on a string.

"What will I give you for them?" asked Miss O'Carroll in the office.

"They're a present," I said.

On my table, that night at dinner, there was a bottle of 1929 vintage Burgundy, and, on a card beside it: "This is a present, too."

⚭

A LETTER REACHED ME. IT WAS FROM A MAN IN THE town of Ennis. He claimed relationship with me on the ground that his aunt had been the second wife of my great-grandfather. He hoped that some day we would be friends as well as relations. And so we were.

It was in Ennis, on a fair day, that one of those peers with a double-barrelled name was seen crossing the square in a somewhat inebriated condition. "Isn't that Lord 'Clare and Galway'?" said one farmer to another. "It is," said the other, "and both of them's drunk."

I had passed through the town many years before, but I remembered little of it. My memories were chiefly of the country round about. In a village a few miles to the west my car had broken down. The bolt in the bottom of the sump had fallen out, and all the oil had gone. The only garage in the village was a small one, and the proprietor could find nothing to replace the missing screw. After two hours on his back on the dusty road he decided to plug the hole with wood which he lashed into place with wire and string. Then he filled up with oil.

"There you are now," he said, "that will carry you on a while."

"How much do I owe you?" I asked.

"Oh, begod, you don't owe me anything."

"And why not?"

"Oh, I couldn't charge you for that. Sure, I only made a temporary job of it."

"But you've spent two hours on it."

"Ah, it was a slack afternoon."

"Well, how much do I owe you for the oil?"

"I couldn't rightly say the price of that."

"I can tell you. It's so much a pint."

"But it's cheaper by the gallon."

Eventually I drove on, and in trying to pick up lost time I ran over a hen that was on the road and killed it. Leaving the corpse beside the car I went to the nearby cottage and knocked. A genial young man came to the door.

"I'm very sorry," I said, "but I've killed one of your hens."

"I'm very much obliged to you," he said.

"And what are you obliged for?"

" 'Twas very nice of you to come back and tell me."

"Well, how much may I pay you?"

"Divil a penny, thin."

"And what will I do with the hen?"

"Take her away with you, you're welcome."

And so to Spanish Point on the coast. An aunt of mine owned a cottage there which she visited each summer with her family. That particular year I had taken a "lodge" for my family. One half of the lodge was a thatched cottage, the other half was a castellated tower. We used to bathe from these houses, which were close to the shore, undressing and dressing indoors, and running to and from the sea in our bathing suits. One day my cousin Kathleen, having returned to her room, on the ground floor, had slipped off her wet garment and was getting busy with the towel when she noticed a shadow by the window. Looking out she saw one of the lads of the village. "Get away out of that, Mickey," she said. "What are you doing there?" "Arrah, Miss Kathleen," said he, "drop down that towel, sure you look lovely in your pelt."

It was one of these men who found in his field of sprouting corn the hoof marks of a mare and foal, and that not on one morning only, but on several. "It seemed to him a queer thing, for he knew well that the only mare and foal in the parish were stabled at night. So he and his son took watch, by turn, and two nights later what should the man hear but a whinny, and it coming up behind him from the sea. It was full moon and, when he turned himself round, there on the rocks was a lovely mare with her foal, and they shaking the salt water off themselves. And, then, up they trotted to the oats, and made a trespass on them. The man was that surprised he kept hidden, and he never said a word that night. But the next day he told a wise man what he'd seen, and the wise man told him the mare was from the enchanted island of Hy Brazil. 'Take with you a halter of sugawn,' he said; 'a straw rope it must be, and throw it over the mare's head and the enchantment will be broken, but mind you never let a common rope touch her neck or the spell will be on her again.' So the man went away and made a sugawn halter, and that night he and his son kept watch, and, sure enough, they heard the whinny again, and this time there was a fine stallion along with the mare and foal, and all three of them trotted up to the oats. And the man was ready and he threw the straw halter over the neck of the stallion and caught him, but the mare and the foal flew back to the sea. Well, that stallion was the grandest animal and the finest worker in the countryside, and always a sugawn halter was used. But one day a new boy was working on the holding and he put a rope halter on the stallion. Up with his heels and a loud neigh he lets out of him and away into the sea with him and none of them was ever seen since."

⟁

FROM GALWAY I PAID MANY VISITS TO CONNEMARA. To Ballynahown on the south coast, and to Maam Cross and Glendalough among the mountains, to Clifden and Ballyconneely in the west. On the day that I left for Ballynahown the bus was full, all except the two front seats, in one of which I sat. The other was taken soon after by an old man whose face was brown and wrinkled as well-worn shoe leather. Two bright blue eyes shone from deep in his head. He wore a bowler hat with a richly curved brim and a ribbon so frayed in front that it suggested a clerical rosette. Just as we were about to start a beggar woman got in. She came down the bus collecting pennies to right and left. As things happened I had nothing in my pocket less than a two-shilling piece. I couldn't be the only one to refuse, so, when it came to my turn, I gave her the silver. Immediately it was as if the heavens had opened, with the flood of blessings that were called down on my head. The whole bus was informed of what I had done. Wasn't I the real gentleman? Didn't she always say a real gentleman was worth a dozen others? Everybody stared at me. The conductor called to her to get out, but she took no notice of him. Saints and angels in scores were invoked on my behalf. The conductor called to her again. Still she paid no attention.

But at last we did get away. The old man on the opposite seat said nothing as we made our way out of the town, but I could see that he was watching me. Suddenly, in a loud voice, he called across the bus: "Have you means?"

"I have not," I said.

"Speak louder! I'm deaf."

"I have not!" I shouted.

"How do you live?"

"Writing books."

"You must have a great brain."

Everybody in the bus was now listening. I tried to break off the conversation by looking out of the window, but there was no escape.

"You write books?" he called again.

"I do."

"Would they bring you much?"

"Sometimes they would; sometimes they wouldn't."

"How much would they bring you?"

Again I could feel the bus agog. "It's hard to say," I said.

"I can't hear you, I'm deaf!"

"It's hard to say," I shouted.

"Would they bring you a pound in the week?"

"They might."

"Would they bring you more?"

"They might, or they might not."

Again I tried to look out of the window, but the inquisition went on.

"Have you been to Ameriky?"

"I have not."

"Have you been to the Indies?"

"I have."

"What took you there?"

"Writing a book."

"You must have a power of learning."

He paused a moment as if in wonder.

"Have you been to Australey?"

"I have."

"How do they live?"

"Same as ourselves."

"Have they sheep?"

"Thousands."

"How many might one man have?"

"Fifteen thousand."

"How can he count them?"

"Don't ask me."

"What did you say?"

"I said, *Don't ask me.*"

"And what took you there?"

"Writing a book."

"Another book! Glory be to God! Have you been to Borneo?"

"Never."

"I'm told they murder you there and hang your scalp on their belt."

"That's true," I said, almost wishing he was there.

"We're better off in Ireland," he said, getting up to go.

After the storm, a calm. The bus rolled on. Stones, stones, nothing but stones in the fields, rough stones, smooth stones, boulders with moss on them, pebbles glinting with quartz. In the road rocks rising like the slate-green backs of monsters from the sea. Wall after wall, so close that you wonder whether they are the boundaries of fields or the sides of ruined houses. Here and there stacks of turf where they could best meet drying winds. And, in the bog-lands, cattle on knolls or rocks to chew the cud.

At last it was time for me to get out. A boy was waiting to carry my bag. "How do you shift the cattle from one field to another without any gates?" I asked.

"Wisha, push a bit of the wall down and build it up again. Isn't it as easy as to be lifting an old gate off its hinges?"

If a man were in search of a wilderness for a scapegoat he couldn't do better than survey the scenery a few miles to the west of Galway. How the cattle and sheep find a picking there it is hard to say. How the human creatures make a living is a greater wonder.

"But, sure, we're the richest people in the world," said an old woman to me; "the priest said that, because, he said, 'we have the faith.' 'Twas a great comfort to us when we heard it, indeed, you'd see the tears of joy in the people's eyes and they goin' down the road after mass."

It was the time of the spring tides and the men were taking advantage of the low water. In their light homespuns they were hardly distinguishable from the rocks, as they gathered weed along the shore. I spoke to several, but they had no English. I could only watch.

A young man sitting on the rump of a pony, behind two panniers, came down a lane at a gallop. The pony's bridle was no more than a rope tied over its head. The panniers hung from pegs in a wooden hames. A waterproof sheet over a thick layer of straw covered the animal's back. The pony stood while the dripping weed was loaded into the baskets, armful after armful alternately to each side. When the panniers were full more weed was piled on top between them, a rope was thrown across and fastened, and more weed piled still higher. Then another rope from the opposite side. As if the pony knew that its load was complete it started homeward across the loose stones before the last knot was tied.

Curraghs, like stranded whales, lay at the head of small beaches, beaches jewelled with shells. A net and a coil of rope, recently tanned, and now resting on a sheet of corrugated iron, drained their superfluous liquid back into the tan tub.

Along this coast it is considered most unlucky to save a man from drowning. "The sea must have its due." If you save a man, you or one of your family will most certainly be taken instead. The same belief is held in the Orkney and Shetland islands, and there are many people, on the east coast of Scotland, who will not even lift a dead body from the sea into a boat. "It belongs to the sea." Among some of the tribes of central and south-east Africa there is a similar reluctance to help a drowning man. To do so will bring misfortune on the rescuer. Closely connected with this idea was the custom among the vikings of Scandinavia, as it was also among many primitive people, to fasten one or more human beings to the rollers over which a ship, or war canoe, was launched. They were offerings to the sea. It was, no doubt, a survival of a similar belief that, till recently, caused two or more of the ship's apprentices to be ducked in the bow wave of the Peterhead whalers as they were launched from the shipyards at Aberdeen. Orkney boys fishing with the line throw back the first fish caught. It will bring luck, this offering of first fruits to the sea-god. And there are parallels to be found all over the world. In Morocco if the water in certain wells is scarce it will suddenly become plentiful if a person or animal falls into it. It may even be seen that the well wants "a kill" by the way its water turns red. Only after some living creature has fallen into it does the water get back its natural colour. "It craves a victim." To-day, in the neighbourhood of Hay, on the Wye, children are warned not to play by the river lest the spirit pull them in. Not long ago, after a boy had been drowned near Ross, on the same river, somebody said that it would be a lesson to his brothers not to go too near the water, but an old man answered: "Let 'em go, let 'em go. The river has had its due." In January 1904 a man was drowned in the Derwent, in Derbyshire, because, it was believed, he had made light of the river. "He said it were nought but a brook. But Darrant got him. Nought but a brook! He knows now." In southern India there are rivers whose spirits must be appeased by offerings of coin before cattle can with safety be driven across. In Peru it was customary to throw maize into a stream as a propitiatory rite before crossing. An even more extreme case of propitiation of the elements comes from County Cork, where an old man would always leave "one little bit of a ridge of spuds for the frost. Sure it must have something to eat," he said.

While I was in Connemara a girl of about eighteen years of age died of consumption. Her mother said to the doctor who was attending her: "Will you tell me, doctor, the moment the soul is leaving the body?" He did so. Immediately the mother got up, closed the door of the room, and plastered half a pound of butter along the crack between the door and its frame. After a while she scraped off the butter and put it in the fire. "Now," she said, "we've caught the evil, and we've burnt it; and it can do no more harm to any one."

On any of the small heather-bounded lakes that dot the bogs swans may be seen, in pairs, in tens, in twenties. These are the true wild swans, the whoopers and the Bewicks, which, unlike the almost domestic mute swans of English rivers and parks, have no black tubercles at the base of their bills. Neither are the bills orange, as in the mute, but lemon-gold, the gold of Lir's coronet; and their singing is like to that of many women humming sadly, a sound weird and mournful, interspersed with sighs and sobs, so that those hearing it, after dark, will flee from the lake, fearing lest it be haunted.

Do you know the story of the children of Lir; how their stepmother, being jealous of the love that was shown to them by their father, Lir, turned them into swans, and how they remained thus for nine hundred years, until the coming of St. Patrick? Two things only she granted to them; that they should retain their human reason, without any grief for being in the shape of swans, and that they should still sing in their own Gaelic tongue. So, through all the centuries, they went from lake to lake, singing sweet plaintive music, the like of which was never heard in other lands. It excelled all the music of the world, and lulled to sleep every tired soul that heard it. And no man lifted a hand to hurt those swans, for the men of Ireland had made it a law that no man should kill a swan from that time forth, and no true man of Erin has ever done so to this day.

It was pouring rain, the day I returned to Galway, and I stood for half an hour, without shelter, waiting for the bus that was late. As if to make it later, we hadn't gone half a mile before a girl ran out of a cottage. "Hold on a while, Taedy, till I do me hair," she called to the driver. And so we tarried in our tracks.

As luck would have it, who should get into the bus at the next stop but my companion on the outward journey. And again he occupied the front seat on the right and I was in my same one on the left. For a while he said nothing, then suddenly he leaned towards me.

"Have you sold many books in Connemara?"

"Not many," I said.

"Not many? That's bad!"

He was silent again for a few minutes, then, as if struck with an idea, "Tell me," he said, "are ye any good at writing love letters?"

"I've been lucky, an odd time," I said.

"I got five pounds once for a love letter," he said. "I wrote it for a man west in Carraroe. He got the girl, and he got seven hundred pounds with her, and, faith then, he gave me five pounds for it. 'Tis a good line, mind you. You should try it."

Before he could tender any more advice we were separated by two portly women in shawls, with baskets. Their conversation was about matrimony, and for the most part it was in Irish, which I did not understand, but every now and again they would break into English. One was apparently telling the other how her son had taken a liking for a girl in the town, "but when I says to him: 'How would she look under a cow?' sure, that finished him. He never threw a thought to her since." Again there was some confidential chat, and then: "But there's Mary Ryan is getting married, and him without as much as you'd jink on a tombstone, and that small you could blow him off the palm of your hand."

"Ah, well, she's got one at last. Every morning for the past five years she's gone to mass, praying for a husband."

And so we reached Galway. That evening the harper was playing again. His wife was there too with her fiddle. If you would hear *The Old Rustic Bridge by the Mill* or *Teddy O'Neil*, played on the harp, across the wide square, in the soft evening light of the west, 'tis better for you to wear a wide-brimmed hat, for you may want to shade your eyes.

&

FOR CONTRAST TO THE WILDERNESS OF STONES AND stone walls of southern Connemara one has only to travel inland a few miles from Galway to find a waste of moorland, with never a fence for mile on mile, and never a stone save the age-worn outcrops of silver granite. The bogs are every shade of brown and gold, the hills are every tint of purple, the only signs of green are a stray holly bush or the twigs of a stunted fir. Black bullocks munch the heather. Wild geese rise from the bog, their steel-grey backs the colour of the wind-swept lakes.

On all sides breath-taking glimpses of hill and pool. A robin sings to running water. Listen. Listen again. Tune your being to the song of streams. Close beside a fir-tree three sheep are grazing. Stand by the tree and think yourself into it. Touch it with the tips of your fingers. Lay the palms of your hands on its rough bark and feel the tremor of its fibres. Stretch up your spirit towards its topmost branches following each changing urge of growth. Sense its growth, for growth is immortality. We all are but cells, forming and re-forming in the elemental tissue, momentary manifestations, glimpses in the microscope of God. What does the chlorophyll cell in the blade of grass know of biology? Just as much, perhaps, as we do of eternity.

The robin is now in the brushwood. The wind has dropped. There isn't a breath to stir the rushes, the cloud shadows stand as they fell on the hills. The road curves like the hollow of a thigh, the mountains rise like the swelling of a breast, the pools are clear as kittens' eyes.

I spoke of geese. Geese, said to be the most faithful to their mates of all living creatures. Among many anecdotes the following, told by W. H. Hudson in his *Birds and Man,* is typical. It was narrated to him by his brother, a sheep farmer in South America. "Immense numbers of upland geese in great flocks used to spend the cold months on the plains where he had his lonely hut, and one morning in August in the early spring of that southern country, some days after all the flocks had taken their departure to the south, he was out riding, and saw at a distance before him on the plain a pair of geese. They were male and female—a white and a brown bird. Their movements attracted his attention and he rode to them. The female was walking steadily on in a southerly direction, while the male, greatly excited, and calling loudly from time to time, walked at a distance ahead, and constantly turned back to see and call to his mate, and at intervals of a few minutes he would rise up and fly, screaming, to a distance of some hundreds of yards; then finding that he had not been followed, he would alight at a distance of forty or fifty yards in advance of the other bird, and begin walking on as before. The female had one wing broken, and, unable to fly, had set out on her long journey to the Magellanic Islands on her feet; and her mate, though called too by that mysterious imperative voice in his breast, yet would not forsake her; but flying a little distance to show her the way, and returning again and again, and calling to her with his wildest and most piercing cries, urged her still to spread her wings and fly with him to their distant home. And in that sad, anxious way they would journey on to the inevitable end, when a pair or family of carrion eagles would spy them from a great distance—the two travellers left far behind by their fellows, one flying, the other walking; and the first would be left to continue the journey alone."

But in fairness to other species of birds I must not omit a story of a peregrine falcon's affection for its mate told by P. H. Bahr in *British Birds* (May 1908). The female had been wounded and had fallen to the ground with both legs broken. It was in January, during a hard frost, and her wings, stretched out, had become frozen to the ground. Around her lay the remains of wild duck, partridges, and pheasants, while above her hovered her mate. From the state of her injuries it was reckoned that she must have been in that position for over a fortnight, yet, thanks to the care of her mate, she was in almost perfect condition when found.

Of the virtues of geese, the late J. G. Millais wrote that of all birds, they are the most intelligent. "Conspicuous, too, are they for bravery and domestic affection. In the particular art of defending themselves against the wiles of the fowler, whether afloat, or ashore, they have absolutely no equal." As an instance of the latter he tells how, on one occasion, when he found himself within about a hundred and fifty yards of a flock of some six hundred birds, a mixture of greylags, pinkfoots, and bean geese, he noticed five or six birds who "kept on the alert the whole time, walking about quickly and suspiciously on all four sides of the main body and never attempting to feed." He goes on to say that after watching them for about ten minutes he saw, distinctly, "a goose which had been busily eating go up to one of the sentinels and touch him on the back with his bill. Immediately the sentry lowered his head and commenced to pick at the grass, while the goose who had just been feeding raised his neck and began to keep watch. It was their mode of changing sentry." After this he "kept particular watch on the sentries, and twice again saw other geese come up, peck them in a friendly sort of way, as much as to say 'I'll do my turn now,' and thus relieve the look-out of his duty." It is told, too, that if a human being, in order to entice them, puts down food in one of their usual feeding places the geese will leave that place instead of staying. But, then, the expression "a wild-goose chase" has become a proverb. So has the watchfulness of geese, ever since the days of Rome, 390 B.C. To-day any farmer will tell you that a goose is the best "watch-dog." In an issue of *The Times* during 1940 we read that before ever the sirens had sounded and before the human ear could catch the drone of an aeroplane there occurred "an outburst of angry cackling from these historic sentinels."

Swans rise heavily and with effort, ducks rise with a flurry, but geese lift themselves majestically into the air. It may be hard to guess how certain collective terms have arisen for other birds and animals, but there can be little doubt about "a gagelyng of geese." "Gaggle-gaggle, gaggle-gaggle" is the sound one hears, high overhead, almost a flock chuckle as they pass far out of range. In this connection I like, too, the terms "a paddling of ducks," in old English "a padelynge of dookysse," "a murmuration of starlings," "a congregation of plovers."

Dotted about the bogs are stacks of brown turf. Here and there the dark walls of peat faces rise from pools of black oily water. In the peat face may be seen the stems and branches of trees long buried. *Vir* or bogwood, they call it. "The best kindling in the world." Almost straight from the bog it will light. A twig when dried will burn as a candle. "It's the oil that's in it from the turf."

Turf is cut with a slane, a narrow spade with an ear at right angles to the blade so that two sides of the sod are cut at the same time from the stepped face of the bog. Each newly cut sod is like a large brick, dark and oily. A good slanesman will cut close on three thousand of them in one day, that is to say, about four tons of turf. But this turf is "raw." It must be spread to dry as hay is spread, cocked as hay is cocked, and stacked into clamps as hay is built into ricks. Finally, it must be thatched with straw even as hayricks are thatched against the weather. A ton of raw turf yields but three hundredweight of fuel. Each year the cutting begins when the winds of March have dried the bogs. If that crop can be saved in time, a second harvest is cut in July.

Bogs hold more than turf and bogwood. It is a commonplace that bronze implements of all kinds have been found in them. Scarcely a museum that has not a specimen of one kind or another, preserved by the bacteria-free soil, of wooden bowls and platters, goblets, spades, spoons, canoes, and paddles; not to mention items of ancient dress such as cloaks and tunics of wool, capes of skin, or shoes of leather. One of the largest dug-out canoes ever found in western Europe, fifty-two feet in length, was taken from a bog in County Galway.

But one of the most surprising, though by no means uncommon, finds is bog butter. This is not, as one might suspect by the name, some strange fungus akin to the yellow jelly-like growth found on trees, and known as witch's butter, but the genuine churn-made product of the milk of cows, sometimes still edible. Knowing the preservative power of bogs its owners had buried it, to await such time as they were going to market, four, five, or six months ahead. Meanwhile, death or accident intervened, and so the wooden firkin, or the skin or cloth container, with its contents, lay undisturbed, fifty, a hundred, maybe two hundred, years.

CHIANG YEE
Going down O'Connell Street, Dublin: 1948

"IT IS A VERY WIDE STREET, AND HAS A LOOK OF
THE CHAMPS ÉLYSÉES MINUS THE TREES OR OF
WHITEHALL WITH SPLENDID SHOPS INSTEAD OF
OFFICIAL BUILDINGS."

"In my books," wrote Chiang Yee, who presented himself as the Silent Traveller, "I record my impressions and experiences, in words and in paint, preserving so far as my powers permit the mood and feeling of the occasion. This is Ching-hua-shui-jueh, reflecting the flower in the mirror or the moon on the water. Flowers fade, the moon wanes, but the reflections were real while they lasted. It is experiences no more substantial than this that I seek to describe."

Yee did just that, in the 1940s and 1950s, in a series of books with titles like The Silent Traveller in London, The Silent Traveller in the Yorkshire Dales, *and* The Silent Traveller in Oxford. *A Chinese artist as well as writer, he filled his books with amusing line drawings and delicate watercolors.*

Yee moved in good circles. In 1938 he had visited with the Earl and Countess of Longford in Dublin. In 1940 he was bombed out of his London flat and moved to Oxford. The Longfords were there too, and the friendship was renewed. He was finally able to take them up on their many invitations in 1948, resulting in The Silent Traveller in Dublin, *published in 1953.*

Originally named Sackville Street, O'Connell Street was laid out in the middle of the eighteenth century. Two of its modern sights are Clery's, a popular discount department store, and the General Post Office, but one of

its oldest sights is gone. The Nelson monument, erected in 1815 to commem-
orate the victory at Trafalgar, was blown up by Irish republicans in 1966 to
celebrate the fiftieth anniversary of the Easter Rising.

I REGRET NOT HAVING MET DR. OLIVER ST. JOHN GO-
garty. The title of his book, *As I was Going Down Sackville Street,*
has suggested to me the title of this chapter. I spent some time vainly
searching for a copy of his book; in the end a kind friend lent it to me.
Having read it, I must admit that it needs a contemporary Irishman to
enjoy every page to the full, though I laughed at passages in which I could
understand the author's wit.

However, it was I, not Dr. Gogarty, who was going down the street;
and it is O'Connell Street now, not Sackville Street. No one who visits
Dublin can avoid going down O'Connell Street and often seeing the
O'Connell Monument, just as no one who goes to Edinburgh can avoid
going down Prince's Street and looking at Scott's Monument. I knew Scott,
however, before I went to Edinburgh, for I had read Chinese translations
of his works. I hope I may be excused my ignorance of O'Connell before
I arrived in Dublin. My inferiority complex prevented me from asking
friends about him, for I realised that he must have been a great figure in
Irish history, and that everybody ought to know about him without asking.
This made me frown a little in the first few days. But one morning my
feelings were suddenly eased when I read the following passage in "An
Irishman's Diary" in the *Irish Times:*

Talking about O'Connell Street, I was sitting in a south-bound
train recently, listening to a native giving a couple of English tourists
a list of places of interest they should see during a projected visit to
the Killarney area. The English tourists had mentioned that they intended to do the Ring of Kerry, and the native suggested that they
should try to fit in a visit to O'Connell's old house at Derrynane.

"We certainly will," said the Englishman, determined not to miss
anything. "Whose house did you say?"

"O'Connell's," replied the native. "You know, the O'Connell Street
O'Connell."

I came to know that O'Connell is called the Liberator of Ireland. I paid a visit to the Daniel O'Connell Exhibition in the National Library, arranged at the request of the Save Derrynane Committee; books, manuscripts, proclamations and prints illustrating the life of the Liberator and his home at Derrynane were on view there. I was very interested to see his first fee-book and some of his early briefs. His first year at the Bar gave no promise of his later fame, for in nine months he earned no more than £2 5s. 6d. Of the proclamations and addresses exhibited, one of the most interesting is the "Grand Address to the Freeholders of Co. Clare" in 1828, which is said to have opened a new door in Irish politics. Though I could not understand the meaning of this address, I liked the way it began "Fellow Countrymen—Your country wants a representative and I respectfully solicit your suffrage to raise me to that station. . . ." He must have been a very self-assured person. Later I read about O'Connell's ingenuity in dealing with a hat case, and also of his talent for vituperative language, as instanced in the case against the fish-woman, Biddy O'Houlihan, a talent well developed early in his life.

The part O'Connell played in Irish history must have been great to have caused such an impressive Monument to him to be erected in the centre of the Irish capital. I know him by this Monument, which I saw every day I was in Dublin. I was perpetually remarking, "I was going down O'Connell Street . . ." Not only did I often pass the Monument incidentally: I treated O'Connell Street as itself one of the chief sights of Dublin and strolled on both sides of it for hours at a time. It is a very wide street, and has a look of the Champs Élysées minus the trees or of Whitehall with splendid shops instead of official buildings. To my nose, what seemed an abnormally large number of ice-cream shops breathed out the smell of Broadway. But such comparisons are invidious. O'Connell Street has a character all its own; I could feel it especially when I stood on O'Connell Bridge. The bridge is as wide as the street. In addition to traffic lanes for buses, trams and cars, it has waiting-stands some yards away from the pavement along the handsome balustrade on either side. Although O'Connell Street is the busiest street in the city and its traffic is always heavy, one can walk quite at ease to the centre of the bridge and stand there near a lamp-post gazing round without fear of being knocked down or thrown over into the river. And the traffic seemed quietened when going over the bridge, though the drivers did not appear to slacken their speed, an impression I have not had on any other bridge in the world. Perhaps Dublin's soft air was responsible for my illusion.

One morning I reached the centre of O'Connell Bridge after the mist had begun to rise. It had already dispersed between the O'Connell Monument and the Nelson Pillar, though the Pillar was not yet quite sharp and clear, and behind it thick swirls veiled the part of the Rotunda which is usually visible. The far end of O'Connell Street seemed to lead into a mysterious infinity, while the thin line of the Pillar rose high above the surrounding buildings. Between the two big monuments other statues occupy the middle of the street, but they were hidden by O'Connell. From one angle I suddenly saw that the Pillar and the Monument were in a straight line, with O'Connell straining to be the higher. Dublin is a seaport, for it has direct access to Dublin Bay, and fifteen minutes' walk from O'Connell Bridge takes one to the end of Sir John Rogerson's Quay. Hence the dense early morning sea-mists spread easily over the city even on an August morning. I once found the whole body of the O'Connell statue and its pedestal completely enveloped in mist. Had it not been for the joking gestures of the few people on the public seat at the foot of the Monument, I should not have known where I was. Their movements seemed to stir the mists to disperse.

The public seats provided on the north and south sides of the pedestal must be a joy to Dubliners. I don't remember ever seeing all the seats empty. There were always some people—men more often than women— sitting there in all weathers except torrential rain. Perhaps they were typical Dublin characters; I did not have the pleasure of knowing any of them. I, too, sat there among them many times, trying to comprehend their jokes, but their quick, rolling tongues were too much for me. Nevertheless, I smiled and laughed when they laughed, for they must have had something to laugh at and would not have been playing a trick on me. Smiles and laughter seldom lead one astray.

The appearance of these leisurely, happy-go-lucky people sitting in the middle of the main street of the busiest quarter of the city banishes the tension otherwise inseparable from metropolitan thoroughfares. It is not merely that pedestrians sit or lounge about: the curious fact is that no one appears to walk fast on O'Connell Street. Dublin seems to retain all its eighteenth-century calm and to get along very happily without any of the fuss and bustle characteristic of modern capitals.

O'Connell Bridge was built on the site originally occupied by Carlisle Bridge. The lowermost of the eight bridges which span the River Liffey, its handsome balustrades invite one to stand and stare over them. Looking down the river, I could see the magnificent bulk of the Custom House, designed by James Gandon and built in 1781–91. No complete view of this famous building is possible from O'Connell Bridge, because it is partly obscured by the lattice girders of the Loop Line railway viaduct. I am no student of town-planning, nor yet an engineer, and I am accordingly powerless to explain why this viaduct has to be just where it is.

The Custom House must have been a very impressive sight to the visitors who sailed into Dublin in the early days. Why are the Customs Houses of the world nearly always built on such magnificent sites and on such a splendid scale? Fortunately, I am not obliged to answer this question. While I stood on the City Quay two small boats anchored beside me, and I followed a number of youngsters who tried to peer into the cabins and other parts of them. A bigger boat, possibly one of the Guinness barges, with a full load of barrels on its open deck, was moored on the opposite side of the water, and there were a lot more barrels piled up in front of the Custom House. There was much activity along the quay—seamen moving about, gawky cranes stooping and reaching like mechanical storks, and large flocks of seagulls, which gave me the feeling that they had some part in the proceedings, wheeling round. About the middle of Sir John Rogerson's Quay I found two more boats lying anchored near the mouth of the river. Their bare, upright masts and hanging ropes looked very picturesque enveloped in soft, sunny haze. I did not manage to reach the Pigeon House Fort, but at the end of the quay I drew a deep breath of sea air: and thereafter I always smelt the sea whenever I looked down the river.

Resting my elbows again on the balustrade of O'Connell Bridge, I stared at the sky. I took a great fancy to the Dublin sky. Like the London sky, it is generally full of cloud, but the clouds are more often separate and do not form that uniform grey ceiling with which every Londoner is familiar. A Dublin cloud formation that particularly appealed to me was like newly combed wool, the strands so fine and light that they furled and unfurled like long, thin pennants. The larger, rounder clouds too seemed to be strung together. Who was holding the strings? Sometimes I was almost persuaded it was me!

Once when towards sunset I stared upstream from O'Connell Bridge, I felt, as the great source of light sank behind the Wellington obelisk in Phoenix Park, the much-darkened dome of the Four Courts and the five or six almost equally spaced Liffey bridges, that it was going to rest for centuries somewhere in the upper reaches of the river. The almost square areas of water between the bridges, and the obelisk standing up like a paint-brush in a jar beside them, recalled the squared paper on which as a child I was taught to write Chinese characters. The obelisk would have done for the brush!

Dublin's sunshine, even in August, is not scorching. The sun's setting rays as they fell on my face on O'Connell Bridge did not dazzle me, but filled me with a gentle electricity of warmth and vitality, not drowsiness or intoxication. This was a magic of sunset which I had not experienced before. Some lines written by Bernard Shaw for an American advertisement came to my mind:

> There is no magic like that of Ireland.
> There are no skies like Irish skies.
> There is no air like Irish air.
> Two years in the Irish climate will make the stiffest and slowest
>   mind flexible and faster for life.

My month's stay in Dublin gave me an exciting inkling of what would happen to me in two years.

Seeing a number of bridges in one glance had a special attraction for me. It recalled the bridges over Soochow Creek, which runs through the city of Shanghai. Soochow Creek is about as wide as the Liffey and its quays on both sides are not very different from Bachelor's Quay, Aston's Quay and the rest. Even its bordering shops look much the same. But Soochow Creek does not run through the centre of Shanghai, nor is Shanghai the capital of China. Nevertheless, the Liffey bridges aroused nostalgic emotions in me.

The sight of some swans dispersed my memories. There are no swans on Soochow Creek. Indeed—if Irish legend is to be believed—there are no swans outside Ireland that have not emigrated to other lands or been deported, all swans being the direct descendants of ancient Irish kings and queens. In a book called *The Irish Mythological Cycle and Celtic Mythology*, by H. D'Arbois de Jubainville, I read the following:

> One fine summer's day, Eochaid Airem, the high king of Ireland, was looking out over the walls of his fortress at Tara, admiring the beauty of the landscape, when suddenly he saw an unknown warrior riding towards him. The stranger was clothed in a pure white tunic; his hair was yellow as gold, and his blue eyes shone like candles. He carried

a five-pointed lance with him, and a shield ornamented with golden beads.

Eochaid bade him welcome, and at the same time expressed a wish to know who he was. . . . "Nothing illustrious about it," answered the stranger. "I am Mider of Bregleith." "What has brought thee hither?" asked Eochaid. "I am come," said the unknown, "to play at chess with thee." "I have great skill at chess," said Eochaid, who was the best player in Ireland. "We shall see about that," said Mider. . . .

"Play," said he to the king. "I will not play without a stake," replied Eochaid. "What will the stake be?" said Mider. "All one to me," replied Eochaid. "If I win," said Mider, "I will give thee fifty broad-chested horses, with slim swift feet." "And I," replied the king, assured of victory, "I will give thee whatever thou demand." But, contrary to his expectation, Eochaid was beaten by Mider. And when he asked his opponent what it was he demanded, the latter replied, "It is thy wife Etain that I demand." Then the king, according to the rules of the game, claimed his revenge, that is, a second game which would finally decide the matter. And he proposed to play this at the end of a year. Mider accepted the delay with ill grace enough, and then disappeared, leaving the king and his court confounded. . . .

At the end of a year, Eochaid was at Tara, surrounded by the great lords of Ireland, when Mider appeared before him, in an angry mood. "Now, to our second game," said he. "What will the stake be?" asked Eochaid. "Whatever the winner demands," replied Mider, "and this will be the last game." "What is it thou demand?" enquired Eochaid. "To put my two hands about the waist of Etain and kiss her," said Mider. Eochaid remained silent; then lifting up his voice, he said, "Come back in a month's time, and we shall give thee what thou askest." Mider agreed, and went away. When the fatal day arrived, Eochaid was in the midst of the great hall of his palace, and his wife with him. . . . Eochaid was determined to resist by force the attempt of his rival to carry off his wife. The day wore out. . . . Night came. Suddenly Mider was in the midst of them. No one had seen him enter. . . . "Here I am," said Mider: "give me now what thou hast promised. It is a debt to pay, and I demand settlement." "I have not given it a thought until now," said Eochaid, beside himself with rage. "Thou hast promised to give me Etain," answered Mider. . . . As he said these words, the blood rushed to Etain's face. "Do not blush," said Mider to her, "thou hast naught to be ashamed of. For a year and more I have not ceased to ask thy love, making thee offer of jewels and treasures. Thou art the fairest of the women of Ireland, and thou wouldst not hear me until thy husband had given his permission." "I have already told thee," said Etain, "that I will not go with thee until my husband yield me up to thee. If Eochaid gives me, I am willing." "I will not give thee," cried Eochaid. "I give him leave to put his two hands about thy waist, here in this hall, as it has been agreed upon between us." "It shall be done," said Mider.

Then he passed his spear into his left hand, and clasping Etain round with his right arm, he rose into the air with her, and disappeared through the hole in the roof which served as a chimney. The warriors rose up ashamed of their impotence, and going out they saw two swans flying around Tara, their long white necks united by a yoke of silver. . . . Later on the Irish often saw wonderful couples like these.

The whole legend is too long to quote in full. But what a lovely and interesting story! I dare say it has been known to Irish people for centuries but I had never heard it, and my ignorance leads me to wonder if it has ever been dramatised. I think it would make an excellent opera or ballet.

There are plenty of ducks and seagulls as well as swans on the Liffey, but the nobility of Dublin's waters are the swans. There are swans on the Thames which can be seen from the Victoria and Chelsea Embankments, but they are insignificant in those wider, roughened waters. On this still surface they are at home. Now that I know the legend, I look upon Etain and Mider as the first ancestors of all swans, and feel sympathy for the many cousins of the Liffey swans who live all over the world and must long for the Dublin air. It is customary in the West for descendants to take the names of their ancestors, and I felt it was inevitable that there should be two swans Mider and Etain among those on the water before me. But when I called their names my Chinese accent must have discouraged them, for they turned away when they found that I had no crumbs. I moved away too. Back in O'Connell Street, I remembered Dr. Gogarty again. I had had a letter from a friend of mine, Sir William Milner, of Parcevall Hall, Yorkshire, who wrote: "Gogarty is very entertaining: I used to know him. He used to tell us how during 'the Troubles' he once escaped by wading down the Liffey with a stuffed swan on his head!" Surely that proves that the swans are a part of Dublin.

Conspicuous among the shops in O'Connell Street are eating places and drapers. At the time of my visit they constituted the chief attractions for tourists, particularly those from England and Scotland smarting under rationing. Most of the visitors to Dublin seemed to be combining their pleasure-seeking with their eagerness for better food and coupon-free clothes. I was better placed than some, for as regards food I was well provided for by my most hospitable hostess with fresh farm produce. However, I could not always go back to Leinster Road for lunch and often had a quick meal in one or other of the eating places. The advantage of choosing a restaurant in O'Connell Street was that I could precede or follow the meal with a stroll in the street, which offers more space for strolling than (say) Grafton Street. This may be why most of Dublin's visitors, as far as I could see, congregate there. In the main streets of other capitals I have seen, people shop or go about their business—seldom just walk. Here it was the reverse. With so many unhurrying people on the pavements and in the centre of the street, with their heads turning in all directions, the traffic, thick though it was, simply could not hurry. I don't think Dubliners are less busy than people in other cities, but they manage to preserve an atmosphere of no-hurry. Three times I saw O'Connell Street more than usually packed with people: once when the news of the death of the Nuncio Apostolic, the Most Rev. Pascal Robinson, had brought crowds to see him lying in state at the Pro-Cathedral; the second time when the funeral procession took place; and the third on a Sunday, when most of the people were wearing rival coloured streamers in their buttonholes for an international football match.

Dublin's General Post Office is so famous that even those who have not been to Dublin know where it is situated. But my foolish but inveterate habit of not taking a guide-book with me put me at a disadvantage, so I had to enquire the reason. I was told that it was the scene of fierce fighting during "the Troubles." When I remarked to my hostess that I found the G.P.O. very easily, she asked if I had been besieged by youngsters anxious to be my guide. I said that indeed two boys had spoken to me, but that neither of them was Flanagan. I did not have to tell her the following story from a little book, *Recitations, Monologues and Character Sketches*, by Val Vousden, which I had picked up:

When Flanagan was a young boy, he used to sell papers on the streets of Dublin. One day an elderly gentleman approached him and said:

GENT.:	My dear young boy, will you kindly show me the way to the G.P.O.?
FLAN.:	I will to be shu-er. Go straight down along dere, take th' first turn to th' right, an' den to th' left, an' yew can't miss it.
GENT.:	Thank you, my boy. Tell me, have you no better clothes to wear?
FLAN.:	Sorra stich, sir.
GENT.:	Oh, that is a pity. Have you no boots?
FLAN.:	Boo-wits, deedin' I haven't.
GENT.:	That is very sad, very sad indeed. Have you no home, my boy?
FLAN.:	Meself and me little bruder, we live in an ow-el garret.
GENT.:	Oh dear, oh dear. Your parents are not living, then?
FLAN.:	No, sir. They're both dead, God rest dere sowls.
GENT.:	Well now, my boy, how would you like to come to a nice home where you would get plenty of food, clothes, boots, in fact surrounded by all the grand things of life?
FLAN.:	Oh begob, dat'd be grand.
GENT.:	Very good, my son. I will take you to that grand place, and not alone will I give you all these splendid things, but at the same time I will show you the way to Heaven.
FLAN.:	Ho! Ho! Is that so? An' sure yew don't know th' way to th' Post Office yerself, yew dirty oul eejit.

The G.P.O. has many functions besides those of dispensing stamps and despatching letters. Its imposing portico and deep overhang, supported by six fluted Ionic columns, make it highly suitable for taking shelter from rain. And the site is so central that if you wish to arrange a rendezvous with a friend, it is sure to be there. Lastly, I could not banish the reflection that with its massive columns for "cover," and with the adjacent Nelson pillar affording the like advantage to the opposition, it was eminently suited to street-fighting.

Close by the G.P.O. is the Nelson Pillar. I felt I could more or less visualise the view from the top, and for some time I resisted the "pull" of the queue outside it and refused to ascend. But one bright morning I found myself following a cheering crowd up the countless spiral stairs—many more than in the Nelson Monument on Calton Hill, Edinburgh, for the

Dublin column is far higher. Before we were halfway up everyone was grunting and exclaiming; the laughing chatter audible lower down had quite died away, though we were all still in holiday mood. The air inside became oppressive as we rose higher. At the top there is a railed platform and I found many people already there, pointing out this and that landmark. As I could not locate places by name, except the Dublin hills, Dublin Bay and the Wicklow Mountains, my moments were spent in enjoying overheard remarks. I had not realised that Dublin was so very cosmopolitan. Several foreign languages were being spoken, but there were a great many more Irish people than tourists. I can distinguish fairly accurately the main languages of the world, though that does not mean that I can speak them: but here were two gentlemen whose language I had never heard before. I suppose they must have come from some small East European country. Somebody pushed me from behind and I was obliged to lean against one of the strangers. He turned his head without saying anything and I apologised hastily. Then I suddenly decided to play one of the tricks employed by London children. I asked him: "Can you tell me the time, Sir?" He smiled, but still said nothing. I made sure that he and his companion had just arrived in Dublin and knew no English. But when in the evening I told my host of the incident he asked if I had noticed a badge on their coats. I was able to tell him that each of them had had a small metal ring in his buttonhole. "Then they were members," replied my host, "of the Irish Language Association. They speak only the ancient Irish language, and refuse even to answer a question in any other language." I listened with respect and thought I could just as easily have spoken to them in Chinese. This reminds me of another passage in the *Irish Times*:

> . . . concerning two English visitors to the Senate, who got into conversation with one of the official stenographers as she was waiting until it was time for her to take over her ten-minute spell. One of the senators had just made a speech in Irish. "I don't know how you can have the nerve to go in there and take notes of that," said one of the tourists. "And with all that Welsh, dear," she hissed. "They call that Irish over here."

At the foot of the Pillar, to the rear, were a few fruit-sellers, mostly women and girls. They had arranged their goods neatly in their baskets, which they rested on rough wooden structures. Always, even in their busiest moments, these women chattered loudly. Despite the passing traffic and the crowd, their cheerful noise was still to be heard, and their coloured dresses and fresh looks took me back to open-air festivals in my Chinese countryside.

At the junction between O'Connell Street and Parnell Street stands the Parnell Monument. It is a towering triangular obelisk of Galway granite. To me it was a new kind of monument. Most of the famous monuments I know are either in the shape of Cleopatra's Needle or of a Greek column. I don't know what inspired a triangular shaft. Its three edges are rather too sharp for visual comfort, but the torch at the top may have been a guiding light in the sharp struggles of Irish history. The row of trees along the middle of O'Connell Street between Nelson's Pillar and Parnell's Monument prevents the latter from looking too small beside the Pillar. A bronze statue of Parnell by Gaudens, with its back to one of the three sides of the shaft, can easily be overlooked. Dr. Gogarty remarks in his book: "The Parnell obelisk dwarfs Parnell." I agree.

HEINRICH BÖLL

Irish Journal: 1954

"IN LIMITLESS PATIENCE TIME AND THE ELEMENTS
HAVE EATEN AWAY EVERYTHING NOT MADE OF
STONE, AND FROM THE EARTH HAVE SPROUTED
CUSHIONS ON WHICH THESE BONES LIE LIKE
RELICS, CUSHIONS OF MOSS AND GRASS."

German novelist Heinrich Böll was born in Cologne in 1917. In 1937 he was drafted into military service, and during World War II he was confined for a time in a U.S. prisoner-of-war camp. After his release in 1947, he began writing and it was soon clear that Böll was going to be one of the great postwar novelists of Europe. Among his best known novels are Billiards at Half-Past Nine *(1959, published in English in 1962),* The Clown *(1963, published in English in 1965),* Group Portrait with Lady *(1971, published in English in 1972), and* A Soldier's Legacy *(1982, published in English in 1985). He won the Nobel Prize in 1972, and he died in 1985.*

In 1954 Böll took a trip through Ireland and recorded his journey in Irish Journal, *published originally in 1957 and in English translation in 1967. His visit to Ireland produced an unusual book, short on sights and places and specifics but rich in poetic evocations of the land itself and the Irish character. The writing is impressionistic but lacks the sunny outlook suggested by that word. But, then, it's a fact that sunshine is itself pretty scarce in Ireland.*

Böll's opening pages, describing his overnight steamer trip across the Irish Sea from England to the harbor at Dun Laoghaire, recall the first chapter of H. V. Morton's 1930 In Search of Ireland. *Here again are the same young people, the families and children, the priest, having a last cup of tea or a last beer, flicking the last cigarette butt over the rail, and bedding down for the night in the public areas or on the windy deck.*

Böll describes few places by name, but one of those happens to be a place that most visitors to Ireland know—the grave of William Butler Yeats in Drumcliff churchyard, under Ben Bulben, north of Sligo—and his description feels absolutely right to me. "Rooks flew up from the old gravestones," he writes, "circled cawing around the old church tower. Yeats's grave was wet, the stone was cold, . . . Rocks in the mist, the lonely church, encircled by fluttering rooks, and three thousand miles of water beyond Yeats's grave. Not a swan to be seen."

Irish Journal is a dark book. Böll's portrait of Limerick is ghostly and surreal, he dwells at length on empty landscapes and lonely lives, and he paints bleak pictures of rainy farewells in the road as sons and daughters board impatient buses that will carry them off to lasting exile in Liverpool, London, Sydney, New York.

Even so, of everything I read in preparing this Reader's Companion, *no other book evoked more vividly my own memories of Ireland, the look and feel of the place, the smell of damp tweed and the snug shelter of indoors, the rocky swellings of the land, the wet streets of stony little villages, and the primitive and haunting scent of burning peat on the wind.*

SKELETON OF A HUMAN HABITATION

SUDDENLY, ON REACHING THE TOP OF THE HILL, WE saw the skeleton of the abandoned village on the slope ahead of us. No one had told us anything about it, no one had given us any warning; there are so many abandoned villages in Ireland. The church, the shortest way to the beach, had been pointed out to us, and the shop where you can buy tea, bread, butter, and cigarettes, also the newsagent's, the post office, and the little harbor where the harpooned sharks lie like capsized boats in the mud at low tide, their dark backs uppermost, unless by chance the last wave of the tide had turned up their white bellies from which the liver had been cut out—all this seemed worth mentioning, but not the abandoned village. Gray, uniform, sloping stone gables, which we saw first with no depth of perspective, like an amateurish set for a ghost film; incredulous, we tried to count them, we gave up at forty, there must have been a hundred. The next curve of the road gave us a different perspective, and now we saw them from the side: half-finished buildings that seemed to be waiting for the carpenter: gray stone walls, dark window sockets, not a stick of wood, not a shred of material, no color anywhere, like a body without hair, without eyes, without flesh and blood—the skeleton of a village, cruelly distinct in its structure. There was the main street, at the bend, by the little square, there must have been a pub. A side street, another one. Everything not made of stone gnawed away by rain, sun, and wind—and time, which patiently trickles over everything; twenty-four great drops of time a day, the acid that eats everything away as imperceptibly as resignation. . . . If anyone ever tried to paint it, this skeleton of a human habitation where a hundred years ago five hundred people may have lived: all those gray triangles and squares on the green-gray slope of the hill; if he were to include the girl with the red pullover who is just passing along the main street with a load of peat on her back, a spot of red for her pullover and a dark brown one for the peat, a lighter brown one for the girl's face, and then the white sheep huddling like lice among the ruins—he would be considered an unusually crazy painter: that's how abstract reality is. Everything not made of stone eaten away by wind, sun, rain, and time, neatly laid out along the somber slope as if for an anatomy lesson, the skeleton of a village: over there—"look, just like a spine"—the main street, a little crooked like the spine of a laborer; every little knuckle bone is there; there are the arms and the legs: the side streets and, tipped slightly to one side, the head, the church, a somewhat larger gray triangle. Left leg: the street going up the slope to the east; right leg: the other one, leading down into the valley, this one a little shortened. The skeleton of someone with a slight limp. If his skeleton were exposed in three hundred years, this is what the man might look like who is being driven by his four thin cows past us onto the meadow, leaving him the illusion that he was driving them; his right leg has been shortened by an accident, his back is crooked from the toil of cutting peat, and even his tired head will tip a little to one side when he is laid in the earth. He has already overtaken us, already murmured his "nice day," before we had got our breath back sufficiently to answer him or ask him about the village.

No bombed city, no artillery-raked village ever looked like this, for bombs and shells are nothing but extended tomahawks, battle-axes, maces, with which to smash, to hack to pieces, but here there is no trace of violence; in limitless patience time and the elements have eaten away everything not made of stone, and from the earth have sprouted cushions on which these bones lie like relics, cushions of moss and grass.

No one would try to pull down a wall here or take wood (very valuable here) from an abandoned house (we call that cleaning out; no one cleans out here); and not even the children who drive the cattle home in the evening from the meadow above the deserted village, not even the children try to pull down walls or doorways; our children, when we suddenly found ourselves in the village, tried it immediately, to raze to the ground. Here no one razed anything to the ground, and the softer parts of abandoned dwellings are left to feed the wind, the rain, the sun, and time, and after sixty, seventy, or a hundred years all that is left is half-finished buildings from which no carpenter will ever again hang his wreath to celebrate the completion of a house: this, then, is what a human habitation looks like when it has been left in peace after death.

Still with a sense of awe we crossed the main street between the bare gables, entered side streets, and slowly the sense of awe lifted: grass was growing in the streets, moss had covered walls and potato plots, was creeping up the houses; and the stones of the gables, washed free of mortar, were neither quarried stone nor tiles, but small boulders, just as the mountain had rolled them down its streams into the valley, door and window lintels were slabs of rock, and broad as shoulder blades were the two stone slabs sticking out of the wall where the fireplace had been: once the chain for the iron cooking pot had hung from them, pale potatoes cooking in brownish water.

We went from house to house like peddlers, and every time the short shadow on the threshold had fallen away from us the blue square of the sky covered us again; in houses where the better-off ones had once lived it was larger, where the poor had lived it was smaller: all that distinguished them now was the size of the blue square of sky. In some rooms moss was already growing, some thresholds were already covered with brownish water; here and there in the front walls you could still see the pegs for the cattle: thighbones of oxen to which the chain had been attached.

"Here's where the stove was"—"the bed over there"—"here over the fireplace hung the crucifix"—"over there a cupboard": two upright stone slabs with two vertical slabs wedged into them; here in this cupboard one of the children discovered the iron wedge, and when we drew it out it crumbled away in our hands like tinder: a hard inner piece remained about as thick as a nail which—on the children's instructions—I put in my coat pocket as a souvenir.

We spent five hours in this village, and the time passed quickly because nothing happened; we scared a few birds into flight, a sheep jumped through an empty window socket and fled up the slope at our approach; in ossified fuchsia hedges hung blood-red blossoms, in withered gorse bushes hung a yellow like dirty coins, shining quartz stuck up out of the moss like bones; no dirt in the streets, no rubbish in the streams, and not a sound to be heard. Perhaps we were waiting for the girl with the red pullover and her load of brown peat, but the girl did not come back.

On the way home when I put my hand in my pocket for the iron wedge, all my fingers found was brown dust mixed with red: the same color as the bog to the right and left of our path, and I threw it in the bog.

No one could tell us exactly when and why the village had been abandoned; there are so many deserted houses in Ireland, you can count them on any two-hour walk: that one was abandoned ten years ago, this one twenty, that one fifty or eighty years ago, and there are houses in which the nails fastening the boards to windows and doors have not yet rusted through, rain and wind cannot yet penetrate.

The old woman living in the house next to us had no idea when the village had been abandoned; when she was a little girl, around 1880, it was already deserted. Of her six children, only two have remained in Ireland: two live and work in Manchester, two in the United States, one daughter is married and living here in the village (this daughter has six children, of whom in turn two will probably go to England, two to the United States), and the oldest son has stayed home: from far off, when he comes in from the meadow with the cattle, he looks like a youth of sixteen; when he turns the corner and enters the village street you feel he must be in his mid-thirties; and when he finally passes the house and grins shyly in at the window, you see that he is fifty.

"He doesn't want to get married," said his mother, "isn't it a shame?"

Yes, it is a shame. He is so hard-working and clean; he has painted the gate red, the stone knobs on the wall red too, and the window frames under the green mossy roof bright blue; humor dwells in his eyes, and he pats his donkey affectionately.

In the evening, when we go to get the milk, we ask him about the abandoned village. But he can tell us nothing about it, nothing; he has never been there: they have no meadows over there, and their peat cuttings lie in a different direction, to the south, not far from the monument to the Irish patriot who was executed in 1799. "Have you seen it yet?" Yes, we've seen it—and Tony goes off again, a man of fifty, is transformed at the corner into a man of thirty, up there on the slope where he strokes the donkey in passing he turns into a youth of sixteen, and as he stops for a moment by the fuchsia hedge, for that moment before he disappears behind the hedge, he looks like the boy he once was.

CHOUGHCS ON IRISH RAIN

THE RAIN HERE IS ABSOLUTE, MAGNIFICENT, AND frightening. To call this rain bad weather is as inappropriate as to call scorching sunshine fine weather.

You can call this rain bad weather, but it is not. It is simply weather, and weather means rough weather. It reminds us forcibly that its element is water, falling water. And water is hard. During the war I once watched a burning aircraft going down on the Atlantic coast; the pilot landed it on the beach and fled from the exploding machine. Later I asked him why he hadn't landed the burning plane on the water, and he replied:

"Because water is harder than sand."

I never believed him, but now I understood: water is hard.

And how much water can collect over three thousand miles of ocean, water that rejoices in at last reaching people, houses, terra firma, after having fallen only into water, only into itself. How can rain enjoy always falling into water?

When the electric light goes out, when the first tongue of a puddle licks its way under the door, silent and smooth, gleaming in the firelight; when the toys which the children have left lying around, when corks and bits of wood suddenly start floating and are borne forward by the tongue, when the children come downstairs, scared, and huddle in front of the fire (more surprised than scared, for they also sense the joy in this meeting of wind and rain and that this howling is a howl of delight), then we know we would not have been as worthy of the ark as Noah was. . . .

Inlander's madness, to open the door to see what's up outside. Everything's up: the roof tiles, the roof gutters, even the house walls, do not inspire much confidence (for here they build temporarily, although, if they don't emigrate, they live forever in these temporary quarters—while in Europe they build for eternity without knowing whether the next generation will benefit from so much solidity).

It is a good thing always to have candles, the Bible, and a little whisky in the house, like sailors prepared for a storm; also a pack of cards, some tobacco, knitting needles and wool for the women; for the storm has a lot of breath, the rain holds a lot of water, and the night is long. Then when a second tongue of rain advances from the window and joins the first one, when the toys float slowly along the narrow tongue toward the window, it is a good thing to look up in the Bible whether the promise to send no more floods has really been given. It has been given: we can light the next candle, the next cigarette, shuffle the cards again, pour some more whisky, abandon ourselves to the drumming of the rain, the howling of the wind, the click of the knitting needles. The promise has been given.

It was some time before we heard the knocking on the door—at first we had taken it for the banging of a loose bolt, then for the rattle of the storm, then we realized it was human hands, and the naïveté of the Continental mentality can be measured from the fact that I expressed the opinion it might be the man from the electric company. Almost as naïve as expecting the bailiff to appear on the high seas.

Quickly the door was opened, a dripping figure of a man pulled in, the door shut, and there he stood; with his cardboard suitcase sopping wet, water running out of his sleeves, his shoes, from his hat, it almost seemed as if water were running out of his eyes—this is how swimmers look after taking part in a lifesaving contest fully clothed; but such ambitions were foreign to this man: he had merely come from the bus stop, fifty paces through this rain, had mistaken our house for his hotel, and was by occupation a clerk in a law office in Dublin.

"D'you mean to say the bus is running in this weather?"

"Yes," he said, "it is, and only a bit behind schedule. But it was more of a swim than a drive . . . and you're sure this isn't a hotel?"

"Yes, but. . . ."

He—Dermot was his name—turned out, when he was dry, to know his Bible, to be a good card-player, a good storyteller, a good whisky-drinker; moreover, he showed us how to bring water quickly to the boil on a tripod in the fireplace, how to broil lamb chops on the same ancient tripod, how to toast bread on long forks, the purpose of which we had not yet discovered—and it was not till the small hours that he confessed to knowing a little German; he had been a prisoner-of-war in Germany, and he told our children something they will never forget, must never forget: how he buried the little gypsy children who had died during the evacuation of the Stuthof concentration camp; they were so small—he showed us— and he had dug graves in the frozen ground to bury them.

"But why did they have to die?" asked one of the children.

"Because they were gypsies."

"But that's no reason—you don't have to die because of that."

"No," said Dermot, "that's no reason, you don't have to die because of that."

We stood up; it was light now, and at that moment it became quiet outside. Wind and rain had gone away, the sun came up over the horizon, and a great rainbow arched over the sea; it was so close we thought we could see it in substance—as thin as soap bubbles was the skin of the rainbow.

Corks and bits of wood were still bobbing about in the puddle when we went upstairs to the bedrooms.

GAZING INTO THE FIRE

IT MUST BE FUN TO HAVE YOUR OWN PEAT DITCH; MR. O'Donovan in Dublin has one, and any number of O'Neills, Molloys, and Dalys in Dublin have them; on free days (and there are plenty of those) Mr. O'Donovan needs only to get on a Number 17 or 47 bus with his spade and drive out to his peat ditch: the fare is sixpence, he has a few sandwiches and a flask of tea in his pocket, and he can dig peat in his own claim; a truck or a donkey cart will carry the peat back down to the city for him. For his compatriot in other counties it is even easier: there the peat grows almost into the house, and on sunny days the bare hills, striped greenish-black, are as busy as at harvest time; here they are gathering in what centuries of moisture have built up between naked rocks, lakes, and green meadows: peat, the sole natural wealth of a country that for centuries has been robbed of its forests, that has not always had its daily bread but almost always its daily rain, no matter how little: a tiny cloud sailing along on a day of brilliant sunshine and—half jokingly—squeezed out like a sponge.

Behind every house the lumps of this brownish cake dry in great stacks, sometimes higher than the roof, and in this way you can be sure of one thing: fire in the fireplace, the red flame licking the dark lumps, leaving pale ash, light, odorless, almost like cigar ash: white tip to the black Brazil.

An open fire renders one of the least attractive (and most indispensable) objects of civilized social intercourse superfluous: the ashtray; when the time the guest has spent in the house is left behind chopped up into cigarette ends in the ashtray, and the housewife empties these malodorous dishes, the stubborn, stickyish, black-gray mess remains. It is strange that no psychologist has yet investigated the lowlands of psychology and discovered the branch of buttology, for then the housewife, in collecting the chopped-up time to throw it away, could turn the butts to her advantage and practice a little psychology: there they are, then, the half-smoked, brutally bent cigarette ends of the man who never has time and with his cigarettes struggles in vain against time to gain time—there Eros has left a dark-red border on the filter—the pipe smoker the ashes of his dependability: black, crumbled, dry—there are the frugal remains of the chain smoker, who lets the cigarette burn almost to his lips before he lights the next one; in these lowlands of psychology it would be easy to find at least a few rough indices as by-products of civilized social intercourse. How kindly a fire is, consuming every trace; only tea-cups remain, a few glasses, and in the fireplace the glowing heart round which from time to time the master of the house piles up fresh black lumps of peat.

And all the meaningless brochures—for refrigerators, trips to Rome, "Golden Books of Humor," automobiles, and investments—this flood that, with wrapping paper, newspapers, tickets, envelopes, is rising alarmingly, here it can be transformed directly into flame; add a few sticks of wood picked up during a walk on the beach: the remains of a brandy case, a wedge washed overboard, dried out, white and clean: hold a match to the pyre and at once the flames leap up, and time, the time between five in the afternoon and midnight, is so quickly consumed by the quiet flame of the fire; voices are low; for someone to shout here he must be one of two things: sick or ridiculous. Sitting here by the fire, it is possible to play truant from Europe, while Moscow has lain in darkness for the past four hours, Berlin for two, even Dublin for half an hour: there is still a clear light over the sea, and the Atlantic persistently carries away piece by piece the Western bastion of Europe; rocks fall into the sea, soundlessly the bog streams carry the dark European soil out into the Atlantic; over the years, gently plashing, they smuggle whole fields out to the open sea, crumb by crumb.

Shivering slightly, the truants put fresh peat on the fire; pieces laid carefully in layers to light the midnight game of dominoes; the needle glides slowly across the radio panel to pick up the time, but all it catches is shreds of national anthems; slowly the light in the panel dies away, and once again the flame leaps up from the peat: there is still one layer there, one hour: four lumps of peat above the glowing heart; the daily rain comes late today, almost with a smile, falling softly into the bog, into the ocean.

The sound of the departing guests' car dwindles toward lights lying scattered in the bog, on black slopes already in deep shadow, while on the beach and over the sea it is still light; the dome of darkness moves slowly toward the horizon, then closes the last chink in the vault, but it is still not quite dark, while in the Urals it is already getting light. Europe is only as wide as a short summer night.

RICHARD CONDON

Making a home at Rossenarra, Co. Kilkenny: 1960s

"MICK JAGGER TOOK A BATH AT ROSSENARRA. THE
ONLY MEXICAN COOKBOOK WRITTEN ON IRISH
SOIL, *THE MEXICAN STOVE*, WAS TESTED AND
FEINSCHMECKED HERE."

*Novelist Richard Condon and his wife spent several decades traveling around
the world, settling for a while in one place, then another: France, Spain,
England, Switzerland, Mexico. Some of these travels were financed by the
success of Condon's best-selling 1959 novel,* The Manchurian Candidate. *He
had great success in later years with the 1982* Prizzi's Honor *and its several
sequels, and with the 1974* Winter Kills.

*Apparently deciding that they no longer wanted to keep any of their
money, the Condons made up their minds to settle in Ireland, where they
bought and began arranging to refurbish a pink Georgian mansion on a hill
in Kilkenny in the southeast of the country. Once they began doing business
with the Irish Building Trades, they quickly realized that they would never
be troubled by wealth again.*

*Other buildings in Kilkenny have colorful histories, too. In 1650 Oliver
Cromwell, who was not the sort of visitor Ireland gets today, stabled his horses
in the Cathedral of St. Canice in Kilkenny city.*

IN A EUROVISION SONG CONTEST RECENTLY A YUGO-
slavian girl sang her country's pop song hit "I Am No Prettier and
No Smarter Than Any Other Girl of My Type." The title happens to be a

shrewd description of a house we bought on the *alta plana* of County Kilkenny in Ireland. It is called Rossenarra, and it is the usual Georgian country house. I was fifty before I understood that Georgian did not necessarily mean something from the State of Georgia or even a Russian prince whose father's farm might have a roof and two cows. Georgian in this story will only mean that which pertains to that bunched group of Germans, all called George, who were kings of England. Rossenarra was built in 1824, about five and a quarter years before the Georgian period ended.

The house has its resident female ghost. The Irish are of the opinion that ghosts show themselves only to people who have Mc or O' in front of their names, but so far our ghost has shown itself only to males of British origin. This does not mean that she is an unfriendly or nationalistic ghost. Or an IRA ghost. More likely it is the wraith of yet another British girl still seeking a husband, because British men do tend to resist marriage even beyond the grave. My wife's parents are British and quite frequently the ghost will move my wife's sweater, or book, or eyeglasses to a different place, requiring that a search from cellar to attic be undertaken. But our ghost has done convenient things as well, such as frightening the wits out of an English domestic couple we had and wished we did not have, thus causing them to quit.

Rossenarra has a family of bats, including a black-rubber baby bat with the anxiety-worn face of a stand-up night club comic. One of the great professional pigeon shooters on the international circuit says he "found his eye" shooting at bats as they emerged from a hole high up in Rossenarra as dusk dropped. The house has one of those extremely rare things, a functioning antique in the form of a shower-spray bath with forty-five jets that deliver the soothe out of five vertical pipes from knee to shoulder. This *objet de virtu* is of course neither Georgian nor Edwardian but Victorian, and is said to have originated in 1882 (may we be here to celebrate the centennial). The shower is a part of the tub, enclosed in glass. The tub—aaaahhhh—is seven feet long and feeds water from the side, so that one does not need to stop reading the threats in the morning newspaper to turn the water off. You don't sit up and strain outward and downward toward faucets beyond your toes. You lift a hand languidly, grasp a tap and turn it.

Rossenarra has the usual sixteen-feet-high ceilings and thirty-feet square rooms, whose ceilings have the plaster-white pie crusts found in any city apartment. It has three stories of such ceiling and a cellar with nine rooms and one bath (for the dogs). It has a safe sunk into the floor of a room (whose location I am too cunning to mention here) where I keep my summer pajamas. There is a grass tennis court, which we keep netless and nicely mown and on which the regal greyhound, Jezebel, does her exercises. The house has two wings. One of these terminates in a garage, presently packed neatly with German cars. The other end is a four-box stable that is empty of thundering hooves. We can account for just over forty of the Irish gentry who avoid us because of this. To have a stable with four horse boxes attached to the building in which you live and not to fill it with *Equus caballus*, their food and their attendants, is something like appearing in the streets of Calcutta with a Holland & Holland shotgun and blasting away at the corner cow. It just isn't done, old man. In Switzerland the first question is, Do you ski? In the United States it is, What do you do? In South Africa it is, Are you white? In Ireland the first question is, Do you hunt? At a press conference on his arrival at the Dublin airport a few years ago they asked the identical first question of a new American ambassador. He replied, "Oh, I shoot the occasional fox."

I was once a twelve-year-old witness in a civil trial against the 104th Field Artillery of New York, which rented saddle horses for trotting through Central Park, because the cavalry has to get exercised somehow. I was summoned to the witness stand because the plaintiff claimed that the twenty-four-year-old horse that I rode most often was the wild, raging thing that had thrown the plaintiff, a Ms., upon the bridle path. I was twelve (then). The sensible horse was twice my age. I am no longer twelve and have grown brittle. I do not ride, nor do I hunt—an insanity that involves balancing oneself upon a horse while it leaps over stone walls. Beyond the film business, I have not greeted either end of a horse for about forty-five years.

Rossenarra is a fat house. Five house painters who began to paint the inside in the first week of March finished painting the outside during the last week of September, spattered and exhausted. When we bought the house a certain amount of gray paint had been slapped over its immediately evident exteriors, in the manner of a tart throwing on ghastly cosmetics in the hope of a sale. All of it had been done, in that "soft" climate, without treating the building wall, so that within days after the title had been closed and passed to us, black spores of fungus began to grow in blotches under the paint. But e'en though the cost of painting a house that fat is cruel, we were glad that the previous paint job had cheated so consciencelessly, because it meant we were rid of that dreadful poor-house gray. It was all repainted in the sort of pinkness that suffuses a bride's cheeks, the loveliest of pinks, trimmed with white windows that will actually remain white for some years to come, because this is rural Ireland where factory smoke is unknown.

Rossenarra is so fat it took a lot of restoring. We had the constant company of as many as thirty-seven members of the Irish Building Trades for one week short of one year. Very few of these men could understand my speech, because I may have left the United States nineteen years ago, but my voice box remains in New York. I had never failed, for example, to make myself understood in Tim Costello's saloon on Third Avenue, which was said to be an Irish home away from home, but perhaps a sea change had set in. During the house-wrecking at Rossenarra most of the gifted restorers stared at me with X's for eyes when I spoke to them, then went straight off to take an early tea break.

Rossenarra's demesne was rather more extensive when it was a farm of about eleven hundred and twenty acres, with a gatehouse at each point of the compass. The Irish Land Commission divided all that into five farms, leaving only the main house and just under twelve acres to lure us in. That is to say, our Irish holdings comprise 1.3 per cent of the original Rossenarra. It sounds cramping when it is stated baldly like that. To us the almost twelve acres are 400.17 per cent larger than any other grounds on which we had ever lived, and the house itself is approximately 812.9321 per cent more ample than any former living machine we had occupied. We had lived on a full acre once (he wrote wistfully) in Switzerland, but it really doesn't count, because almost all of it was steeply downhill. Of even more clanging importance, Rossenarra was the first immovable thing we had ever owned, and almost twelve acres is bigger than anyone's Monopoly board.

It is large enough to support a walnut tree, two Irish-born Airedale terriers named Mona and Fiona, one guest greyhound on loan from Wendy (the right greyhound lends feudal style to a country house by reposing mostly in doorways, so that when one trips over her, one has the chance of running headlong across an entire room before falling), a few hundred rhododendron bushes, offering three colors, more laurel leaves than all the heroes of the entire Roman Empire ever wore, and about one hundred and seventy tall trees that are not walnut.

As the fortunate automobile enters across the cattle grid and through the unstately cement gates built by our handyman, Vincent Murray, then rolls down the avenue toward, but not yet upon, the house, on either side it is possible to gaze out upon what is called by the kindly "a lawn," which undoubtedly does resemble a lawn when spotted from a moving helicopter (unlike the hopelessly real emerald green on the west of our near twelve acres). All our savings go into trying to grow grass in that harsh shale. We have planted three hundred pounds of grass seed upon the land. It seems like a shockingly unnecessary thing to worry about—whether or not grass will grow in Ireland, but aside from my years as a press agent, this was the first thing I had ever planted. The arrival of the coming spring will tell. La! Glass those four acres in, give them a few thousand pounds of peat and nitrogen fertilizers, cover them with quilts through the winter, and, bejabbers, within three years you'll see a lawn as good as anything in Death Valley.

The almost twelve acres also have a ruined Temple of Diana. Someone who feared that the Irish Land Commission would not appreciate it sheared off its classical façade and its three stately pillars and carted them away to rest for a mere eleven years in their dismounted pieces all astrew across the ground of a contractor's front yard (where it would be quite impossible for the Land Commission or anyone else to appreciate it). It's just as well that this chap cared that much about beauty, because there is something not quite fitting about a stately Temple of Diana standing on twelve acres—which is a fraction of Forest Lawn. Now that the trees have gone around it, it would stand there like Grant's Tomb, if General Grant had been a much shorter man.

Rossenarra has a skulk of foxes to enrage the dogs. The man who owned Rossenarra in its heyday was Master of the Kilmoganny Harriers Hunt, and the foxes liked to be near their work. We still have the grossly adequate stone kennels that once housed the hunting hounds. We have a plentitude of wells, which we have covered over lest a strolling guest disappear instantly, as though he had fallen down a well or something. There is a prudently small area that we hope will become a kitchen garden next spring. All city people do that reflexively when they move into the country, because they see it as a duty. No one plants more than one vegetable, of course, because any vegetables can be bought so much more cheaply than they can be grown by city people. We have planted shallots. I suppose when our grandchildren take over they will plant marijuana. We talk about planting red currants to make a chartreuse of hare, or some parsley to temper the beef and kidney soup—but it is not likely.

None of the foregoing inventory is unusual for a Georgian house on the Irish pampas. What does make Rossenarra prettier and smarter and more personally regarded than any other house of its type was what was transfused into it from the very veins of our bank by the solicitous Irish Building Trades. When the Fates met on the occasion of the birth of a son to a king of ancient Greece, the first prayer wafted to Olympus was, "Save this infant from ever having to deal with the Irish Building Trades." Later, at the age of two months, the infant was put before the court hypnotist to begin conditioning it from ever emigrating.

As for us Condons, we have lived in Paris, Madrid, New York, Mexico City, Paris again, London, Geneva, Locarno and Kilmoganny in the course of these years, spending a minimum of fourteen months in Spain (leaving with sorrow) and a maximum of nine and a half years in Switzerland (leaving with grief) along the way. Each country was different—which is the reason for emigrating regularly. There are certain requirements. Being able to speak the language is important when the plumbing needs fixing or to orient a dentist. But communications are not all that effective when confined to speech. The vital interest in emigrating is to try to understand the people in a new country. Clearly, the emigrant has failed to understand the people in his own country, so he moves into areas where he can pretend to try to understand foreign habits of living that he has never encountered before. It is doubtful whether this is ever successful, but the operative words are "to try." It is a pleasant game. Natives tend to give the emigrants much larger scoring handicaps than they would give their own people and to make impossible allowances. Local food habits are a sound way through which to begin to approach understanding. Also bathtubs, mirrors, hotels, some books, and some traffic patterns.

Understandings and misunderstandings in the seven countries we lived in, and the thirteen other countries to which we contemplated emigrating, should be a part of this record, as well as trying to remember why we stayed longer in some countries than in others. However, most of all, this book hopes to be a warning against anyone ever, ever trying to restore/renovate/recreate an old house anywhere, and a tale of what happened to us when we defied the gods of the building contractors and began to do just that at Rossenarra.

A story is told about God making Ireland. When it was finished, all the people of the world in such places as Las Vegas, Calcutta, McMurdo Sound, New York, Milan, Glasgow and other garden spots cried out bitterly because he had made Ireland so unutterably beautiful. "Ah, yes," He acknowledged, "but I haven't put in the Irish Building Trades yet." They were well installed when we got there. They were waiting around the corner when we found Rossenarra.

And why Ireland—considering the fact that the Irish themselves are world-champion emigrants? Well, Ireland for a lot of good reasons, as follows. I am a novelist. That means that my own way of earning bread, roof and clothes is big enough to fit on my knee or to carry wherever we choose to go. No catching the 8:17 in the morning. No plotting to push a large Mosler safe off a balcony onto a division rival. No hopes of becoming a vice-president; no pension plan, no retirement funds from Our Patron Employer. We have sacrificed all that, but in return we have been issued rights to live anywhere in the world we choose to live. It's hard, folks, but that's the way it is.

Evelyn and I have been married for thirty-five short years and have, as issue, Deborah, age thirty, and Wendy, age twenty-five (or thereabouts, as I am not getting into hot water to pacify my publisher's copy-editor). They each have one child. Debo's daughter bears the Dickensian name of Jemma Jupp and uses a British passport. They live in London, where ex-husband and father is a playwright, and also in Hampshire where Debbie has been licensed as a full-fledged trainer of race horses and Jemma owns a pony a/k/a Humpty Dumpty. Wendy's son, Benito-Juarez Bennett, wears a Mexican passport, even though the Mexican government has begun to take a dim view of dual citizenship, even for five-year-olds. Their ex-husband and father lives in New York. Though Wendy now lives in Aspen, Colorado, her greyhound stays in Ireland with us. If she had been taken to the United States when Wendy re-emigrated, quarantine laws would have made it impossible for her to return to these exotic islands if Wendy were to change her mind about living in America. (And she has changed her mind. In the year since I began writing this book, Wendy and Nito have emigrated from London to Fort Worth, Texas, to Aspen. In the fall of 1973 Wendy will re-emigrate to London from Fort Worth.) Professional dog racers destroy greyhounds that aren't winning money. At three years old. Jezebel was luckier. She was taken to the outskirts of London in someone's automobile and thrown away like an old banana skin. Wendy found her at the dog pound. It isn't something anyone would be likely to think about, but, unexpectedly, greyhounds make sweet house dogs and pets.

My wife has red hair, green eyes. Debo has blond hair and very blue eyes. Wendy has hazel eyes. When Debo was five she described my eyes accurately as being pink-and-blue. Debbie is tall and slender. Wendy has mahogany hair; is smaller and rounder. Evelyn is tall and has had the same figure for thirty years. Through a contrasting series of never-ending diets of wine and pasta on one side and the calm advice of Professor John Yudkin on the other my weight has swung from two hundred and thirty-six pounds down to one hundred and seventy-five pounds in one year. Evelyn and Wendy speak English, French and Spanish. Debbie speaks those plus Italian and working Russian. Miss Jemma Jupp, at six, is learning French. Benito-Juarez Bennett is learning English. All are master emigrants and I am their tour leader, pursuing the illusion that a regular change of scene, sounds, people and food keeps improving my chances of improving as a writer. All of us are very fond of what we like. Contrasting places are what we have liked best, favored most.

Place is the most important component of the novel. Readers of such formalized fantasies must be able to see and understand totally the terrain in which the story takes place. Fantasy or not, we all need to know where we are.

Our present place, in fact, is Ireland. Because of the extraordinary number of writers who have emigrated to Ireland and who will continue to set up shop here, Ireland may well become a place seen by many different sorts of eyes. In the year 2020, writers who emigrated to Ireland in the 1970s will be seen as part of a Major Literary Migration. Everything literary that has happened fifty years before becomes Major, because belles-lettrists must make a living too. By sinking my heroic fortune into Rossenarra I may have become a part of the future Bloomsday set, in the manner of the Bloomsbury layabouts who freeloaded on that nice Mrs. Woolf. The clan is congregating. The lady who wrote *Mary Poppins* and the man who created The Saint, Len Deighton, and, at present count, some two hundred and fifty-six other writers, composers, painters and sculptors have emigrated to Ireland. The Irish Republic made such a booming typewriter market possible by absolving all those emigrants from the sin of paying Irish income taxes. Writers are employing other writers as actors. Actors are writing. All are painting the culture in roseate hues. All but one of these (me) so far are British for the reason that Britain—like other rational nations—has laid down sane and humane taxation laws by which a national staying outside his country for one year pays no taxes to his own government.

In World War II the government of the United States of America revised the tax law as it applied to royalties paid to inventors because the government needed self-steering torpedoes and other gadgets (if not Art)—

it has yet to change the law in relief of taxes on royalties paid to writers, because beyond the need for an occasional speech, politicians have no use for writers. They are deeply suspicious of the arts, and even go so far in their invective as to call all artists intellectuals. Politicians find writers too critical, too independent; and it is hard to keep a rope on them. So although Evelyn and I, two working writers who could not be considered intellectuals even by George Wallace, have lived outside the United States for nineteen years, we have had to pay full, fuller, fullest income taxes to the American government every year. Furthermore, the Internal Revenue Service "reviews" our income statements every year faithfully.

My books are published in nineteen languages. They can be published, by copyright law, in the American language only in the United States. That leaves eighteen other languages, in hard-cover and paperback editions, which (one hopes) might earn money outside the United States. Further, the income from the sale of rights, such as film rights, to utter one example, are defined in the booklet issued by the Internal Revenue Service as being the same as the sale of a used car. Writers are allowed no capital-gains taxation on the sale of property, which is far more perishable than oil, from a source that depletes itself much faster than any source of petroleum. Once and for all: Evelyn and I don't use American pavements, and certainly don't want to use the United States Army, but we pay for them just the same, in the form of annual income taxes, to an absentee tax collector; for which steady, constant, nineteen years of payment we do not get the right to vote. And the new Irish tax law was really no lure to us. No matter where we had lived before, the American tax treaties with the countries in which we lived had permitted us—at least—the deduction of any foreign taxes paid. In short: we don't have to pay any Irish taxes though we do use their roads, laws, hospitals and serenity because such taxes are deductible from the American taxes which we do have to pay though we don't use American roads, laws, hospitals or lack of serenity. It is as silly as politicians can arrange things, short of drafting taxpayers to be shot in Asia because it is good for national business.

My grandfather was born in Ireland, and therefore the Irish law states that I may become an Irish citizen in an hour or so of any afternoon. If I did so, this would so enrage the American government that they would tax all my American income, a mere 90 per cent of the total, at the source and at punitive rates. But the fact is that one becomes triste about paying taxes only when one lives where one isn't required to pay any. The government by politicians here in Ireland values all arts as the only characteristic of any nation after one, two or three millennia that they are thrilled to invite the strangers of the world into their country to live as their guests. The resident novelist, Constantine Fitzgibbon, had the original inspiration. He took it to Charles Haughey, Irish Minister of Finance, who refined the idea, and caused it to be made into a law. Today any painter, composer, sculptor or writer who earns his living entirely from any of those activities can, upon making application after establishing Irish residence, be pronounced legally free of the payment of Irish income taxes—a considerable bite. This is an immeasurable accomplishment by a modern government. It is a prodigious revelation of national character. It would be impossible for any American government to conceive of a program of tax relief for its artists, even though they are the main messengers delivering the meaning of American culture to present and future, so that the nation may be recognized for what it is, whatever it is.

Another reason for our seeking to live in Ireland was that Switzerland, where we had been living most recently (and everywhere else in Europe south of the Stockholm airport), had become so crowded, it took three months' waiting time to get a dental appointment. Excepting northern Scandinavia, there is no country in Europe less crowded than Ireland. Further, according to the World Health Organization, which is affiliated with the United Nations, Ireland is the best-fed country in the world.

Living in the last uncrowded country means good, wide highways on which one might not see another car for a dozen miles. It means an easily obtained seat in the theater. The only places in Ireland that seem really crowded are racetracks, bars and airports. Further, crime is scarce. My mother-in-law has just escaped from New York, where, in her eighty-fourth year, she had been mugged twice (off Fifth Avenue in open daylight) and where her eighty-year-old husband had been held up once at the point of a knife by needy youths trying to raise money for heroin.

Ireland could be the last of the countries. Ireland is not only remote from places, it is remote from time the present, as anyone waiting for the delivery of carpets well knows, and as any country whose people are part Phoenician, part Viking should be. Wilfrid Sheed noted that the status of the writer in Ireland is equivalent to that of a priest except that it is impossible for the writer to lose his status once attained. I have some cause to doubt that. An Irish neighbor proposed that he put me up for membership in the Kildare Street Club, because it has exchange privileges with Boodles in London, and Boodles is the only place outside Perth where one can get Old Grouse Scotch whiskey, said (by him) to be the finest Scotch whiskey ever distilled. However, he confided to a mutual friend that he was having doubts about proposing me, because he had read one of my books in the meantime. Lurking in the shadows of that sentence is the most blatant sort of literary criticism.

I had revenge, however. I asked a friend who runs a fleet of oil tankers if, the next time one of them touched port at Perth, he would ask one of the crew to buy me a case of the Old Grouse. When it was in hand I invited the critic to Rossenarra and left a bottle of the ambrosial stuff in clear presence on the bar. Agog, he asked where on earth I had got it. I looked mystified, then, recovering, told him I had bought it at our local store in Kilmoganny. He had the elegance to weep.

The soft fact is, whether one is a professional writer with long-time, built-in motor habits and prejudices, or whether one is an amateur who would choose the name before the game, Ireland is completely a writer's country. Chances are that if one were to ask twelve boys and girls in Ireland what they would like to become a majority of them would answer "writer." That could also happen in Mexico. It might happen in France. It would not happen in the United States.

Another startlingly convenient fact for emigrants is that no foreigners seem to exist for Ireland after the seventeenth century. One might have the speech of a Bulgarian mustache engineer and saunter into a pub he had never seen before in some faraway Irish county, murmur, "I am Sir Vaginal Bliss, essayist and poetaster" and immediately settle down to an entertaining listen.

My friend James Nolan is an emigrant Pennsylvanian who lives in London. He is one of the remaining scholar monks of the twentieth century (a man who covers all of Europe spending contented nights under the roofs of former mistresses, eating at dinner tables vibrating from overtense husbands). Nolan says I bought Rossenarra just to have it over my fickle grandfather, who left all this grass and serenity behind. I don't agree, because I am more sparsely informed about my grandfather than most people. The only dimensional fill-in I ever had about him was from Grandmother, who, in a valiant reach to find something endearing, told me, "He was a neat, little man who never had a crack in his shoes." I think I know why we bought Rossenarra. It has to be the logical reason, because it is inane enough and far enough from any grasp of reality.

We had been working steadily for ten weeks in Locarno, and every ten weeks it was our practice to go somewhere (Switzerland being equidistant from everywhere) for ten days and cool it. This time, instead of going to Athens or Copenhagen, Madrid or London, we decided to look at Ireland. It must be clear that when we travel we travel behind our main interest, which is emigrating. Golfers investigate golf courses. Policemen look up old lags. Famous beauties seek yet new mirrors to conquer. We look for houses and "conditions." We had been to Ireland once, years before, and then only for a weekend, to visit a film star whose lady had just had bosoms packed with gel and who insisted that everyone, including the room-service waiter, test their impressive firmness.

We took off to Dublin from Zurich on Sunday, May 3, and, mysteriously, got ourselves into the only wrong hotel in the entire capital. The hall porter lost no time in hiring the only wrong car livery service—it belonged either to his brother-in-law or perhaps to a chap he had grown up with when they had both trained with Fagin as boys.

The car hire worked out at about $2.40 a mile for a 1945 Mercedes, with a driver who had been born ten years later and amazing tires made out of some native pasta. However, if one can get the two major mistakes out of the way early, usually the remainder of an emigration reconnaissance will go smoothly. We toured across the tiny country and back again and had a lovely time, even though we had found nothing that a championship emigrant would pass. After the next ten weeks of work went by we returned again and set out to drive south, a different direction from the explorations of the first journey. Within a week we had exhausted all realty listings but one, and this one had the advantage of a lovely name and of being very difficult to find—a vital factor to discourage the casual dropper-in.

As we came upon it around the bend in the rutted dirt road (which we were destined later to have paved, providing the sort of drainage for it which would have inspired Victor Hugo to a sequel), the back of the Rossenarra house looked like a department store that had been teleported from the Dublin of a hundred and forty-seven years ago—when Dublin was the second city of the British Empire—filled with exotic and pleasuring merchandise, roamed by foam-bosomed ladies and hard-eyed Regency bucks. The only recurring dream of my life, at least when asleep, is one in which I roam through an enormous, crowded department store. It is what we of Vienna and Matteawan call the greed dream. My life has been characterized by greed. I have no sloth, no casual lust, no envy, avarice or false pride, but only three out of the seven deadly sins: greed, wrath and gluttony. The wrath is the result of having played that ridiculous game of American football when I was in my teens, suffering a concussion, and not being made to stay on my back in bed for three weeks. Later findings show that old concussions are the cause of most of the sudden, unaccountable rages of the baffled men of the world. As for gluttony, that family heirloom called angina pectoris has made the old-time delights of feeding and wining out of the question. As a matter of desperation I am left bereft of all the deadly sins but greed.

Really, I am not outstandingly greedy. I know a film director who has two Rolls-Royces and who will drink only Dom Perignon. Driving two Rolls-Royces is entirely logical and normal. But Dom Perignon is utterly unnecessary when Pommery '53 is available, don't you think? This director is simply too greedy. He wears vicuña underwear and carries eighty-nine pieces of Vuitton luggage, including a sock case. But I am certainly as greedy as my resources permit me to be. I try harder. Emigrating is an exercise in greed, a greed for new experience, possessions, impressions and serenity. And almost anything that is sold in department stores.

Halfway down the hill to that illusion of an ancient emporium we paused beside the largest of Rossenarra's three ponds. They lay one below the other, connected by a glittering necklace of brook. We sighted between a weeping beech and a weeping willow over the world's most diminutive waterfalls and saw the house. We all hear a lot of blather about Victoria Falls and Niagara. Or Angel Falls in Venezuela, which crashes down 3,212 feet from the river Carrao and is therefore the highest waterfall in the world. Or about the sheer volume of the Salto das Sete Quedas on the Alto Paraná River between Brazil and Paraguay, whose normal flow could fill the Yankee Stadium to the top in three-fifths of a second.

No one until now has bothered to write about the world's smallest waterfalls, but they are part of the minute Rossenarra chain of three, as advertised in the estate agent's brochure. From peak to trough the greatest of these falls is 1.2 inches, and we have so advised the *Guinness Book of Records*.

As we gaped down the hill our hearts filled at the gallantry of the television aerial straining eastward vainly, trying to steal license-fee-free BBC pictures from England, 190 miles away. From that view the house seemed to be wearing an enormous gray Norfolk jacket with darker gray panels. Plonked on all that grass, four-square, it was assurance that time stood for something more tangible than bifocals and snapped arches; that there might be a serenity in years that we could acquire with strokes of the pen. Leave Tara and Manderley to David O. Selznick, I thought. Rossenarra was kith and kitsch with the greatest architectural eccentricities of Cecil Blount DeMille.

The house's very name—Rossenarra—made Tara sound like Sammy's Bowery Follies or something naughty in the Filipino language. Craftily I set out to learn what Rossenarra meant in Gaelic. We wormed a translation out of one of the plumbers: Rossenarra, a veritable invitation to the waltz, for it meant (the plumber said) Rosse=rosy, Narra=narrow—i.e., the Primrose Path. Months later, when we had fixed a far grimmer bead upon the plumber, we quickly sought another translation. A red-bearded Irish scholar connected with the Tourism Board swiftly translated Rossenarra as: a place or hill or fort or river or ski lift near woods or a road or grass or a supermarket. I have no knowledge of the baffling Irish language beyond the fact that Dr. David Hanly says my own name is spelled Risteard O'Conduin—not that it can be pronounced. When watching Irish being spoken on the Vulgar Tube in the days when I still believed that a glass or two of wine was good for my heart, I was convinced that they were just teasing. Gaelic is a language that has the quality of suggesting that the speaker is making the sounds up as he goes along in order (a) to satisfy government regulations and (b) to meet a deep nationalistic urge in the viewers at home, who have not been able to remember a word of it. Gaelic could be the most noncommittal language. It has no words for either "yes" or "no." We are researching "maybe." In the end we did our own translation of Rossenarra. Rosse has to mean rosy. Narra must mean nose. Because of that belief we have caused the house to be painted a soft, blushing pink.

Rossenarra is (about) eighty miles south-southwest of Dublin, sixteen miles due south of Kilkenny town and two miles east of Kilmoganny, the great crossroads of the Western hemisphere for people going from the Hare and Hounds pub to Tom Moore's or P. J. McDonald's.

In the Irish language Kilmoganny means the church of St. Mogeanna, despite the fact that no saint called Mogeanna is to be met with in the Irish martyrologies, therefore similarly fanciful, says *The History and Antiquities of the Diocese of Ossary*, is naming the twenty-third of August as his feast day. Originally the townland of Kilmoganny belonged to the branch of the Butler family that came from Rossenarrow, which is one reason why such scholars of Gaelic as Dr. Hanly and Noel Speidel have such difficulty in translating the word "Rossenarra." For centuries, in the Rossenarra demesne, the chief seat of the Walshes, Lords of the Mountain, was the castle at Castlehale. It stood near the summit of a high hill that forms the culminating point of the townland, built soon after the Anglo-Norman invasion.

At the time of the Cromwellian oppressions of the Irish, The Walsh chose as his *nom de guerre* the name Bhaitear Breathnacht, which seems so self-defeating. If he tried to check into a hotel with three successive girls and signed in as Mr. and Mrs. Bhaitear Breathnacht, one would think the room clerk would be onto him at once. Breathnacht means night breath, a combination of John Jameson's and Guinness.

About 1824 a Mr. Morris Reade, who lived in Rossenarrow and had a large estate in that locality, finding his new residence not quite up to date, built a new one in the townland of Castlehale. Because of veneration for the old family homestead he transferred its name of Rossenarra House to the new house at Castlehale, and changed the name of the townland of Castlehale itself from Castlehale to Rossenarra demesne.

Rossenarra has many unexpected handles. The beautiful lady who appears on all Irish paper currency, wife of the portrait painter, Sir John Lavery, was part of the family who owned Rossenarra. She was a great and good friend of that endomorphic bricklayer, Winston Churchill, and other statesmen of the time, and was the last lady to have dined with Michael Collins, a leader of the struggle that made Ireland a free republic.

Mick Jagger took a bath at Rossenarra. The only Mexican cookbook written on Irish soil, *The Mexican Stove,* was tested and feinschmecked here. Len Deighton cooked in the Rossenarra kitchens. The house has been painted by Sir John Lavery and James Richard Blake, photographed by John Bryson, Ferdinand Fairfax and the Columbia Broadcasting System, recorded in needlepoint by F. Marx Heller, and has new central heating by a consortium of the furthest flung experts ever to disperse themselves across a nation guerilla-fashion to achieve the job: always on the run between telephone calls from Dublin to Kilkenny to Clonmel to Castle Comer, to Cork and to Limerick as though to prove the essence of what the Bard of Rockrimmon wrote: "It takes a heap o' money/To make a house a home." If I complete fifty-odd more novels or two screenplays, the abacus people say I will come even with our investment gain.

Nonetheless the indirect costs of finding Rossenarra over a nineteen-year period may have gone beyond buying and restoring the house itself. The bulk of the costs was spent following the thirty-five years of travel-through-marriage, journeys that finally led to this large building we now occupy.

DEBORAH LOVE

From Cork to Killorglin: 1969

"THE ROADS BELONG TO THE ANIMALS AND
PEDESTRIANS MORE THAN THE MOTORIST. SHEEP
LIE DOWN AND TAKE NAPS IN THEM, COWS ARE
DRIVEN DOWN THEM, CHILDREN WALK TWO AND
THREE ABREAST ALONG THEM."

*One summer in the late 1960s, writer Peter Matthiessen and his wife, Deborah
Love, rented Annaghkeen, one of the many small islands in Lough Corrib in
Co. Galway. With them were Peter's son, Luke, and Deborah's daughter, Rue.
Love's reflective account of the experience,* Annaghkeen, *was published in 1970.*

The following selection from Annaghkeen *traces their route from Cobh
to Killorglin through the south of Ireland, later continuing up through Limerick and Clare to Galway, a route followed by many visitors to Ireland. Cobh
is the port from which generations of Irish young people have sailed away to
seek their fortunes in other, richer lands.*

*Two years later, back home in New York, Love was teaching at the New
School for Social Research when she was diagnosed with cancer. She died
early in 1972. Matthiessen, a Buddhist monk, wrote movingly about her death
and his own return to meaningful life through Zen in his 1985* Nine-Headed
Dragon River.

LAST NIGHT, BEFORE GOING TO SLEEP, WE SAW LIGHTS
on the coast. The lighter *Killarney* came alongside at three-thirty
this morning to take the baggage off for Cóbh. Hundreds of steamer trunks

were going over the side, two and three at a time in nets or canvas slings, and then set in rows on the after deck of the *Killarney*. The forward deck was filling with suitcases and hand luggage carried over a narrow gang plank by an ant-like stream of *commis* boys, assistant stewards, pages, bellboys (many of them looking not sixteen), from our ship. The steamer trunks must be those of the nuns and priests coming home from missions to America.

The steward banged on the door at six and by eight we were break-fasted and waiting in the lounge for landing cards and passport clearance. After waiting in a line filing past an official table we were told to return until our section was called. At this weary moment Donald and Carol Braider came through the lounge doors. They are old friends of P and had come from Dublin, where they have been living for the past two years, to meet us and welcome us to Ireland. And welcome they were. Functioning where our sleep-deprived minds stalled, they seemed to know everything, including the way off the *Sylvania* to the lighter that would take us across the harbor to Cóbh.

The *Killarney* had returned for the passengers and we were all on the deck in the fine rain looking at Ireland, as green as the photographs prom-ised. A little island to the west presented its dazzling slopes and all round the harbor the hills lay in shades and patches of green. Carol said, "*There* is the green of Ireland."

Seen from the lighter's deck, the *Sylvania* seemed too small for the voyage she had just made over those wide seas. Now as we looked back at her swinging around to the harbor's cleft, she seemed as high as the great barricading hills that stanchioned her passage back out to sea. She had wasted no time weighing anchor and had disappeared long before we docked in Cóbh.

Cóbh is Queenstown of pre-Republican Ireland and it was from this harbor that so many Irish boys and girls, superfluous to their families and country, said good-bye and boarded ships for New York and Boston.

We walked off the tender onto the cobblestones of Cóbh with as little ceremony as getting off the Staten Island ferry to go to work in Manhattan. Customs was an uncomplicated affair which took place in a huge shed. We gathered our bags under the letters LMNOP, where they were marked and released. Outside Donald had drawn up their Volkswagen bus and we drove away out of the streets of Cóbh to the road that followed the River Lee to Cork. The tide was out, and the river here so near the sea was a tiny rivulet parting a wide mud flat. Ruined towers and ancient stone forts went by, muffled in ivy; I saw them, silent as scenery, scarcely believing as we rode along that they were there at all.

In Cork the two oldest Braider children waited in front of the Intercontinental Hotel to greet us. Susan and Christopher had been Lukie's first playmates long ago and the children greeted one another with enthusiasm.

In the hotel bar, listening to the Braiders tell about Ireland, we drank Bloody Marys and discovered that Blarney Castle, where they had never been, was just down the road.

The castle looks down from a mountainside onto daisy-drifted meadows where cows graze, their backs looming like fallen logs in the tall grass. A small stream becomes a corridor through the dark boughs of overhanging trees, and warned too late by Carol to skirt the invidious nettle, we walked through it along the bordering path. Actually the nettle stings are rather pleasant on one's legs, not unlike the pleasure of eating hot curry or peppers.

The castle keep is eighty-five feet high and the stone to kiss is in the outer rim of the machicolation at the very top. Two rods cross this hole through which stones, hot oil, and other lethal materials were poured on assailants, yet a child could slip through, and I was glad to have got there too late to witness Luke and Rue kissing the Blarney Stone in the perilous position required. The photographer who is there to record this moment had kindly held the children's feet while, on their backs, they descended, head first, into the hole.

There are several theories about the origin of kissing the Blarney Stone and thereby getting the "gift of the gab," one being that it had its roots in the bardic school that existed at Blarney in the Gaelic times, and even into the Norman, before the English banned it in their remorseless attempt to render the Irish into aliens on their own soil.

We returned the children to the Intercontinental and with Carol and Don set off for Bandon, twenty miles south and west of Cork, to find Maizie Mulhern. Twenty-eight years ago she said good-bye in America to three children whose nurse she had been since they were babies, and returned to Ireland to marry Dominic, the garda she had met on a trip home.

On a corner in Bandon, three old men leaned against a wall, silent, watching us as we pulled into the curb and Donald called out, "Do you know where Convent Court is?" One of them straightened while the other two looked on. Hearing his answer, I heard an Irish voice for the first time, rising and falling, soft and beautiful. He subsided again to the wall and we drove to the top of the hill and let P out on the corner of Convent Court Street while Donald turned the car around. The door of the corner cottage opened and we saw the upper part of P disappear inside when he leaned forward to kiss his former nurse.

He brought her out to meet us and we were all invited to come in. The house was old and made for smaller folk and we ducked under a low door passing from the front hall through walls two feet thick to a tiny square living room lit by windows looking both to the southwest and toward the back of the house. Maizie plugged in the electric fire in the fireplace. Dominic, a tall, bald genial man, greeted us warmly and brought out Irish whiskey and an unopened bottle of Scotch. Glasses were waiting on the table. "I think Scotch is always nicer," Maizie said, but we all chose Irish and water, not wanting Dominic to open the Scotch. She asked P to fix the drinks and after we were all seated kept on standing until P asked her to sit down.

Her voice was even and her face expressionless as she remembered P's family, and the house in Irvington, and their life there and at Fishers Island, but her eyes never forsook the eyes of the child of memory.

To me she said, "I first held him as a baby," and showed with her two hands his length. Her eyes returned to gather him in again. "Did you recognize me, Peter?"

"In the doorway you saw that I knew you immediately. Did you know me?"

"Yes, yes, you're just the same." She had known when our boat would dock and had spent this day by the window until P came to the garden gate.

We promised to bring Luke the following morning. Maizie put a package wrapped tightly in brown paper and string in P's hands. "It's Waterford glass. I thought you might like to have some."

Outside she kissed P solemnly and shook our hands and stood looking after our car going down the street, and P looked back and waved again before we reached the bottom of the hill and turned into the main street of Bandon, where the three old men still leaned against the wall.

The next day cups were set out for tea and beside them a photograph album and newspaper clippings lay on the table. Together we all looked through the album as Maizie slowly turned the pages identifying guests and friends of the family and in the baby pictures we guessed which ones were P. One of them, when he was three, was torn from the album and was for me.

Maizie said it refreshed her to see P because it brought the past back more vividly. "You'll know that the best days are when the children are young. When they grow up there are only memories."

I thought of Dominic yesterday saying with a smile and a twinkle in his eye that Maizie could never have gone back to America "because she got so fond of me," and Maizie sucking in her breath and holding on to P with her eyes.

She brought the tea in and we sat in the four places and she to the side. "Do you remember, Peter," she would begin while we ate from the plates piled with cookies and cake, and then P would say, "Do you remember, Maizie . . . ?"

"Do you remember, Peter, when you scratched your brother Carey's face?" She ran her fingers lightly over her cheeks. "I told you I was going to tell your teacher about it, and I did, I did."

P told about the time Carey chased him with a knife and he had run for his life. Then Maizie began again, in her sober voice, to tell about the scratches, all the way through to her last words, "And I did, I did." P countered with another story and still one more until things seemed even and the character of one not worse than the character of the other. Most of the pictures in the album were of P, the memory of him perhaps more poignant than that of her own son. For it was a younger Maizie whose love he was, a Maizie who had not yet chosen and whose future could still turn out anyway at all. We saw the son's picture, taken with his fiancée, both very handsome and the girl gay-looking.

The conversation turned to crime. It wasn't only New York City that had become a terrifying place to live. Even in Ireland, in the country, life was getting dangerous. Luke told about women being raped in the city, and Rue reached for cake.

It was time to go. In a red Volkswagen we hired yesterday we would drive to Waterville and in four days we should be at Annaghkeen Island, in County Galway, which is ours for the month of July. The Braiders have gone back to Dublin and will come to the island later.

In the tiny yard before the house, thyme grew in clumps against the wall and a circle of bright flowers grew in the center outlined by cement and packed earth. Maizie kissed us each, slowly, a kiss I felt upon my cheek and remembered.

We waited in the car while P said good-bye and I watched the short figure with ruddy cheeks and a solemn mouth, and watched the sober eyes take leave of a tall child of ten.

She waved, her arm held straight out, the hand rising and descending slowly from the wrist, until we were down the hill and out of sight on the road to Macroom.

Coming from Kenmare to Waterville on the Iveragh Peninsula, I first *saw* Ireland, that is, it suddenly became clear and became mine. There are moments when a town, a landscape, the world belongs to you, is dazzlingly familiar. I do not know what causes these shocks of recognition, what state of mind it is when the outside is the inside, but I remember the exact place; it was where the road began a long descent into a valley and the mountain plunged into armlets of the sea reaching into the land, that I realized I had not, until that moment, known I was here.

We spent two nights in Waterville and I remember a picnic with the sun coming out on the island in Lough Currane where Pat O'Shea had rowed Rue and me in his lake boat. P and I were angry and I would not go with him to see Staigue Fort, a prehistoric structure with walls thirteen feet thick. So he and Luke had gone and afterwards went fishing.

The boy who worked in the garage behind the hotel drove us to the end of a road where the lake boat lay in the reeds. Pat is a gillie and had no fishing party this day so spent it with this party of two, having our lunch behind the stones of a monk's cell, tucked away out of the wind.

Once there was a monastery on this island of five acres, and now there remains the walls of St. Fionan's and three clochans—beehive-shaped huts of stone where the monks lived. Earthworks, strewn with stones, mark out a plan—the monastery walls and enclosures of small gardens.

An island is a monastery. Look across the water or look up at sky, or down at the earth. There is nothing to say, there is nothing; eventually it becomes God. There is no human voice to call it otherwise.

In the towns and villages, witnessing men avoiding or confronting one another, one must also eventually see God. But it takes much more imagination, and a lifetime mightn't be enough time.

Most of the ruined abbeys, oratories, and friaries in Ireland are still sacred ground, from time to time reconsecrated so they may be used as burial grounds. One is likely to find, shining above the weeds flooring a chancel opened to the sky for centuries, a marble slab inscribed to one born and dead in the last fifty years.

Outside of the enclosed ground of St. Fionan's is a startlingly imposing monument: a gray, sharply cut granite sarcophagus, bearing the date 1886, and enclosing the body of the twenty-seven-year-old son of William Wake, Baron of Courteenhall of Northamptonshire, erected in loving memory by his brothers and sisters. Besides being a Protestant, he was a suicide, two reasons, if one weren't enough, for being outside the holy ground. Pat O'Shea could tell nothing more of him. Committing suicide is romantic enough, but to be buried, in addition, next to ancient cells of holy men on an island in a wild Irish tarn is beyond all expectation; poor English boy, keeping his dreams.

Two cows graze around the stones. They have left their mark on every bit of the island, among the nettles, the foxglove, and blackberry vines, and even behind the altar in an inaccessible rough depression. They are curious and gaze at us, their pretty heads adorned by long, graceful, curling horns. Like dogs they sniff our baskets and nose among the sweaters and the books. The island will feed two cows for two months and then must have a six weeks rest. I would like to see those animals going away in their boat.

We lay in the sun while Pat talked about fishing, and the life of the salmon and the sea trout. He told us how the salmon spawn in late October and November, digging out a nest in the gravel with their fins. By spring the young grilse go down the rivers to spend the next two years in the sea. "It's a fascinatin' thing to read a book about the salmon. And do you know, it's only in the last ten years they know anything at all, and still they don't know where they go in the sea, though there's one found in Greenland that was tagged as a baby in Galway."

The mountains rise around us and far away on the southern slope a house squats halfway up the mountainside, the only dwelling in the radius of the eye. Pat says the farmer has sold it to an Englishman to spend his summers in, and built himself another at the bottom of the hill, so now there are two on the mountain.

I asked Pat if he thought Ireland was beautiful. "No," he said, "it seems just what I always see. To see the beauty I'd have to look upon something I'd not seen before."

I remember the incredible beauty of Sagaponack, where potato fields run down to the dunes, and privet moving in the wind lines the road to the sea, the first two years we lived there. Now I remember how it struck me, but cannot find again the *impact* of beauty. But the children's faces never dull: their beauty bursts upon me daily. The children are acutely aware, and therefore changing, so we see them new whenever we look. But to perceive old landscapes as quick-moving as children's faces, we need to be new ourselves, aware at once of what we see and ourselves seeing. Double awareness destroys the distance, and there is no viewer to distort a view. We do not know the dancer from the dance.

Beds of wild yellow iris grew by the shore and yellow gorse blooms scattered over the grass amid the white buttercups. Foxglove bearing speckled "fairy fingers" made lavender lights everywhere. In the crevices of the corbeled stones of the clochan grew small bunches of ferns, and penny-leaves fell down the walls. Pat said, peel the penny-leaves and they will cure a burn. His missus burnt her hand baking, and the inflammation spread up her arm, and since the doctor only made it worse Pat persuaded her to try penny-leaves. Within twenty-four hours the infection had disappeared. I peeled one and indeed, underneath the integument, it was wet, shining, and viscous, the very thing for a burn, and I lay the cool leaf on my forehead.

A lone merganser passed us as we rowed back across the dark water; it splashed into the shore. A bright tern dipped and bounced above us, a lark descended suddenly from the sky; Rue lay in the stern watching the springing reeds come back from the water where the boat, passing, had laid them low.

Sea trout for dinner: three small ones caught by Luke, and the big one by P. In the evening, in the entrance hall of the hotel, the fishermen lay out their catch in pans and a piece of paper placed on top of the fish tells who caught them. Yesterday there were two pans, one with two beautiful silver salmon, the other with a mess of trout. This custom would seem to preclude any fish stories in the bar. Most of the fishermen, and fisherwomen, here now are English. The only boat seen this afternoon on Lough Currane contained two ladies, outfitted in standard fishing attire with brimmed canvas hats, casting slowly from each end of the boat with the gillie sitting quiet in between.

The fish were excellent. Being so fresh it would have been hard to hurt them, but they were well-prepared. As for the rest of the cuisine, what makes the soups and stews good, boiling for hours, makes the rest bad. On sweets, one word—glutinous—covers the variety of trifles, surprises, snows, and delights. The fresh fruit from Portugal, Spain, and Italy is delicious. Even the big strawberries have a wonderful flavor, the pears are crisp and sweet, and tomatoes might be warm from the garden.

In a few years, when most fruit and vegetables will be grown from seeds developed for machine harvesting and yield rather than taste and nourishment, American gourmets will jet to these places for a meal, perhaps of a single delicacy, an apple. In the future, grande cuisine may simply be real food.

It may well be that the fault of Irish cooking is traceable not only to the English, but to the potato. As it was eaten in place of bread, they had no need to bake and therefore no oven, and the Irish got the habit of throwing everything in a great pot of water.

☙

THE RING OF KERRY IS A COASTAL ROAD CIRCLING the Iveragh Peninsula from Kenmare, in the east, to Killorglin, at the western end; Waterville is halfway around. Killorglin is the town of the famous Puck Fair, and I looked to see evidences of orgiastic townsfolk, who for three days every August cavort and carouse while an enthroned male goat, raised high on a scaffolding, presides over the marketing and trading of horses, sheep, and cattle. But no person did I see the length of the quiet narrow street that slopes with the town to the edge of the pretty River Laune.

That there are so few people is a striking feature of Ireland. In all this country which comprises 32,595 square miles, there are only four million souls. Another tour for the future: to places where one can stand in a natural area, turn a full circle, and not see a human or hear a sound derived from humans.

Once I lived in the Berkshires in country that to the eye could not have been more pleasing, yet the sound of diesel trucks from the valley floor was never absent. In summer I would go up to the top of the hill and sit among the black-eyed Susans looking far down the green valley to where the turnpike wrapped it from west to east in a white ribbon. As the deep-throated gargle of the diesel began to fade in the east, I would hold my breath in anticipation of a silence. It was a challenge to Life to give it to me, like the bet a child makes on the way to school: that the bird will fly from the branch before he counts ten, or a car will go by before he reaches the corner. It is a gamble because one throws oneself entire into the risk and the secret stakes are an affirmation of one's own mysterious progression and so all life; or the feared "No." But never did I win. Long before the sound of the diesel had truly died, without echo, and long before the next behemoth showed itself, again came the terrible roar, and my heart sank and my anger rose.

"You owe me silence," I shouted silently to the beautiful green valley. It answered with the great drawn-out fart of man's twentieth-century effort.

In Ireland, the ear and the eye have luxuries everywhere. The roads are narrow country lanes, and as petrol costs three times as much as in the United States, few cars travel them. The roads belong to the animals and pedestrians more than the motorist. Sheep lie down and take naps in them, cows are driven down them, children walk two and three abreast along them.

Coming up behind a cyclist you are often treated to a wild conflagration of movement. While the coat or shirt billows sideways in the wind, the folds of the skirt ripple up and down from the pumping legs and forward motion of the bike.

And one time we came around a curve suddenly behind a pedestrian going along full in the middle of the lane. An old, old man, he hobbled steadily, letting his full weight fall, at every other step, against his cane, taking his rightful place on a road he knew before anyone had seen a motor car.

TIM ROBINSON
The Aran Islands: 1972

"ON THE DAY OF OUR ARRIVAL WE MET AN OLD MAN
WHO EXPLAINED THE BASIC GEOGRAPHY: 'THE
OCEAN,' HE TOLD US, 'GOES ALL AROUND THE
ISLAND.' "

Tim Robinson is an Englishman who studied mathematics at Cambridge, then moved and taught around the world for a few years before going to the Aran Islands in 1972 to write and make maps. Some of his new mapmaking techniques have influenced later mapmakers. After the Aran Islands, he lived in Galway and wrote two books about Connemara. His Stones of Aran: Pilgrimage *was first published in 1986.*

In the opening pages of his book, Robinson pays tribute to earlier explorers of the islands, all of them Irish: the nineteenth-century scholars, Lady Gregory, W. B. Yeats, and J. M. Synge, whose The Aran Islands *appeared in 1907.*

Then he writes a bit about Man of Aran, *the 1932 documentary film by American director Robert Flaherty. "The images Flaherty dealt us," he says, "of Man as subduer of sea-monsters, of Wife anxiously looking out for his return while rocking Babe-in-the-Cradle, and of Son eager to follow him into manhood—the perfect primal family in unmediated conflict with a world of towering waves and barren rocks, as if eternally in silhouette against the storm— . . . will not be brushed aside by subsequent knowledge of the subtle actualities of Aran life."*

AS WITH THOUSANDS OF OTHERS, IT WAS A MILD CU-
riosity engendered by Flaherty's film that first brought us (my wife
and myself) to Aran, in the summer of 1972. On the day of our arrival we
met an old man who explained the basic geography: "The ocean," he told
us, "goes all around the island." We let the remark direct our rambles on
that brief holiday, and found indeed that the ocean encircles Aran like the
rim of a magnifying glass, focusing attention to the point of obsession. A
few months later we determined to leave London and the career in the
visual arts I was pursuing there, and act on my belief in the virtue of an
occasional brusque and even arbitrary change in mode of life. (I mention
these personal details only as being the minimum necessary for the definition of the moment on which this narrative will converge, the point in
physical and cultural space from which this timescape is observed and on
which this book stands.) On that previous summer holiday Aran had presented itself, not at all as Flaherty's pedestal of rock on which to strike a
heroic stance, but rather as a bed of flower-scented sunlight and breezes
on which one might flirt delectably with alternative futures. But on our
definitive arrival in November we found that bed canopied with hailstorms
and full of all the damps of the Atlantic. The closing-in of that winter,
until the days seemed like brief and gloomy dreams interrupting ever in-
tenser nights, was accompanied by an unprecedented sequence of deaths,
mainly by drowning or by falls and exposure on the crags, that perturbed
and depressed the island, quite extinguished the glow of Christmas, and
ceased only with the turn of the year, the prayers of the priest and the
sinister total of seven. It was a severe induction but it left us with a knowledge of the dark side of this moon that has controlled the tides of our life
ever since.

For my part (Máiréad's being her own story), what captivated me in
that long winter were the immensities in which this little place is wrapped:
the processions of grey squalls that stride in from the Atlantic horizon,
briefly lash us with hail and go sailing off towards the mainland trailing
rainbows; the breakers that continue to arch up, foam and fall across the
shoals for days after a storm has abated; the long, wind-rattled nights,
untamed then by electricity below, wildly starry above. Then I was dazzled
by the minutiae of spring, the appearance each in its season of the flowers,
starting with the tiny, white whitlow-grass blossoms hardly distinguishable
from the last of the hailstones in the scant February pastures, and culminating by late May in paradisal tapestry-work across every meadow and
around every rock. The summer had me exploring the honeysuckled bo-

reens and the breezy clifftops; autumn proposed the Irish language, the blacksmith's quarter-comprehended tales, the intriguing gossip of the shops, and the discovery that there existed yet another literature it would take four or five years to begin to make one's own. This cycle could have spun on, the writings I had come here to do having narrowed themselves into a diary of intoxication with Aran, but that some way of contributing to this society and of surviving financially had to be found.

A suggestion from the post mistress in the western village of Cill Mhuirbhigh gave me the form of this contribution: since I seemed to have a hand for the drawing, an ear for the placenames and legs for the boreens, why should I not make a map of the islands, for which endless summersful of visitors would thank and pay me? The idea appealed to me so deeply that I began work that same day. My conceptions of what could be expressed through a map were at that time sweeping but indefinite; maps of a very generalized and metaphorical sort had been latent in the abstract paintings and environmental constructions I had shown in London, in that previous existence that already seemed so long ago, but I had not engaged myself to such a detailed relationship with an actual place before. The outcome, published in 1975, was a better image of my ignorance than of my knowledge of Aran, but it was generously received by the islanders, prospered moderately with the tourists and brought me into contact with the specialists in various fields who visited Aran. During the subsequent years of accumulation towards the second version of the map, published in 1980, I have walked the islands in companionship with such visiting experts as well as with the custodians of local lore whom I sought out in every village, and have tried to see Aran through variously informed eyes— and then, alone again, I have gone hunting for those rare places and times, the nodes at which the layers of experience touch and may be fused together. But I find that in a map such points and the energy that accomplishes such fusions (which is that of poetry, not some vague "interdisciplinary" fervour) can, at the most, be invisible guides, benevolent ghosts, through the tangles of the explicit; they cannot themselves be shown or named. So, chastened in my expectations of them, I now regard the Aran maps as preliminary storings and sortings of material for another art, the world-hungry art of words.

However, although the maps underlie this book, the conception of the latter dates from a moment in the preparation for the former. I was on a summer's beach one blinding day watching the waves unmaking each other, when I became aware of a wave, or a recurrent sequence of waves, with a denser identity and more purposeful momentum than the rest. This appearance, which passed by from east to west and then from west to east and so on, resolved itself under my stare into the fins and backs of two dolphins (or were there three?), the follower with its head close by the flank of the leader. I waded out until they were passing and repassing within a few yards of me; it was still difficult to see the smoothly arching succession of dark presences as a definite number of individuals. Yet their unity with their background was no jellyfish-like dalliance with dissolution; their mode of being was an intensification of their medium into alert, reactive self-awareness; they were wave made flesh, with minds solely to ensure the moment-by-moment reintegration of body and world.

This instance of a wholeness beyond happiness made me a little despondent, standing there thigh deep in Panthalassa (for if Pangaea is shattered and will not be mended by our presence on it, the old ocean holds together throughout all its twisting history): a dolphin may be its own poem, but we have to find our rhymes elsewhere, between words in literature, between things in science, and our way back to the world involves us in an endless proliferation of detours. Let the problem be symbolized by that of taking a single step as adequate to the ground it clears as is the dolphin's arc to its wave. Is it possible to think towards a *human* conception of this "good step"? (For the dolphin's ravenous cybernetics and lean hydrodynamics induce in me no nostalgia for imaginary states of past instinctive or future theological grace. Nor is the ecological imperative, that we learn to tread more lightly on the earth, what I have in mind—though that commandment, which is always subject to challenge on pragmatic grounds if presented as a mere facilitation of survival, might indeed acquire some authority from the attitude to the earth I would like to hint at with my step.) But our world has nurtured in us such a multiplicity of modes of awareness that it must be impossible to bring them to a common focus even for the notional duration of a step. The dolphin's world, for all that its inhabitants can sense Gulf Streams of diffuse beneficences, freshening influences of rivers and perhaps a hundred other transparent gradations, is endlessly more continuous and therefore productive of unity than ours, our craggy, boggy, overgrown and overbuilt terrain, on which every step carries us across geologies, biologies, myths, histories, politics, etcetera, and trips us with the trailing *Rosa spinosissima* of personal associations. To forget these dimensions of the step is to forgo our honour as human beings, but an awareness of them equal to the involuted complexities under foot at any given moment would be a crushing backload to have to carry. Can such contradictions be forged into a state of consciousness even fleetingly worthy of its ground? At least one can speculate that the structure of condensation and ordering necessary to pass from such various types of knowledge to such an instant of insight would have the characteristics of a work of art, partaking of the individuality of the mind that bears it, yet with a density of content and richness of connectivity surpassing any state of that mind. So the step lies beyond a certain work of art; it would be like a reading of that work. And the writing of such a work? Impossible, for many reasons, of which the brevity of life is one.

However, it will already be clear that Aran, of the world's countless facets one of the most finely carved by nature, closely structured by labour and minutely commented by tradition, is *the* exemplary terrain upon which to dream of that work, the guide-book to the adequate step. *Stones of Aran* is all made up of steps, which lead in many directions but perpetually return to, loiter near, take short-cuts by, stumble over or impatiently kick aside that ideal. (Otherwise, it explores and takes its form from a single island, Árainn itself; the present work makes a circuit of the coast, whose features present themselves as stations of a *Pilgrimage*, while the sequel will work its way through the interior, tracing out the *Labyrinth*.) And although I am aware that that moment on the beach, like all moments one remembers as creative, owes as much to the cone of futurity opening out from it as to the focusing of the past it accomplished, I will take it as the site of my book, so that when at last it is done I will have told the heedless dolphins how it is, to walk this paradigm of broken, blessed, Pangaea.

BEFORE BEGINNING

THE CIRCUIT THAT BLESSES IS CLOCKWISE, OR, SINCE the belief is thousands of years older than the clock, sunwise. It is the way the fireworshipper's swastika turns, and its Christianized descendant St Bridget's cross. Visitors to holy wells make their "rounds" so, seven times, with prayers. This book makes just one round of Árainn, though seven could not do justice to the place, and with eyes raised to this world rather than lowered in prayer. On Easter Fridays in past centuries the Aran folk used to walk around the island keeping as close to the coast as possible, and although nothing has been recorded on the question it is inconceivable that they should have made the circuit other than in the right-handed sense. This writing will lead in their footsteps, not at their penitential trudge but at an inquiring, digressive and wondering pace.

I start at the eastern end of the island. The road from Cill Rónáin through Cill Éinne continues past the last village, Iaráirne, and then makes a sharp turn north to a little bay; there is a stile in the wall at that turn from which a faint field-path continues the line of the road eastward, across smooth turf in which hosts of rabbits are digging sandpits, to the exact spot I have in mind. Here one can sit among the wild pansies and Lady's bedstraw with the low rocky shore at one's feet, and get one's bearings. Behind and to the left is level ground of sandy fields, and dunes in the distance. To the right the land rises in stony slopes to the ruins of an ancient watch tower on the skyline. A mile and a half ahead across the sound is Inis Meáin; the third island, Inis Oírr, is hidden behind it, but the hills of the Burren in County Clare appear beyond, a dozen miles away. Since the three islands and that north-western corner of Clare were once continuous—before the millions of years of weathering, the glaciers of the Ice Ages and the inexhaustible waves cut the sea-ways between them— the landforms visible out there, a little abstracted as they are by distance, can be seen as images of Árainn itself in the context of its geological past, and it is valuable to read them thus before going on to clamber among the details and complexities of the way ahead, so that an otherwise inchoate mass of impressions may find an ordering and a clarification.

Since this opposing, western face of Inis Meáin is cliffed it is in fact like a cross-section of Árainn. The highest land lies across the centre, and from there to the south the skyline declines evenly to sea level, giving the southern half of the island the appearance of a long dark wedge driven in between sky and sea. The cliffs' ledges and the great platforms of rock along their feet all have the same slant as the skyline, so that the island is visibly made up of a small number of thick parallel layers slightly canted to the south. But if this is an image of Árainn, it is from a time before its southern range of cliffs was formed, for Inis Meáin's coast is low on the south and stands well out beyond the general line of Árainn's Atlantic cliffs. Why the ocean has been able to cut back just one of the three islands into south-facing cliffs is a question to which certain features of the extreme western tip of Árainn may suggest an answer—but that is as yet a dozen miles of walking and a hundred pages of reading ahead.

While the profile of Inis Meáin's southern half is simple to the point of monotony, that of the northern half has a wild vigour recalling one's experience of that strange island; it hops and jumps down from the central heights, and then reaches the north in two long strides with a sharp fall between them. The land is enlivened by these little scarps; the houses are in their shelter, the wells at their feet, the boreens wind up and down them. Árainn is the same except that the aprons of bare rock below the terraces that carry the villages are not so wide; here, as in Inis Meáin and Inis Oírr, the terrain south of the ridge-line is uninhabited, severe, disconcertingly open to nonhuman immensities, while the northern flank of the island is at least raggedly shawled with the human presence. In fact over parts of the north the fabric of history is so closely woven that it can be as oppressive as the more elemental spaciousness of the south, and for all their beauty neither landscape is a forgiving one.

This side-view of Inis Meáin shows the formation of the terraces with diagrammatic clarity: first the topmost of the great beds of limestone slanting up gently from the south is broken off short by a north-facing scarp; the next layer continues a little farther north before being similarly ended, the next runs still farther north to form another tread of the stair, and so on. There are five such terraces, with three less distinct ones below them, and they can be traced the length of the island chain and indeed matched with similar terraces in the hills of the Burren—at least the geologist can match them, by means of slight variations in the composition of the limestone and in the fossils to be found in each stratum. In some places the scarp-faces separating them are considerable cliffs of up to twenty feet in height, in others they dwindle to broken slopes so that the terraces are not immediately distinguishable and it would be hard to count them, while elsewhere minor subdivisions become more prominent than these major ones—and in the face of these, the usual and generous ways of reality, any diagram having done its work goes on to demonstrate its own inadequacy.

Beyond and above the northern tip of Inis Meáin as viewed from this spot stands the outline of the Burren, which can be seen—through a bewitching gauze of sunshine and cloud-shadow—as a further, more inclusive diagram of Árainn's geology. The northernmost end of the sequence is the promontory on the south of Galway Bay called Black Head, a great rounded hill rising to about a thousand feet. A well-marked terrace, showing from here as a long streak, silvery below and dark above, crosses the face of this hill, strikingly parallel to the general slant of Inis Meáin. Above this level the profile of Black Head rises in indistinct steps, which elsewhere in the Burren are very clear but here have been rounded off by glacial action. These are the strata that correspond to and were once continuous with those of the Aran Islands. The unterraced hillsides below them in the Burren represent the roots of Aran below sea level. To see what once lay above these strata one has only to follow the Burren skyline south to a long dark plateau the southern end of which falls away out of sight behind the heights of Inis Meáin; this is Slieve Elva, a high bog-covered tract of shales that dominates the bright limestone slopes below it. These great thicknesses of shale once covered much more of the area, and above them were further depths of flagstone, still extant a little farther to the south where they form the Cliffs of Moher. All these rocks, laid down as sediments under various conditions and heaved up into a gently sloping plain by slow earth-movements, have been worn away piecemeal by the two hundred-odd million years of exposure to climates varying from the tropical to the arctic. The process may seem so hugely unimaginable as to be irrelevant, but many features of the ground directly underfoot here are only comprehensible in terms of the pressure of the thousands of feet of rock that once bore down on it. And the process of stripping, not just to the bone, to the bare rock, but of the rock itself and its fossil bones, continues today. Rainwater swilling across the surface has washed an inch or two off its thickness even in the comparatively brief span of man's presence here. Unless vaster earth-processes intervene Aran will ultimately dwindle to a little reef and disappear. It seems unlikely that any creatures we would recognize as our descendants will be here to chart that rock in whatever shape of sea succeeds to Galway Bay.

THE ARCHITECTURE OF DESTRUCTION

BUT WHERE IS ALL THE RUBBLE FROM THESE GIGANTIC demolitions? Finer than dust, most of it, and dispersed by solution into the sea whence it came. The particles sifted and sorted out by currents into muds, sands and shingles along the sheltered north coast are another remnant of it, while the results of the sea's most recent and crudest hammer-work lie along the coast south of the point this book starts from— the tumbled blocks of stone shouldered above high-water mark by the waves that broke them out of the layers of rock immediately seaward, leaving a shore of steps and ledges, convenient fishing-seats for the lads of Iaráirne. Among them is a slab about twenty feet square and four or five feet thick which always catches my attention as I walk that way, because its upper surface is curiously webbed with what look like lengths of petrified rope. These are traces of burrows made by some invertebrate mud-dweller of the ancient sea-bed. Deposits of sediment have filled in the burrows and then, under the pressure of further accumulations, hardened to preserve their form. But these fossil casts are now outgrowths of the *top* of the limestone block, which itself was formed by a continuation of that sedimentation; therefore the block is lying upside-down. As I pace out its canted deck, and later on at home when I calculate its weight at a hundred and twenty tons or so, I begin to acquire a sense of the forces that shook it free from its bed and overturned it.

This "storm beach" or "boulder beach," as such banks of broken stone above high-water mark are called, fades out a couple of hundred yards to the south in the lee of a rising cliff, the beginning of Árainn's precipitous Atlantic face. The cliff is a continuation of a little scarp, the riser of one of the island's terraces, that comes down to the coast here and turns south along it. One can begin to understand how these terraces were formed by looking at the face of this cliff near the coast. The lowest three feet of it are composed of soft shales and clays, which have been eroded back to leave the more resistant limestone overhanging above them. If this under-mining continues, a cliff-fall will follow, and then, if and when the fallen and shattered rock weathers away or is swept aside by waves, undercutting of the cliff will begin again, and stage by stage it will slowly be eaten back into the hillside.

The process can be seen at its most dramatic by following the shore southwards under the cliff. It is possible, if the tide is out and the seas not too high, to reach the easternmost angle of the cliff and look round it at a spot where the swells coming up the channel from the open ocean thrust into a cave they have excavated in this same shale stratum, and columns of foam are blasted out through them by the air trapped and compressed by their inrush. Over on the coast of Inis Meáin the same thing is happening at a point halfway along the cliffs, where if there is any pulse in the ocean at all it is timed by the repeated building-up and falling-down of a tower of white water against a perpetually drenched and black-ened rock wall. The two places are both called Poll an tSéidéain, the cave of the blown spray. After a south-westerly gale the Inis Meáin example is a superb sight, a gleaming space rocket launching itself out of solemn turbulences up the one-hundred-foot cliff face, to be mysteriously trans-formed into a great vague fading bird and swept inland by the wind. Seen from Inis Meáin, and responding to a south-easterly, its Árainn partner is almost equally impressive, and the cliff above and beyond it so smooth, grey and apparently indestructible with its long sheer walls and massive square-cut overhangs that it has the grandiose inhumanity of a space-age fantasy fortress of steel, artillery thundering at its base. In reality, the cliffs are extremely vulnerable. In 1980 a livid scar appeared on Inis Meáin's face just opposite this point, where a piece like the façade of a three-storey house dropped off one night. And here in Árainn the cliff's clean facets show that it is breaking up along a threefold system of weaknesses: the partings between the almost horizontal strata, and the vertical fissures deeply dividing the limestone, one set of which run parallel to the coast at this point, with the other at right-angles to them. So under the blows of the sea the coast is shedding great rectangular blocks and slabs, and owes its style of awesome impregnability to a triple predisposition to failure.

CONNOISSEURS OF WILDERNESS

THE RUINOUS STONE TOWER THAT TOPS THE HILL HERE was perhaps a lookout post, as it commands such a fine view of the seas to north and south as well as of the channel below, but how old it is nobody knows. It is called Túr Máirtín, Martin's Tower, as it was when the first Ordnance Survey was made in the 1830s. There is a path leading in this direction from the village of Iaráirne called Bóithrín Mháirtín, Martin's "boreen" or little road, which suggests that at some period this forgotten Martin owned the land around the tower, but again nobody knows. The ruin, which has recently been overzealously reconstructed by the Board of Works men, measures seventeen paces round and stands to a height of about ten feet. At the time of the first Survey it was described as being solid, but it looks to me as if it was always hollow, and the original masonry on the north side includes some long blocks that protrude into the interior like a crude stairway. Otherwise its stones are as uncommunicative as its history.

Legend, however, has more to say about it: this then is the tomb of a saint from Inis Meáin called Gregory of the Golden Mouth, Gríóir Béal an Óir. The site of this hermit's sojourn in the wilderness of Inis Meáin can be seen from the tower; beyond the little bay and its bright shinglebank on the opposite coast is an inland cliff that has collapsed into a line of huge stone blocks like the carriages of a derailed train, and St Gregory's cave is a burrow among these. There the unhappy recluse gnawed off his lower lip in a spasm of anguish over the sins of his early life (according to the chronicler monks) or simply because he was hungry (as I was told by a more down-to-earth Inis Meáin native)—and a golden lip grew in its place. When St Gregory felt death approaching, regarding himself as unworthy of burial in the holy soil of St Enda's Árainn, he asked the monks of that island to abandon his body to the sea in a cask, which they did, and found on their return that the cask had reached Árainn before them. The little bay, just north of the starting-point of this book, called Port Daibhche, the harbour of the barrel, was its landfall. So the humble saint was buried in Árainn after all, high on this proud headland overlooking the barren island of his lonely struggle and the Sound named after him, Sunda Ghrióra.

In its drift through time Gregory's story has become entangled with others. Thus, when dying in Rome as Pope Gregory he ordered his body to be launched on the Tiber, a tablet on its breast, and eventually came floating home to burial in his native Aran. As Gregory the Fairheaded, Grióir Ceannfhionnadh, he was beheaded by a tyrant at Cleggan in Connemara, the name of which town derives from *cloigeann*, a head; and then (as if to harmonize this tale with his Aran legend) he rose up, cursed the people of that locality, carried his head to a spring (now a holy well named after him), washed and replaced it, and came home to Inis Meáin.

These legends are all faded now. Fishing boats used to dip their sails to the tomb of St Gregory of the Golden Mouth, but nowadays the lobsterboats that come throbbing by below regard it only as a useful sea-mark; an Iaráirne man remembers hearing that the old folk used to come here looking for gold teeth; a touch of golden lichen illuminates the tower's lee side, and that is all.

The slopes falling south from the tower to the coast where it turns to face the full power of the Atlantic are scaly with loose stone, and as harsh and desolate as any in Aran. It is a wild spot to which the magnetism of sanctity steered the desert father from Inis Meáin, and it seems that as such it appealed to another connoisseur of wildernesses, the English artist Richard Long, who in 1975 left his mark, a small stone circle, nearby. It still stands in part, a group of limestone splinters jammed upright into crevices of the rocky ground, about three hundred yards south of the tower. Long's work takes him to the remotest parts of the earth, where he makes some construct like this out of what is to hand—stone, of necessity, in this instance—frequently impermanent, often circular or spiral, a passing shadow cast on nature by a restless culture, and then photographs it and exhibits the photographs with accompanying trophies of maps, stones and words in the air-conditioned, neon-lit art galleries of capital cities. I first saw this circle depicted on the poster of an exhibition in Amsterdam, and later made finding it the object of an hour's wintry loitering about this deserted corner of Aran.

THIS VALE OF TEARS

IN THE LAST CENTURY EMIGRANT SHIPS SAILING OUT OF Galway for America used to come through Sunda Ghrióra and sometimes had to wait for days in the lee of the south-east point of the island for a favourable wind. Then if there were Aran people on board their relatives and friends who had already said goodbye to them and may even have held a wake for them, knowing that in most cases the parting was forever, were given another sight of them by this chance that was perhaps more cruel than kind, but at a distance that must have made it an unreal, wordless and ghostly reappearance. The way by which the bereaved came down to the shore to wave and weep is a little valley called Gleann na nDeor. This phrase is the Irish equivalent of the old preachers' platitude for this world as a place of sorrow, "the vale of tears," and even if the traditional account of the origin of the name I have given is perhaps uncertain, a weight of bitter truth about Aran's past hangs about the place now because of it.

There was another cause for mourning here once, on the 15th of August 1852 (a date every Aran man, woman and child seems to know), when fifteen men were drowned, fourteen of them from Cill Éinne and the other from Iaráirne. They were fishing from the great rock terrace under the cliffs around the point, at Aill na nGlasóg, known in English as the Glasson Rock (the *glasóg* or *glasán* is the black pollack, a type of shorefish for which the spot is well known). It seems that a freak wave rose out of a calm sea and swept them away; the misfortune occurred on the Feast of the Blessed Virgin and was seen as a consequence of working on the holy day, for rock-fishing was then a livelihood, as it still is for a few men of the eastern villages. The ballads, one in English and the other in Irish, that commemorate the tragedy mention Gleann na nDeor as the way by which the bereaved came down to the shore, and it is often supposed that the place-name refers to the tears shed over the bodies of the drowned there. In fact it anticipates the event, for it was recorded by the Ordnance Surveyors in the 1830s. (Misrecorded, rather, since the map has it as Illaunanaur, anglicizing Oileán na nDeor, island, instead of glen, of tears. The error has imposed itself on one or two islanders who reverence the written and official word more than the spoken folk memory, and on my first attempt at a map of Aran.)

Finally, an islander has suggested to me that the name refers to the dew which early morning fishermen sailing by see sparkling on this grassy plot among the grey stones—the dew, proverbially both fresh and fleeting, which still out-cries all human tears.

OCEAN WALLS AND WINDOWS

IN THE DAYS WHEN ALL VISITORS WERE ASSUMED BY the islanders to be of superior birth, the rock-fishermen at Aill na nGlasóg often had a genteel audience watching them from the clifftop, and the big triangular boulder perched on the very tip of the point that served as a seat for these observers became known as Cloch na nDaoine Móra, which an Aran man would translate as "the big-shots' stone." Some day a wave is going to climb the cliff with enough residual power either to shift the stone a little farther inland or drag it back into the sea. All the more exposed coasts of Aran carry a rock-bank above the levels of the highest tides, and where, as here and elsewhere on the south coast, this "storm beach" actually lies above cliffs thirty to eighty feet high, is composed of vast numbers of blocks it would take many men to move, and furthermore is separated from the cliff's edge by a clear space of ten or twenty feet or more, then the impression given of the sea's power is overwhelming.

It is indeed difficult to find a vocabulary for the combination of the prodigious and the orderly that such natural phenomena display. Most accounts of the Aran Islands, including my own first attempt, give one the idea that these stones have been hurled up over the cliffs from the bottom of the sea, whereas in fact they have been stripped off the rim of the cliff and moved inland by small degrees. Revisiting this spot after the winter of 1981–82, I found startling evidence of this process. A block of freshly broken rock, white with the unweathered calcite of innumerable fossils, caught my eye just a few paces east of the boulder described above. The detached piece was about two feet square and five feet long, and lay askew along the mouth of a trough-like recess of exactly the same dimensions running in from the cliff's edge. There was half a fossil coral in the lower left-hand face of the block, and the other half of it was in the right-hand wall of the recess; clearly a wave had knocked the piece like a splinter out of the rim of the cliff, spun it on its axis and dropped it almost upside down back into its place. No doubt it had been detached from its substrate before this happened, by long ages of shocks and blows, and the unremitting discreet persuasions of daily temperature changes and trickling solvent waters; no doubt too in some future winter storm a wave will mount the sixty or seventy feet of cliff and flip it out of its present awkward rest, and then someday another wave will slide it inland and add it to its accumulated predecessors on the storm beach. By such repeated touches a rampart up to ten or fifteen feet high has been assembled all along this next three miles of south-facing cliff, so that the interior of the island is invisible from the broad promenade of ground swept clear of loose rock along the cliff edge.

On Inis Meáin around the low-lying south-western point there are two or three hundred yards of smooth, cleared rock terrace between high-water mark and the gigantic storm beach, and as the cliffs rise from there towards the north the storm beach gradually approaches them and fades out on their brink at a height of a hundred and sixty feet above sea level. Inis Oírr too has an impressive storm beach, topped off by the hull of a freighter wrecked off the coast some years ago. These mighty works have been done partly by gale-by-gale, winter-by-winter processes as described above, and partly no doubt by more drastic events like the "Night of the Big Wind" of 1839 which is said to have buried in boulders the prehistoric stone huts on the peninsula of Dúchathair two miles west, or by such combinations of equinoctial tides and millennial storms as may only have occurred a very few times since the Ice Ages left Aran a bare slate, as it were, for the compilation of this reckoning. The only force tending to the destruction of the storm beach once formed, apart from the slow weathering of individual stones, is cliff-fall, which in places has overtaken the retreat of the storm beach; for instance at Dúchathair it is interrupted by deeply carved inlets, and on the western side of the bay next to the Glasson Rock boulders of the storm beach are tumbling off a cliff that has been cut back under their feet.

This little bay of which the Glasson Rock forms the eastern arm is divided into two amphitheatral halves by a narrow peninsula with a rock terrace below it, and in the deeply undercut recesses of either half is a sea-cave leading back to a blow-hole or "puffing-hole." The more spectacular of these chasms, which one comes across with casually horrific suddenness if not forewarned, is the eastern one, a rectangular opening in the ground about thirty-three yards from the clifftop, a dozen yards across and rather more than that from front to back. On its inland side one can scramble down natural steps and ledges to where it opens out sideways into black dripping vaults like some waterlogged upside-down Piranesi dungeon. On calm days a tongue of green and light-filled water mutters below, but when the tide is high and the wind in the right direction waves come breaking up these steps and strew the ground inland with sand and shreds of seaweed. The power with which water has now and again been funnelled up and jetted out of the opening can be judged from the storm beach which here loops back from the cliffs and lies sixty yards inland of the hole, the intervening sheets of rock having been swept bare and the stone skimmed off it or smashed out of the slope of the puffing-hole heaped up in a ten-foot bank. That is not all, for a few yards outside that bank is a second, smaller one, and a third beyond that again. These outer banks must be relics of very ancient commotions of the sea, for no wave could reach them now over the inner bank, which itself was not built in recent days. Immediately to the north-west a little meadow very different from its barren surroundings has come into existence where sand, blown up the puffing-hole and carried across by the south or south-easterly winds that would drive waves directly into the sea-cave below, has accumulated in a slight hollow. It is called Muirbheach na gCoiníní; the first word means a stretch of sandy coastal land, and this is the "*muirbheach* of the rabbits," which are softly housed here by grace of this freak outfall of the storm.

The western puffing-hole is much smaller and lies inland of the storm beach; it is about a hundred yards from the clifftop. Its opening is a ragged grassy funnel above a narrow cleft of rock in which the sea spleenwort fern grows. Occasionally a sigh of spray hangs in the air over it, the sea can always be heard in its depths, and sometimes in spring a nesting chough explodes out of its rocky muzzle as one peers down, and flaps black and screaming overhead until one moves on.

RICHARD HOWARD BROWN

Belfast: 1970s

"I HAD A WHISKEY IN THE GRILL, WHICH WAS
CROWDED AND NOISY . . . ALTHOUGH SIX BLOCKS
AWAY ON DONEGALL STREET THEY HAD NOT YET
FINISHED LIFTING BODIES INTO TRUCKS AND
AMBULANCES."

*Richard Howard Brown, an American marketing executive, was three gener-
ations removed from his Irish origins. In the early 1970s he traveled to both
the Republic of Ireland and Northern Ireland, seeking some personal connection with his cultural and ethnic roots. His journal of discovery,* I Am of
Ireland, *was widely praised when it was first published in 1974.*

The following excerpt from I Am of Ireland *reports on Brown's arrival
in Belfast in the immediate aftermath of a terrorist bombing.*

*A new edition of Brown's book, published in 1995, includes an intro-
duction by Tim Pat Coogan, author of* The IRA: A History. *Writing of the
struggle for peace in Northern Ireland, Coogan celebrates the promise of the
Downing Street Declaration of December 15, 1993, and the subsequent IRA
cease-fire of August 31, 1994.*

That cease-fire ended. As I write this, there is talk of another.

*Things looked promising for a while. Finally, in the summer of 1998,
both sides signed the Northern Ireland Peace Accord, negotiated with the help
of American diplomat George Mitchell and the encouragement of President
Bill Clinton.*

*Within weeks, when the traditional "marching season" came around and
Protestant groups were prevented by police and army forces from marching
through Catholic sections of Belfast (commemorating a victory over Catholics
that took place nine hundred years ago), the news was filled with images of*

fights, fires, riots, a weeping mother, and a funeral for three young Catholic boys who died when their house was firebombed.

The images looked very much like those Richard Howard Brown saw on his visit to Belfast.

WHEN THE STOLEN GREEN FORD CORTINA WITH A HUN-dred pounds of gelignite in the trunk was driven into Donegall Street and parked in front of the shopping arcade across from the Belfast *News-letter,* I was on the train from Dublin, looking out at the passing countryside and farmhouses and thinking that I could rent my home, leave my job and find another, move my family across the sea three thousand miles and live in Ireland for a while, where everything seemed different. It was only the first day of spring, but in Balbriggan, Drogheda, and Dundalk, the warm winds off the Gulf Stream had already made the fields as green as the end of April.

A dark-haired girl with sad gray eyes sat opposite me reading a paperback copy of *The Godfather,* and as I looked out of the window I kept stealing glances at her and finally, on some small pretext, we began to talk. When she recognized my speech as American, she nodded toward her book and asked me if it really was like that in the United States, with gangsters shooting each other in the streets. I told her that it happened all the time, but that there were twice as many people in New York as there were in all of Ireland, so you hardly noticed it. I told her there were as many people and more murdered for one reason or another each year in New York as were killed in the war in the North, but again, it was a big city. I enjoyed making New York big and bad and exciting for her, the best and the worst of all the cities. She said she'd like to see it sometime but she didn't think she'd want to live there with so many people and all that violence, and that at least the killing at home had some point to it.

After a while she turned back to *The Godfather* and I closed my eyes and wondered what it would be like to live down in Kerry by the sea. There had been an American from Chicago staying in the hotel in Dublin whom I'd had breakfast with a couple of mornings, and he lived there in a room behind an inn on the Dingle peninsula where *Ryan's Daughter* had been filmed. He had come up to Dublin for the St. Patrick's Day weekend and was wearing a suit and tie for the first time in seven months. Before that he had been in business in Rome, but his affairs had become very tangled and in the various cities of Europe there were two ex-wives and four children and some former mistresses whom he had loved more than his wives. There were also debts and some business opportunities that he was no longer capable of handling, so he'd turned his back on it all and taken what was left in his savings account and bought a ticket to Ireland.

Except for the fact that there were no women in Dingle such as he had known in Europe, he was happy for the first time in many years. His room behind the inn was next to a small barn and a cow was tethered in a stall on the other side of the wall from his bed, and he said that over the months he had come to feel very close to the cow. He could hear its heavy breathing and movements about the stall at night and he was beginning to feel love for it as another living being that shared a point in time with him.

I laughed at what he said about the cow, but the more he told me about it and about sitting by turf fires and visiting each day with farmers and their wives and walking the country lanes and watching the ocean waves crash against the rocks, sending up huge sheets of spray, the water swirling up and around and changing colors, the more I could see it his way that all the movement he had known in life was right there in Dingle whenever he wanted to look at it, and it all began to sound good to me, too.

I enjoyed listening to him because he had made one of those wild, open-ended, life-changing decisions that a lot of people sometimes think they'd like to make, but I suspected he was living through some sort of breakdown and I shouldn't have been surprised at his reaction when I asked him to come to Belfast with me. We were sitting over coffee in the dining room and he pushed back from the table and shook his head several times and there was something like real fear on his face. He said there were too many things inside him that he could barely cope with and he could not handle the things he had heard about in Northern Ireland, "You're inquisitive," he said. "I'm not. Go if you want to, but I can't."

I dozed and thought I was in Dingle and we were well past the border when I awoke and I didn't realize we were in the North until I saw the graffiti—REBELS BEWARE! NO IRA HERE! FUCK THE POPE!—on the brick-walled backs of Protestant houses and factories as we approached the Belfast outskirts. As soon as we were standing in the station, a porter, a sunken-cheeked old man in a blue work shirt and one of those black leather-brimmed hats that seamen wear, boarded the train and came down the aisle, wild-eyed, leaning into seats with the news of the explosion. I couldn't understand his old man's thick accent and I thought he was telling me of a place to go like some Paris pimp with dirty post-cards. Again he said it: "There's dead all over Donegall Street," and moved on down the aisle.

The first phone call had come at quarter to twelve, advising a business firm on nearby Church Street that there was a big bomb on its premises. It was common practice for both wings of the IRA to give advance warning and to acknowledge responsibility afterward if a bombing was their doing. At that time the Officials were still bombing, though more selectively than the Provisionals, and it was important to both that the public knew where to assign credit or blame. The warnings were sometimes not reliable because the fuses in the bombs did not always function properly.

There was a second call seven minutes later which, the police said, also reported a bomb on Church Street. The police claimed it was not until eleven fifty-five that they were notified of a bomb in a building on lower Donegall Street, and by that time the street itself was filled with people evacuating stores and offices in the Church Street area.

Because bombings were almost a daily happening then in Belfast, and hardly a block was not marred in some way, scares occurred frequently. Many of those who mingled with Donegall Street shoppers that day must have had the same impatient "here we go again" attitude I saw in the days after, watching people crowd curiously across from some bank or department store, not fifty yards from where a bomb was thought to be. Some were uneasy, I'm sure, but others undoubtedly welcomed the sense of excitement and the relief from office boredom.

The last warning was still vague, according to the police, and there was almost no time to act on it or do anything about clearing the sidewalks because three minutes later the green Ford Cortina exploded.

Two policemen were approaching it when it went up and the blast tore their bodies apart. Most of a garbageman who had just returned an ash can to the curb in front of the car was blown over his truck. The heavy truck itself came apart in huge twisted pieces, killing two other garbage workers who were in the cab. A salesman driving through the street on his way to an appointment was killed instantly and a crowded bus, caught in the jam of people on the street, was mangled. Blood and smoke were everywhere and then people began screaming.

That had all happened before I told the girl on the train about the gangsters shooting each other in New York. After the old man had passed through our car and gone on to the next one with his news of the explosion, we left the train, passed through the customs check, and walked out together onto the station plaza facing Great Victoria Street. It was she who suggested the Europa, the modern concave-fronted hotel adjacent to the rail-road station. It was convenient and perhaps she thought its newness and elaborate security precautions would make it more impregnable to IRA attack, and thus a safer place to stay.

There were attached metal fences across the front and around the sides of the hotel. Just in from the sidewalk I was stopped at a temporary wooden shack, the kind you see on construction sites, where they searched my luggage and frisked me from thigh to armpit and across the back before I was able to proceed up the curved driveway that had been converted into a maze of metal stanchions leading to the main revolving door of the hotel itself. A bellboy unlocked the door and locked it again as soon as I was in the lobby.

I had a whiskey in the grill, which was crowded and noisy still with lunching businessmen, although six blocks away on Donegall Street they had not yet finished lifting bodies into trucks and ambulances. I felt guilty and irresponsible for not being where that was happening. I had come to Belfast because it was where the trouble was; because people were killed there every day. I had no ties to Northern Ireland. The dreary Protestant city of Belfast, which was to remind me of Albany, satisfied no inner need of mine, except that the IRA was waging a war there. But the war that day had happened on Donegall Street, and I was afraid of what I would see. It was like the magnetic draw that a highway accident has when you're driving by it, and I was fighting not to look. I ordered a sandwich and a cup of coffee, checked into my room, took a shower, and changed my clothes.

They had cleared the bodies and the wreckage by the time I found my way there in the late afternoon. The firemen had hosed the blood away and a work force of carpenters was nailing sheets of plywood across the dozens of blown-out storefronts and open doorways and up and down the street there was the grating sound of broken glass being swept and shoveled into piles that looked like gravel.

A stationery store was open and people were buying cigarettes and candy while workmen boarded up the empty windows. I asked the proprietor what happened. His eyes were still glazed and he told me that when the garbageman had blown over the truck, his boots, with the feet and lower shins still in them, lay like two overturned containers emptying his blood onto the street where he had been standing; that even with all the ambulances from Belfast's four main hospitals, and ambulance trucks from the Army, there still were not enough stretchers and the ambulance men and paratroopers had used tarpaulins to carry away the injured, and that they'd also used the tarpaulins to wrap the larger pieces of bodies, while the smaller portions, the hands and fingers and bits of flesh, were gathered up in plastic bags.

The proprietor was an alcoholic, away from whiskey only eleven months, and that day he'd helped move torn bodies and had guided hysterical office girls to the room behind his store so they wouldn't have to look any more at what it was like out on the street. He had not yet had a drink but he was frightened that he would not be able to survive the night ahead without one.

"What kind of an animal could have done this thing?" he asked me. "How can he face himself and pretend that he's a hero for any cause? Who will he ever be able to tell that he did this?"

I went outside again and watched the young men sweeping up the glass. It was Monday and the business day was ending and people who had been at work were beginning to pass normally through the street on their homeward route as if the bombing had never happened. A bus drove through, then an Army jeep and two cars, then, slowly, a tank. I walked up to the Cathedral Church of St. Anne at the end of the street and stood at the foot of the steps, thinking crazily, and with no memory of the outrages committed in the cause of religion throughout history, that it was wrong that there had been such horror so close to a church; that it was somehow improper, more than that, a desecration, and that greater respect should have been shown for life so near the temple of the God these Christian adversaries were supposed to worship.

There was no mark of the explosion on the church and I walked the few yards to the first building with windows shattered. There was a lumber office on the ground floor. I started to count my steps until I came to a building with no visible signs of damage. There were two hundred and forty-eight. I crossed the street and walked back up, this time passing the arcade where the bomb had gone off. The concrete facing around the entryway and the adjacent building fronts had been blasted away and parts of the girders and internal metal mesh supports showed through as if some huge tool had hacked and gouged the masonry. On the other side of the street, the hollowed-out remains of a large two-sided clock projected out over a balcony above the entrance to the *Newsletter*. The steel hands were still attached to the remnants of its inner works and they just missed marking noon in empty space.

There were two hundred and forty-three steps when I'd finished walking to the end of the street near the church. I had probably lost my count passing the wrecked arcade and the debris that lay in front of it that second time, but the totals were close enough. My stride was somewhat short of a yard and therefore the shattering effects of the explosion, at least in terms of blown-out windows, had extended for more than a hundred yards on either side of the car. I calculated that a sprinter would take just over twenty seconds to cover that distance, which had nothing to do with the torn bodies and the mangled garbage truck and bus, or the flying glass that had cut like a hatchet. All that had happened simultaneously. Measuring horror in terms of the space it had occupied was a way of accounting for the fact that I was there.

That night after a late dinner I drank expensively with some television newsmen and a BBC man I'd met in Dublin. We sat in the large, softly lit private bar and lounge on the Europa's mezzanine floor, all comfortable low chairs and sofas aligned in squares, and I looked out through curtained plate glass windows at the patroling armored cars and tanks on the street below. There was a dispute over which bars were safe and which were going to go up one night soon for sure, and I thought of the movie *Dead End* with the rich apartment house at the very edge of the slums and the dock where the gang of poor kids played. My room was in the hotel's rear and from it I could see the concentration of chimneys and occasional lights in the Catholic ghetto on the Falls Road only a few hundred yards away.

The two television men, one a news director, a big man with protruding eyes, and the other a bearded newscaster for one of the British services, had closed the pubs and were finishing off the night in the Europa, where guests could drink until breakfast if they wanted to, and where they were sure to find other newsmen, who were almost the only people who visited Belfast any more.

The news director said he had laughed when he knew he had to put together five minutes on Donegall Street for the evening's newscast. "I bloody well did, I can tell you. My horror threshold has disappeared entirely." Because there had been more than two hours' worth of film to edit, and because ninety seconds of the five minutes allotted to the bombing had to be given over to interviews with the Chief of Police and a Government Minister, "both of them talking shit," he hadn't had time to do anything about the other two explosions where no one was killed, or the British soldier who had been shot that day in Derry.

The BBC man said to stop Bogarting it, that the moral depravity of the people who had placed the bomb was beyond comprehension. The news director told him to come off the righteous indignation. "Any one of us at this table could have placed that bomb and you know it." The BBC man said that he certainly couldn't have done it.

"Don't give me that. It's a simple matter of disassociation. You don't even have to be a member of anything. We've all of us been indifferent to suffering and death a thousand times over."

While the BBC man argued that there was a distinction between indifference to an existent state and being the direct cause of that state, I remembered once when I was a boy placing a small flat stone on the railroad track across the golf course from where I lived. We used to do that with pennies and the next day they would be lying between the ties, misshapen and as thin as razor blades. I hadn't thought of that time in all my years as an adult. Why had I put a stone there? Had I lain in bed that night frightened that I would hear a train tumble down the embankment, and if it had, that they would find out I had been the cause? I couldn't remember.

The news director was saying, "All you care about is that it wasn't you, and don't tell me different. What are you going to give me, stories about the sorrowing wives and mothers and the little kiddies at home? Can't you see that nobody really cares?"

The BBC man was sober and this man wasn't, so allowances had to be made. Still I resented his badgering, even though it wasn't directed at me. Just walking through that street had made me feel uneasy all evening. I was afraid of sudden shattering calamities where all the little strengths of mind and character, built up and cultivated for a lifetime, might prove useless. It wasn't only that one could be killed or maimed in a moment; one's sense of person could be undone as easily.

"You mean you don't care about this," I said, folding out from an inside page of the evening paper a photo that had haunted me and handing it across the cocktail table. It showed an old man with his leg blown off. A soldier was trying to comfort him but the old man was in shock and he didn't know the leg was gone. The photo had been shot head on and you saw the torn trouser leg and the stump and the blood spreading on the sidewalk. The news director hardly looked at it. He threw it back at me and it fell on the carpet. "I couldn't give fuck all," he said.

Perhaps to cover for his friend's rudeness, the bearded newscaster with the tinted glasses asked me why I cared. The news director interrupted and said he hoped I didn't think there was a simple solution sitting there in the middle somewhere between the Orange and the Green, if only people would see it. When he talked it was as if he spoke in waves because his body and head moved forward and back and his eyes seemed to protrude more with each new sentence. I shrugged and told them I didn't know, and that I was numb with impressions that were not new to them any more and that I was having a great deal of difficulty knowing what was important and what wasn't, and that my past kept coming in on top of those new impressions, muddying them still further. I told them that walking back from Donegall Street I kept thinking about the Christmas week back home when the showroom and offices of an automobile dealer I knew had blown up in a chemical fire, and I had felt that same vague, uneasy frightened vulnerability that I felt now, and that the feeling had stayed with me all night and the next day, and that I had remembered the automobile dealer running a sensational anchor leg in a relay race many years ago when we were both in high school.

"Was it a big explosion, tell us," the man in the tinted glasses asked, and the other one started to laugh, and I felt like a fool for telling such a story; as if they would care about an ordinary accident that had happened in another country.

A group of English and European journalists came upstairs noisily and joined us. There were five men and two women and they were all tight. One of the women sat on the side of a sofa and let herself fall back onto the cushions with her legs kicking over the arm. "God, I'm tired," she said. "I've absolutely had it."

"Where the hell is the waiter?" one of the journalists asked us. The BBC man told him he was back getting us drinks. "Well, he can bloody well get us a round as well."

"One round at least," another of them said.

"My God, you'd think they could at least put two men on at night. We've come here and saved their bloody country for them and you can't even get a bloody drink."

JAN MORRIS
Dublin: 1970s

"ARE THERE ANY URCHINS LIKE DUBLIN URCHINS, GRUBBY AS SIN AND BOUNCY AS PING-PONG BALLS? ARE THERE ANY MARKETS LIKE DUBLIN MARKETS, SPRAWLING ALL OVER THE CITY STREETS LIKE GIPSY JUMBLE SALES?"

Jan Morris, often named as the greatest travel writer of our time, was born in Wales in 1926 as James Morris and lived and wrote as a man until a gender change in 1972, an event recounted in her best-selling autobiographical volume, Conundrum.

James Morris served in the British Army in Italy and the Middle East, attended Oxford, and worked for ten years as a foreign correspondent for the Times *of London and the* Manchester Guardian. *He was the first European to cross the Arabian desert from the Indian Ocean to the Persian Gulf, a journey reported vividly in* Sultan in Oman. *He was also the only correspondent to accompany Edmund Hillary's Mount Everest expedition in 1953; his news report that the summit had been conquered reached England on Queen Elizabeth's coronation day.*

Among Morris's greatest works is the Pax Britannica *trilogy, a vivid history and meditation on the British Empire in the nineteenth century, consisting of* Heaven's Command, Pax Britannica, *and* Farewell the Trumpets.

Jan Morris has spent most of her life traveling and writing—and, in recent years, supporting the cause of Welsh nationalism. She has written books about Oxford, Hong Kong, Sydney, Manhattan, Canada, Spain, and Wales, three about Venice, and half a dozen volumes of collected essays, most notable of which is Among the Cities. *In 1997 she looked back over the enormous changes in Europe in* Fifty Years of Europe: An Album.

153

Another selection by Jan Morris, a view of the city of Durban, is included in The Reader's Companion to South Africa.

Morris has visited Ireland often, though not always with enormous pleasure. The following impressions of Dublin are warmer than others.

WHEN I WENT TO DUBLIN ONCE, I FOUND THAT THE very next morning the fifth President of the Irish Republic, the *Uachtarán*, was to be installed in the Hall of St. Patrick in Dublin Castle. Hastening out to buy myself a proper dress ("I congratulate you," said the maid at my hotel in some surprise, "you've got excellent taste"), and procuring an official pass (*Preas, Insealbhu an Uchtaráin*), promptly in the morning I presented myself at the Castle gates, made my way through the confusion of soldiery, officialdom and diplomacy that filled the old yard, and found my place beside the dais in the elegantly decorated hall ("No place for purple prose," murmured my cicerone pointedly, "more the Ionian white and gold.")

It was a delightful occasion. All Eire was there, among the massed banners and crests of the ancient Irish provinces, beneath the stern gaze of the trumpeters poised for their fanfare in the minstrels' gallery. All the Ministers were there, with their invisible portfolios. All the Ambassadors were there, with their distinctly visible wives. *Both* Primates of All Ireland were there, side by side in parity. There were judges and surgeons, old revolutionaries and new politicians, clerics by the hundred, professors by the score. There was Conor Cruise O'Brien. There was John Lynch. There was Sean MacBride the Nobel Laureate. There was Cyril Cusack the actor. It was like seeing the Irish Republic encapsulated, dressed in its newest fineries, sworn to its best behaviour, and deposited in the building which, more than any other in Ireland, speaks of Irish history.

The new President, Cearbhall O Dalaigh, seemed a dear man indeed, and gave us a gentle rambling speech much concerned with what the removal men said when they packed his possessions for the move. Some of it was in Gaelic, some in French, some in English, and I confess my mind did wander now and then, towards the Ruritanian Ambassadress's fur coat, towards the twin smiles of the Archbishops, towards the fierce survey of the bandmaster high above, who might easily have stepped from the ranks of the old Connaught Rangers. One phrase in particular, though, and not alas the President's own, caught my attention. It was a quotation from Thoreau, and it ran thus: "If a man does not keep pace with his companions, perhaps it is because he hears a different drummer."

A different drummer! What drummer beat in Dublin now, I wondered, where the best were always out of step? What pace would the bandmaster set today? Was the drum-beat different still, in this most defiantly different of capitals?

That evening, when the dignitaries, officials and soldiers had dispersed to their celebratory banquets (all except the poor military policeman who, vainly trying to kick his motor-bike to life, was left forlorn in the Castle yard to a universal sigh of sympathy), I drove along the coast to Howth, and then the Joyceness of Dublin, the Yeatsness, the pubness, the tramness, the Liffeyness, the Behanness, in short the stock Dublinness of the place seemed to hang like a vapour over the distant city. It was one of those Irish evenings when the points of the compass seem to have been confused, and their climates with them. A bitter east wind swayed the palm trees along the promenade, a quick northern air sharpened that slightly Oriental languor, that Celtic *dolce far niente*, which habitually blurs the intentions of Dublin. Over the water the city lay brownish below the Wicklow Mountains, encrusted it seemed with some tangible patina of legend and literature, and fragrant of course with its own *vin du pays*, Guinness.

This is everyone's Dublin, right or wrong, and if it is partly myth, it is substance too. There is no such thing as a stage Dubliner: the characters of this city, even at their most theatrical, are true and earnest in their kind, and Dublin too, even today, lives up to itself without pretence. Are there any urchins like Dublin urchins, grubby as sin and bouncy as ping-pong balls? Are there any markets like Dublin markets, sprawling all over the city streets like gipsy jumble sales? Are there any buses so evocative as Dublin buses, lurching in dim-lit parade towards Glasnevin?

Certainly there are few more boisterous streets on earth than O'Connell Street on a Saturday night, when a salt wind gusts up from the sea, making the girls giggle and the young men clown about, driving the Dublin litter helter-skelter here and there, and eddying the smells of beer, chips and hot-dogs all among the back streets. And there is no café more tumultuous than Bewley's Oriental Café in Grafton Street, with its mountains of buns on every table, with its children draped over floors and chairs, with its harassed waitresses scribbling, its tea-urns hissing, its stained glass and its tiled floors, its old clock beside the door, the high babel of its Dublin chatter and its haughty Dublin ladies, all hats and arched eyebrows, smoking their cigarettes loftily through it all.

It is an all too familiar rhythm, but it beats unmistakably still, hilariously and pathetically, and it makes of Dublin one of the most truly exotic cities in the world. One still finds shawled beggar women on the Liffey bridges at night, huddling their babies close, attended by wide-eyed small boys and holding cardboard boxes for contributions. One still hears the instant give-and-take in Dublin pubs and parlours. "Ah, me rheumatism's cured," says the old lady quick as a flash when the landlord pats her kindly on the knee, "you should advertise your healing powers." "Sure it was only my left hand too," says the landlord. "Well and it was only my left knee—try the other one, there's a good man." I experienced the tail-end of a bank robbery in Dublin one day, and only in this city, I thought, could I observe the principal witness of a crime interviewed by the police in a butcher's shop—between whose ranks of hanging turkeys, from the pavement outside, I could glimpse his blood-streaked face enthusiastically recalling the horror of it all.

Dublin's gay but shabby recklessness, too, which so infuriated its English overlords, brazenly survives. If there is a public clock that works in Dublin, I have yet to find it, and I was not in the least surprised when, calling at a restaurant at a quarter to five to arrange a table for dinner, I found several jolly parties concluding their lunch. The Irish honour their own priorities still. "It's not very satisfactory just to tell your customers," I overheard a lady complaining at the G.P.O., "that the mail's gone up with a bomb, it's not very satisfactory at all." "He'll make a fine President," somebody said to me of Cearbhall O Dalaigh, "nobody knows what his name is." "Enjoy yourself now!" everybody says in Dublin, and they mean enjoy yourself *notwithstanding*.

Dublin is very old—old in history, old in style. If there is no such thing as a stage Dubliner, in a curious way there is no such thing as a young one, either. The dry scepticism of the Dublin manner, the elliptical nature of its conversations, the dingy air of everything, the retrospection—all conspire to give this city a sense of elderly collusion. Everyone seems to know everyone else, and all about him too. Go into any Dublin company, somebody suggested to me one day, and present the cryptic inquiry: "Do you think should he have gone over?" Instantly, whatever the circumstances, there will be a cacophony of replies. "Sure he should, but not without telling his wife"—"And why shouldn't he have, was he not the elected representative?"—"Well it wasn't so far as it looked"—"It didn't surprise me, his father was just the same." Such is the accumulated familiarity of the city that to any inquiry, about anybody, about anything, every Dubliner—every true Dubberlin man, as the vernacular has it—possesses an infallible response, usually wrong.

Such a sense of commonalty curdles easily into conspiracy, and of course history has helped to fuse your Dubliners, making them feel far more homogeneous than the people of most western capitals. This is not only a classless society, at least in externals, it is an indigenous one too. Your Italian waiter, your Chinese take-away *restaurateur*, your Jamaican bus conductor, even your Nigerian student of computer technology are all rare figures in Dublin still, and the consequent unity of method and temper gives the city much of its exuberant punch.

It also gives it a special pride, for this is not only the capital of a nation, but the capital of an idea. The idea of Irishness is not universally beloved. Some people mock it, some hate it, some fear it. On the whole, though, I think it fair to say, the world interprets it chiefly as a particular kind of happiness, a happiness sometimes boozy and violent, but essentially innocent: and this incradicable spirit of merriment informs the Dublin genius to this day, and is alive and bubbling still, for all the miseries of the Irish Problem, in this jumbled brown capital across the water.

Sometimes I could hear other drummers, though. I rang up the *Dáil* one day and asked if there was anything interesting to observe that evening. "There's always me," said the usher, "I'm interesting." For if on one level Dublin is a world capital, to which subjects from Melbourne to the Bronx pay a vicarious or morganatic allegiance, on another it is the day-to-day capital of a little state. In this it is very modern. Ireland seems to me the right size for a country, the truly contemporary size, the size at which regionalism properly becomes nationhood, and the parliamentary usher answers the telephone himself. Small units within a large framework offer a sensible pattern for the world's future, and beneath the fustiness of the old Dublin, the world's Dublin, a much more contemporary entity exists.

Old Dublin is averse to change, but this smaller, inner Dublin welcomes it. "If I know the Brits," said a genial enthusiast at a Ballsbridge party, holding my hand and talking about London, "they'll soon be having St. Paul's down to make way for a new ghastly office block." Well, the Micks are not much better when it comes to urban development. Visual taste is hardly their forte, and they have done little to improve the look of

Dublin since the end of the Ascendancy. Wide areas of the Liberties are in that melancholy state of unexplained decay that generally precedes "improvement," there are frightful plans for the Liffey quays, the Central Bank is building itself a structure which is not only grossly out of scale with the time and the city, but seems in its present state of completion to be made of Meccano—"an awful thing in itself," as a bystander observed to me, "and terrible by implication."

More often the implications of change are merely sad. They imply a deliberate, functional rejection not perhaps of tradition or principle, but of habit. Gone is many an ancient pub, anomalous perhaps to a condition of progress, but beloved in itself. Crippled is many a Georgian square. Doomed and derelict is J. J. Byrne the fish shop ("This Is The Place"). Fearful ring roads threaten. No good looking in for Dublin Bay prawns at the old Red Bank: it was long ago converted into a Catholic chapel, where in the Dublin manner the local girls slip in for a moment's supplication before rejoining their boy friends on the pavement outside for a stout in the corner bar.

There are worse things to worry about, too. There are the Troubles, those endemic mysteries of Ireland, which are inescapable in Dublin if only by suggestion—*Beál Feirste*, as the road signs say, is only 100 miles to the north. A fairly muzzy security screen protects the offices of the Irish Government, and sends the unsuspecting visitor backwards and forwards between the guards—"Did you not see this young lady when she came in?" "I did not, she must have walked by like a ghost." When I saw a big black car with two big men in it, standing outside my host's suburban house, I knew a Minister was calling, and I looked more than once over my shoulder before, in a spirit of pure enquiry, I entered the house in Parnell Square where they sell Christmas cards and *objets d'art* made by the internees of Ulster.

But far more immediate than the bomber is the rising price. In Britain inflation is merely another blow to the punch-drunk: in Ireland it is an unfair decision. For so many centuries a loser, in recent years Eire has found a winning streak, finding its feet at last, establishing its place in the world, evolving a mean between the practical and the ideal, forgiving and even half-forgetting the tragedies of the past. With change, it seemed, prosperity was coming. Many of the new buildings of Dublin might be unlovely, but at least they were earnests of success.

Now the poor Dubliners find themselves haunted once again by the prospect of failure. The Irish economy is less than hefty, and could not long resist a world recession. Then the brief holiday would be over, the cars would be sold, the colour televisions sold, the plump young Dublin executive would no longer be lunching at a quarter to five. You might not guess the possibility from the Grafton Street stores, which are among the most charming and fastidious in Europe, but your Dubberlin man sees it plain enough, and often speaks of it with cheerful foreboding, as he chooses a third sticky cake at Bewley's, or summons a second bottle of hock.

For luckily Dublin's rueful optimism survives, and pervades the Republic too. They said some fairly gloomy things in the *Dáil* that evening, and discussed some daunting prospects, but when they adjourned for a vote, and the deputies hung over the rail of the Chamber waiting for the tellers, with their rubicund laughing faces, their stocky country frames, their irrepressible chatter and their elbows on the rail, I thought they looked for all the world like convivial farmers at a cattle sale, looking down towards the Speaker's chair as towards the auctioneer, and waiting for the next Friesian to be led in from the robing chamber. "Didja enjoy yourself now?" said the usher when I left, and the security man in his little lodge waggled his fingers at me as I passed.

I suppose there are terrorists plotting in Dublin, and bombers preparing their fuses, but it remains, all the same, pre-eminently the innocent capital of a star-crossed state—for the luck of the Irish is a wish more than a characteristic. One of its greatest charms is its intimate completeness. There are only 3 million people in Eire, scarcely more than there are in Wales, but Dublin has its diplomatic corps and its Government departments, its *Uachtarán*, its *Taoiseach* and all the trappings of a sovereign capital. Irish pictures, Irish plays, Irish artefacts, Irish heroes—Dublin is obsessed with itself and its hinterland, giving the little capital a character introspective perhaps but undeniably authoritative, for it is certainly the last word on itself.

Half its pleasure lies in its pride. Ten columns of the Dublin telephone book are needed to list the 660 institutions which boast the prefix "Irish." Like the Welsh and Scots, but unlike the hapless English, the Irish are still frankly affectionate towards their nationality, and this gives Dubliners an unexpected balance or serenity. I went one night to the Abbey Theatre, where Mr. Cusack was playing the Vicar of Wakefield as to the manner born, and thought as I looked at the audience around me how enviably *natural* they looked. The burden of their history did not show, and they were not entangled by inhibitions of power or prestige. They had never been citizens of a Great Power, and never would be. They talked in no phoney accents, pined for no lost empires, and laughed at Goldsmith's gentle humour without much caring whether the world laughed too.

For if Dublin is parochial, it is not provincial exactly, for it remains original. British influences are ubiquitous, it is true, from the Aldershot drill of the Presidential guard to *Coronation Street* on Monday evening, but there is no sense of copy-cat. Dubliners are their own men still. Even when a concern is foreign owned, as so many in Dublin are, it acquires a distinctively Irish flavour, so that even Trust House-Fortes' Airport Hotel coffee-shop, physically a carbon of every airport coffee-shop ever built anywhere, will give you eggs and bacon at lunch time if you ask nicely, "for sure the chef's a kindly man."

And though it is small, still Dublin feels like a true capital. Like Edinburgh, it deserves sovereignty. It is a fine thing to walk through the Dublin streets on a Sunday morning, say, when the sun is rising brilliantly out of the Bay, and to see the monuments of Irish pride around you—the fire on Parnell's column, O'Connell the Liberator on his plinth, the great columns of the Customs House, the delicate dome of the Four Courts. Over the great bridge you go, where the wind off the Bay sweeps up-river to blow your hair about, and there is Trinity before you, where Congreve and Swift and Burke were educated, where Goldsmith stands on his pedestal and the *Book of Kells* lies for ever open in its case. On your right is the old Irish Parliament, on the left is the City Hall, and soon, turning the cobbled corner at the top, you are—

Soon you are where? Why, back in the yard of Dublin Castle, where Presidents of Eire are installed indeed, but where for 800 years, in a presence far more monstrous, far more stately, the power of the English inexorably resided.

For like it or not, whatever your opinions, the drums of tragedy sound still in Dublin, muffled but unavoidable, as they sound nowhere else on earth. For eight centuries the Irish struggled against the dominion of the English, and it takes more than fifty uneasy years to silence the echoes.

The most compelling of all the figures at that Presidential occasion was that of Eamon de Valera, who arrived in an aged Rolls, and whose stiff blind figure, depending upon the arm of a veteran officer, leaning slightly backward as the blind sometimes do, and tapping with his stick between the silent lines of the diplomatic corps, cast a somewhat macabre hush upon the assembly. "The skeleton at the feast," whispered an irreverent observer somewhere near me, but I found the spectacle very moving;

and when with difficulty the old rebel climbed the dais and sat ramrod-stiff on his chair a few feet away from me, holding his stick between his knees and sometimes decorously applauding, I envisaged all he had seen in the progress of the little state, the Easter Rising, the war against the British, the horrible Civil War, and so by way of plot and revolution, ob-stinacy and courage, deviousness and boldness, to the installation of the fifth *Uachtarán* there on the bright blue carpets of St. Patrick's Hall.

When I first knew Dublin, in the early 1960s, I thought the old fer-vours of revolution were fading, and that the memories of that sad struggle would die with its own generation. But the drum beats still, a drum to the treble of the Ulster fifes, and the presence there of Mr. de Valera did not seem an anachronism to me, only a grave reminder. The terrible beauty lingers still, tainted perhaps but inescapable. That evening, after dinner, I wandered alone among the back streets behind the General Post Office, where little more than fifty years ago the fated visionaries of the Rising fought and died among the blazing ruins.

It is smart in Dublin to denigrate the Easter Rising now, and to say that it achieved nothing after all, but still those streets seemed haunted ground to me. The glow of the burning Post Office lit the night sky still, the Soldier's Song sounded above the traffic, and at the end of every street I could see the barricades of the British, and hear the clatter of their rifles and the clink of their tea-mugs. Sometimes machine-guns rattled, and the awful smell of war, of death and dirt and cordite, hung all about the build-ings. I wept as I remembered that old tragedy, and thought of those brave men so soon to be shot at dawn, and of the ignorant homely English at their guns behind their sandbags, and I turned towards home in a sad despair, contemplating the deceits of glory.

But when I turned into O'Connell Street I looked up into the plane trees, swaying above me in the night wind, and dimly I discerned there the grey shapes of the pied wagtails, those miraculous familiars of Dublin. Every winter those loyal country birds come back to roost in the trees of O'Connell Street, settling down each day at dusk, fluttering away to moun-tain and moorland when the dawn breaks. They calmed and comforted me at once, and I saw in their silent presence a figure of my own gratitude—for the gaiety that takes me back to Dublin year after year, for the melody that sounds always above the drums and bombs of Ireland, and for the old comradeship of this city, which transcends all bitterness, ignores time and is the truest of Dublin's contradictory truths.

PAUL THEROUX

Discovering Dingle: 1976

"NO ONE MENTIONS RELIGION. THE ONLY
INDICATION I HAD OF THE FAITH WAS THE
VALEDICTION OF A LADY IN A BAR IN
BALLYFERRITER, WHO SHOUTED, 'GOD BLESS YE!'
WHEN I EMPTIED MY PINT OF GUINNESS."

Paul Theroux's career as a traveler began when he answered President John F. Kennedy's call for volunteers and was among the first young Americans to join the Peace Corps. He was assigned to teach English in Mali and received, let us say, mixed notices during his service, having inadvertently become involved in local politics. He was quickly recalled to Washington but soon returned to Africa to teach at Makarere University in Uganda. There, he and his English wife were married. They later lived for some years in the Far East and then in London, although Theroux continued to spend time in Cape Cod and Massachusetts, where he grew up. At present, he lives in Hawaii.

His literary career began with several novels and dozens of short stories, most set in the places where he lived and often fictionalizing his experiences as a traveler. Indeed, his own life has been the major source of his best and most controversial fiction, notably his novels My Secret History *and* My Other Life. *His other novels include* The Black House, The Mosquito Coast, Half Moon Street, *and* Millroy the Magician.

His career as the most popular travel writer of our time began on September 19, 1973, when he rolled out of London on a four-month train journey through the Orient that was later recounted in the best-selling The Great Railway Bazaar. *To a large degree, it was this book that sparked a huge new wave of interest in travel writing in the last quarter of the century. Theroux's later travels have taken him to South America (*The Old Patagonian Express*),* *around the coast of Great Britain* (The Kingdom by the Sea), *China* (Riding the Iron Rooster), *the Pacific* (The Happy Isles of Oceania), *and the Mediterranean* (The Pillars of Hercules).

Theroux is an acerbic traveler. Nothing escapes him, he doesn't try to be liked, he's brutally honest, and he doesn't give a tinker's damn what people think.

Here he is in Dingle.

THE NEAREST THING TO WRITING A NOVEL IS TRAVELING in a strange country. Travel is a creative act—not simply loafing and inviting your soul, but feeding the imagination, accounting for each fresh wonder, memorizing and moving on. The discoveries the traveler makes in broad daylight—the curious problems of the eye he solves—resemble those that thrill and sustain a novelist in his solitude. It is fatal to know too much at the outset: boredom comes as quickly to the traveler who knows his route as to the novelist who is overcertain of his plot. And the best landscapes, apparently dense or featureless, hold surprises if they are studied patiently, in the kind of discomfort one can savor afterward. Only a fool blames his bad vacation on the rain.

A strange country—but how strange? One where the sun bursts through the clouds at ten in the evening and makes a sunset as full and promising as dawn. An island which on close inspection appears to be composed entirely of rabbit droppings. Gloomy gypsies camped in hilarious clutter. People who greet you with "Nice day" in a pelting storm. Miles of fuchsia hedges, seven feet tall, with purple hanging blossoms like Chinese lanterns. Ancient perfect castles that are not inhabited; hovels that are. And dangers: hills and beach-cliffs so steep you either hug them or fall off. Stone altars that were last visited by Druids, storms that break and pass in minutes, and a local language that sounds like Russian being whispered and so incomprehensible that the attentive traveler feels, in the words of a native writer, "like a dog listening to music."

It sounds as distant and bizarre as The Land Where the Jumblies Live, and yet it is the part of Europe that is closest in miles to America, the thirty mile sausage of land on the southwest coast of Ireland that is known as the Dingle Peninsula. Beyond it is Boston and New York, where many of its people have fled. The land is not particularly fertile. Fishing is dangerous and difficult. Food is expensive; and if the Irish Government did not offer financial inducements to the natives they would probably shrink inland, like the people of Great Blasket Island who simply dropped everything and went ashore to the Dingle, deserting their huts and fields and leaving them to the rabbits and the ravens.

It is easy for the casual traveler to prettify the place with romantic hyperbole, to see in Dingle's hard weather and exhausted ground the Celtic Twilight, and in its stubborn hopeful people a version of Irishness that is to be cherished. That is the patronage of pity—the metropolitan's contempt for the peasant. The Irish coast, so enchanting for the man with the camera, is murder for the fisherman. For five of the eight days I was there the fishing boats remained anchored in Dingle Harbor, because it was too wild to set sail. The dead seagulls, splayed out like old-fangled ladies' hats below Clogher Head, testify to the furious winds; and never have I seen so many sheep skulls bleaching on hillsides, so many cracked bones beneath bushes.

Farming is done in the most clumsily primitive way, with horses and donkeys, wagons and blunt plows. The methods are traditional by necessity—modernity is expensive, gas costs more than Guinness. The stereotype of the Irishman is a person who spends every night at the local pub, jigging and swilling; in the villages of this peninsula only Sunday night is festive and the rest are observed with tea and early supper.

"I don't blame anyone for leaving here," said a farmer in Dunquin. "There's nothing for young people. There's no work, and it's getting worse."

After the talk of the high deeds of Finn MacCool and the fairies and leprechauns, the conversation turns to the price of spare parts, the cost of grain, the value of the Irish pound which has sunk below the British one. Such an atmosphere of isolation is intensified and circumscribed by the language—there are many who speak only Gaelic. Such remoteness breeds political indifference. There is little talk of the guerrilla war in Northern Ireland, and the few people I tried to draw on the subject said simply that Ulster should become part of Eire.

Further east, in Cork and Killarney, I saw graffiti reading BRITS OUT or UP THE IRA. It is not only the shortage of walls or the cost of spray cans that keep the Irish in Dingle from scrawling slogans. I cannot remember any people so quickly hospitable or easier to meet. Passers-by nod in greeting, children wave at cars: it is all friendliness. At almost three thousand feet the shepherd salutes the climbers and then marches on with his dogs yapping ahead of him.

Either the people leave and go far—every Irishman I met had a relative in America—or they never stir at all. "I've lived here my whole life," said an old man in Curraheen on Tralee Bay; and he meant it—he had always sat in that chair and known that house and that tree and that pasture. But his friend hesitated. "Well, yes," this one said, "not here exactly. After I got married I moved further down the road." It is the outsider who sees Dingle whole; the Irish there live in solitary villages. And people who have only the vaguest notion of Dublin or London, and who have never left Ballydavid or Inch, show an intimate knowledge of American cities, Boston, Springfield, Newark or San Diego. The old lady in Dunquin, sister of the famous "Kruger" Kavanagh—his bar remains, a friendly ramshackle place with a dark side of bacon suspended over one bar and selling peat bricks, ice cream, shampoo and corn flakes along with the Guinness and the rum—that old lady considered Ventry (her new homestead, four miles away) another world, and yet she used her stern charm on me to recommend a certain bar on Cape Cod.

I did not find, in the whole peninsula, an inspired meal or a great hotel; nor can the peninsula be recommended for its weather. We had two days of rain, two of mist, one almost tropical, and one which was all three, rain in the morning, mist in the afternoon, and sun that appeared in the evening and didn't sink until eleven at night—this was June. "Soft evening," says the fisherman; but that is only a habitual greeting—it might be raining like hell. In general, the sky is overcast, occasionally the weather is unspeakable: no one should go to that part of Ireland in search of sunny days. The bars, two or three to a village, are musty with rising damp and woodworm, and the pictures of President Kennedy—sometimes on yellowing newsprint, sometimes picked out daintily in needlepoint on framed teatowels—do little to relieve the gloom. The English habit of giving bars fanciful names, like The Frog and Nightgown or The White Hart, is virtually unknown in Ireland. I did not see a bar in any village that was not called simply Mahoney's, or Crowley's, or Foley's, or O'Flaherty's: a bar is a room, a keg, an Irish name over the door, and perhaps a cat asleep on the sandwiches.

The roads are empty but narrow, and one—the three miles across the Conair Pass—is, in low cloud, one of the most dangerous I have ever seen, bringing a lump to my throat that I had not tasted since traversing the Khyber. The landscape is utterly bleak, and sometimes there is no sound but the wind beating the gorse bushes or the cries of gulls which—shrill and frantic—mimic something tragic, like a busload of schoolgirls careering off a cliff. The day we arrived my wife and I went for a walk, down the meadow to the sea. It was gray. We walked fifty feet. It rained. The wind tore at the outcrops of rock. We started back, slipping on seaweed, and now we could no longer see the top of the road, where we had begun the walk. It was cold; both of us were wet, feebly congratulating ourselves that we had remembered to buy rubber boots in Killarney.

Then Anne hunched and said, "It's bloody cold. Let's make this a one-night stand."

But we waited. It rained the next day. And the next. The third was misty, but after so much rain the mist gave us the illusion of good weather: there was some promise in the shifting clouds. But, really, the weather had ceased to matter. It was too cold to swim and neither of us had imagined sunbathing in Ireland. We had started to discover the place on foot, in a high wind, fortified by stout and a picnic lunch of crab's claws (a dollar a pound) and cheese and soda bread. Pausing, we had begun to travel.

There is no detailed guidebook for these parts. Two choices are open: to buy Sheet 20 of the Ordnance Survey Map of Ireland, or climb Mount Brandon and look down. We did both, and it was odd how, standing in mist among ecclesiastical-looking cairns (the mountain was a place of pilgrimage for early Christian monks seeking the intercession of St Brendan the Navigator), we looked down and saw that Smerwick and Ballyferriter were enjoying a day of sunshine, Brandon Head was rainy, and Mount Eagle was in cloud. Climbing west of Dingle is deceptive, a succession of false summits, each windier than the last; but from the heights of Brandon the whole peninsula is spread out like a topographical map, path and road, cove and headland. Down there was the Gallarus Oratory, like a perfect boathouse in stone to which no one risks assigning a date (but probably 9th Cent.), and at a greater distance Great Blasket Island and the smaller ones with longer names around it. The views all over the peninsula are dramatic and unlikely, as anyone who has seen *Ryan's Daughter* knows— that bad dazzling movie was made in and around the fishing hamlet of Dunquin. The coastal cliffs are genuinely frightening, the coves echoic with waves that hit the black rocks and rise—foaming, perpendicular—at the fleeing gannets; and the long Slieve Mish Mountains and every valley— thirty miles of them—are, most weirdly, without trees.

We had spotted Mount Eagle. The following day we wandered from the sandy, and briefly sunny, beach at Ventry, through tiny farms to the dark sloping lake that is banked like a sink a thousand feet up the slope—

more bones, more rabbits, and a mountain wall strafed by screeching gulls. We had begun to enjoy the wind and rough weather, and after a few days of it saw Dingle Town as too busy, exaggerated, almost large, without much interest, and full of those fairly grim Irish shops which display in the front window a can of beans, a fan belt, a pair of boots, two chocolate bars, yesterday's newspaper and a row of plastic crucifixes standing on fly-blown cookie boxes. And in one window—that of a shoe store—two bottles of "Guaranteed Pure Altar Wine"—the guarantee was lettered neatly on the label: "Certified by the Cardinal Archbishop of Lisbon and Approved by his Lordship the Most Reverend Dr Eamonn Casey, Bishop of Kerry."

But no one mentions religion. The only indication I had of the faith was the valediction of a lady in a bar in Ballyferriter, who shouted, "God Bless ye!" when I emptied my pint of Guinness.

On the rainiest day we climbed down into the cove at Coumeenoole, where—because of its unusual shape, like a ruined cathedral—there was no rain. I sent the children off for driftwood and at the mouth of a dry cave built a fire. It is the bumpkin who sees travel in terms of dancing girls and candlelight dinners on the terrace; the city-slicker's triumphant holiday is finding the right mountain-top or building a fire in the rain or recognizing the wildflowers in Dingle: foxglove, heather, bluebells.

And it is the city-slicker's conceit to look for untrodden ground, the five miles of unpeopled beach at Stradbally Strand, the flat magnificence of Inch Strand, or the most distant frontier of Ireland, the island off Dunquin called Great Blasket.

Each day, she and her sister-islands looked different. We had seen them from the cliffside of Slea Head, and on that day they had the appearance of sea monsters—high backed creatures making for the open sea. Like all offshore islands, seen from the mainland, their aspect changed with the light: they were lizard-like, then muscular, turned from gray to green, acquired highlights that might have been huts. At dawn they seemed small, but they grew all day into huge and fairly fierce-seeming mountains in the water, diminishing at dusk into pink beasts and finally only hindquarters disappearing in the mist. Some days they were not there at all; on other days they looked linked to the peninsula.

It became our ambition to visit them. We waited for a clear day, and it came—bright and cloudless. But the boat looked frail, a rubber dinghy with an outboard motor. The children were eager; I looked at the high waves that lay between us and Great Blasket and implored the boatman for reassurance. He said he had never overturned—but he was young. On an impulse I agreed and under a half-hour later we arrived at the foreshore on the east of the main island, soaking wet from the spray.

No ruin in Ireland prepared us for the ruins on Great Blasket. After many years of cozy habitation—described with good humor by Maurice O'Sullivan in *Twenty Years A-Growing* (1933)—the villagers were removed to the mainland in 1953. They could no longer support themselves: they surrendered their island to the sneaping wind. And their houses, none of them large, fell down. Where there had been parlors and kitchens and vegetable gardens and fowl-coops there was now bright green moss. The grass and moss and wildflowers combine to create a cemetery effect in the derelict village, the crumbled hut walls like old gravemarkers.

I think I have never seen an eerier or more beautiful island. Just beyond the village which has no name is a long sandy beach called White Strand, which is without a footprint; that day it shimmered like any in Bali. After our picnic we climbed to Sorrowful Cliff and discovered that the island which looked only steep from the shore was in fact precipitous. "Sure, it's a wonderful place to commit suicide," a man told me in Dunquin. A narrow path was cut into the slope on which we walked single file—a few feet to the right and straight down were gulls and the dull sparkle of the Atlantic. We were on the windward side, heading for Fatal Cliff; and for hundreds of feet straight up rabbits were defying gravity on the steepness. The island hill becomes such a sudden ridge and so sharp that when we got to the top of it and took a step we were in complete silence: no wind, no gulls, no surf, only a green-blue vista of the coast of Kerry, Valencia Island and the soft headlands. Here on the lee side the heather was three feet thick and easy as a mattress. I lay down, and within minutes my youngest child was asleep on his stomach, his face on a cushion of fragrant heather. And the rest of the family had wandered singly to other parts of the silent island, so that when I sat up I could see them prowling alone, in detached discovery, trying—because we could not possess this strangeness—to remember it.

ELIZABETH SHANNON

The Ambassador's residence, the Dublin Horse Show, Phoenix Park: 1977

"I FINALLY QUERIED MICHAEL ABOUT IT TODAY: 'WHY
IS IT SO WILD AND UNKEMPT?' I ASKED. 'IT'S THE
FAIRY HILL,' SAYS HE, EXPLAINING ALL."

On May 4, 1977, President Jimmy Carter named William Shannon, then
editorial writer for the New York Times, as Ambassador to the Republic of
Ireland. By July 15, the Shannon family—five strong, counting sons Liam,
Christopher, and David—were getting their first look at the American Ambassador's residence in Dublin's Phoenix Park.

Shannon served as ambassador until 1981. From the day his nomination
was announced, Elizabeth Shannon, who is now at Boston University, kept
a journal of the whole experience. The book that resulted in 1983 was called
Up in the Park.

The early-August Dublin Horse Show, held annually since 1868, is the
high point of the Dublin social season.

Phoenix Park, northwest of the center of Dublin and stretching three
miles along the bank of the River Liffey, covers five times as much area as
Hyde Park in London. Within its 1,760 acres are lakes and woods and playing
fields; the zoo, opened in 1830; the People's Garden, a flower display designed
in 1864; and the official residences of both the American ambassador and the
president of the Republic. These grounds have seen duels, political assassi-
nations, and a 1979 visit by Pope John Paul II, who greeted a million people
here.

Phoenix Park was the closest my grandmother ever got to Ireland's green *and lovely hills. It was her only happy memory of late nineteenth-century Dublin.*

THERE IS AN HOUR'S WAIT AT SHANNON FOR PASSENgers going on to Dublin. I went into the ladies' room and reconstituted myself. It's amazing how much a change of clothes and new makeup will convince you that you aren't jet-weary. I put on slacks, a plaid shirt and a white wool blazer. Women in Ireland seldom wear slacks, but I often do, and I decided that I would arrive as myself.

We took off from Shannon on time and began the final lap of our long journey. It's just a twenty-five minute flight from Shannon Airport, in the west of Ireland, to Dublin, on the east coast. The soft, rounded green hills and stone fences of the Irish midlands, rich farm and grazing country, rolled by under me. I turned from the window to look at my gang of four. Bill looked fresh and excited, although as always he hadn't slept a wink on the plane. Poor David was still woozy after being awakened from a sound sleep, and was grumpy and apprehensive. Liam was excited, eager and smiling, and Christopher looked thoughtfully out the window, not reacting until he could appraise the situation. I knew that the minute we stepped off the plane in Dublin we would cease to be the people we left behind last night. We would be playing a role as long as we stayed in Ireland, and that role would define us.

I took out my small purse-sized diary and wrote: "My Eight Commandments" (to be changed later according to circumstances):

1. I will play my role with energy and try to leave my mark. I will *not* leave Ireland known merely as "the American ambassador's wife."
2. The children will have to come before official duties, no matter how important those seem.
3. I will not allow the children to be treated differently from their friends, and they will not ride around town in a limousine (Liam's dream).
4. I will write in my journal every day. (Well, every other day.)
5. I will try to be at Bill's side when he needs me, and definitely *not* be at his side when he doesn't.

6. I will not be lazy about trying to learn all I can about Ireland, by reading, traveling, meeting people and listening.
7. I will not complain about the weather.
8. I will have fun.

The plane landed with the tiniest of bumps and sped smoothly down the runway. In seconds, we were saying good-by to the crew and waiting for the heavy doors to slide open. I stepped out first, with the boys close behind, and Bill bringing up the rear. There was a platoon of men standing outside the door of the plane. The first hand I shook belonged to Jack Rendahl, the voice behind so many helpful telephone calls. Suddenly, seemingly out of nowhere, the cameras appeared. Bulbs began popping, TV lights turned on, journalists were walking alongside us, asking questions. David tucked his head behind my back and wouldn't look at anyone. I remembered, too late, that I hadn't explained about the cameras to him before he deplaned so that he would be prepared. I also remembered, too late, that I had not brought a "sick bag" off the plane for him. He has an unorthodox habit of throwing up when he gets *off* a plane. I smiled at the flashing cameras and whispered to Bill: "Did you bring a bag for David?"

"No." He smiled back. David looked beige, which is his pre-throwing-up color. We all just smiled.

We were taken into the small VIP waiting room, which was hot and stuffy, and filled with cigarette smoke. I began to feel beige myself. It's an embassy custom for the American staff and their spouses to come to the airport to greet the new ambassador. They were all there this morning, and we shook hands with each of them. It gave the effect of an immediate rapport and warmth surrounding our welcome. Bill was whisked off into another room for a television interview. Poor fellow, no sleep and no breakfast and a TV appearance.

Finally, we went outside to two waiting cars. No limousines, thank goodness. The ambassador's car was a small black Holden; I had never seen one before. We started to pile in, when the boys and I were gently disengaged from Bill and led over to another waiting car. Several men from the embassy staff got in with Bill; he gave me a wistful smile as I walked away. He had wanted to "see my face" when we pulled up in front of our new home, and, once again, we weren't to share a special moment.

The ride from the airport to our house in the Phoenix Park was not memorable, and it was a gray, damp, chilly day, raining lightly; a "heavy" day, the Irish would say. (Mind you, I'm not complaining, only stating the facts.) Our driver, Joe Lewis, chatted about the neighborhoods we were driving through: Drumcondra, Phibsboro, Cabra, the Navan Road, and finally, the Cabra Gate, into the Park.

"That's the home of your nearest neighbor, the papal nuncio," Joe added, as we glimpsed a large white house through the trees on our right. I knew from reading about the Park that we had only two neighbors, the papal nuncio and the president of Ireland. "No dashing out to borrow a cup of sugar," one of my neighbors in Washington had warned.

We crossed the Main Park Road and turned into a short drive which led to two white stucco gate houses framing the large black wrought-iron gate of our new home. The flags, one Irish, one American, were flying above the gate for our welcome. Two polished hardwood plaques on the white stucco pillars read, in gold lettering: "Home of the American Ambassador," and, in Irish, "Áras an Ambasadoir Amurcain."

Slowing down to drive through the opened gates, we saw a dozen children of all sizes lining the driveway, waving little American and Irish flags and smiling at us. David immediately perked up when he saw them and waved back.

"They're children of the staff," Joe explained. "They all live here, and they've been waiting to give you a proper welcome."

We drove up the broad avenue toward the house; a white iron fence lined the meadows on either side of the drive, keeping in the herd of black and white Friesian cattle that munched the thick green grass and looked up lazily as we drove past. A dozen huge chestnut trees along the drive shaded them.

The big white house stood at the end of the drive, facing a circle of green lawn hedged by miniature boxwood. A bust of Abraham Lincoln stood opposite the front door against a high garden wall, looking gravely down on all who passed his way. We pulled up to the porticoed green front door, and as we all got out, we were greeted by Dennis Buckley, the chief butler and general manager of the house, and his wife, Maeve, the embassy social secretary.

My first impression as we went into the house was of flowers everywhere: multicolored sweet peas trailing over table tops; Japanese iris, roses, daisies, snapdragons, petunias and dahlias—blues and yellows, pinks, reds, rainbows of color and scent. Bouquets on every table. I've never seen so many flowers.

The rest of the household staff came in to meet us: Maureen Sharkey, who did all the lovely flower arrangements; Anne O'Brien, the cook; Kitty Horgan, in charge of the family quarters. They are all a blur of friendly, smiling faces and blue eyes at the moment. We needed to retreat into the baths and beds to get our second wind. Bill and I went upstairs to our beautiful, large, light bedroom at the end of the hall. Its three floor-to-ceiling windows look out over our lawn and the Park beyond. The boys were down the hall in two adjoining rooms. I had a cup of tea and fell into bed.

We came downstairs just in time for our first meal here. Anne's roast lamb and tiny potatoes were marvelous. I will happily, eagerly, enthusiastically give up my culinary efforts to her for the next few years. We sat at a small round table at one end of the large dining room, in the bay of three huge windows with the same view as our bedroom. The table must have been in that place for a long time; its dark mahogany finish has been bleached and mellowed to pale gold by years of sunshine.

During dinner the sun broke through dark rifts of clouds and sent flames shooting through the western sky. Shafts of light fell across the smooth green lawn that stretches from the house to the edge of the Park. It was my first experience of the magic of Irish light.

Cows and deer grazed silently in the Park, staring up at the house as we stared back at them. There is a peace and stillness here as the sun still rides high in a long Irish summer evening. Even the cattle seem to have fallen into a reverie of their own.

After dinner we walked slowly through each of the large rooms. The house is graceful and handsome. Now we have to make it home.

July 17

We awoke to a dull, gray sky, but I feel rested and excited and keen to get going. Maureen has unpacked all my bags and put everything away, which is a marvelous luxury, except that I can't find anything.

After a huge breakfast—eggs, thick Irish bacon, sausage, brown soda bread and scones, tea (they can't believe that we Americans are tea drinkers)—we went to mass at our neighborhood church in Chapelizod, just outside the Park gate. The pastor, Father McCarthy, welcomed us to the parish in his sermon, and that embarrassed the boys mightily. They hung their heads and smirked and nudged each other. The parishioners eyed us shyly as we filed out, but the Irish have far too much dignity to intrude on one's privacy. No one came up to say hello.

After an enormous Sunday lunch (this can't go on; in fact, tomorrow I will tell Anne that we are a two-meal family on Sundays), we took a ride around Dublin with Gerry Noctor, Bill's driver. Downtown Dublin looked awful in the gray Sunday mist. There are great gaping holes in blocks of buildings that make one think of postwar bombed-out Munich or Vienna. Destruction and demolition seem rampant. Where are the pretty Dublin squares I saw last summer in the sunshine? Surely all this destruction couldn't have happened in a year?

Then we passed a most appalling encampment of broken-down cara-vans parked in an empty lot right in the city center. Litter was strewn with to-tal abandon; cans, rags, old mattresses, car seats, rusty tins, papers, garbage and a gaggle of dirty, laughing children playing in the midst of it all.

"Tinkers," Gerry told us. Tinkers to me conjure up gaily painted wag-ons with dark-haired, pretty boys and girls frolicking about on a grassy verge. This looked like a West Virginia hillbilly scene moved to a New Delhi slum, with a few rusty car parts thrown in for good measure.

Our spirits lifted as we headed out through Ballsbridge toward Dun Laoghaire* ("God's country," Gerry explained, being a Dun Laoghaire man himself). The Vico Road, high over Killiney Bay, with the Wicklow moun-tains rising in the distance, was remote and mysterious in the mist.

This evening, Jack Rendahl had us all over to his house for dinner. We talked about Dublin, and Ireland, and the embassy and the people here we would want to get to know. Jack is an accurate and observant reporter and good company, and Bill is grateful to have such a cool and professional diplomat to guide him through his first weeks here.

We came home early. Tomorrow Bill has to "go to work."

"What are you going to do when you sit down at your desk tomorrow?" I asked him, as we were getting ready for bed. He thought for a moment, and smiled. "Ask me that tomorrow. What are you going to do?"

"I'm going to walk through the house from top to bottom with Dennis. I'm going to ask a lot of questions and make a list and try to look as if I know what I'm doing."

July 18

I did wander all over the house today with Dennis. It's big and beau-tiful, but my first impression of it is that it's bland and colorless, despite

*Pronounced "Dun Leary."

the lovely flowers everywhere. The walls and carpets are pale gray, elegant and cool, but I like warm houses, filled with color. It was built in 1776, but no one, either here or at the State Department, seems to know much about its history. I want to do some research on it, to know why it was built here in the Park, and who has lived in it.

The downstairs has two small entry halls, which open out into a lovely oval foyer, two stories high, with a graceful Adams-style skylight in the ceiling. Dennis told me that some past ambassador's teenaged son was climbing on the roof and crashed through that skylight, falling two stories to the hall floor. He lost an eye in the accident. I made a mental note to the boys; warning number two thousand and three: Don't climb on the roof and fall through the skylight.

An American flag and an ambassadorial flag flank a large marble table in the foyer where we put our picture of President Carter. It's our "official" reception room. On either side of the marble table, two doors lead into the two drawing rooms. The house is well designed for entertaining. Four large rooms along the back open into each other. The ballroom is on one end, the two drawing rooms in between, and the large, handsome dining room at the far end. All the rooms have floor-to-ceiling windows looking out over the lawns of the residence and the Park beyond.

The furniture is mostly eighteenth-century American reproduction, or traditional American "all-purpose." Some of it looks good, some is in need of repair, and some of it should find its way to the nearest garage sale. The draperies in the ballroom and the drawing rooms are lovely. The dining room drapes are so old they are beginning to shred.

Workrooms and storage rooms line the back passage and one of them will make a good crafts/playroom. The end of the house has a sunny, large, old-fashioned workable kitchen. Pantries, a store room, a staff lounge and the laundry make up the rest of the wing.

All the staff live here. I've gone to visit their quarters; Dennis and Maeve are above the kitchen in a lovely apartment they share with their two small boys; the single women are in rooms over a wing to themselves; Gerry, with his wife and children, live in a spacious apartment over the garage.

My first priority will be redecorating the staff bedrooms. They need more storage space, new dressers, paint and curtains. Do I present a list to the general services officer at the embassy, requesting the changes? Do they like ambassadors' wives who initiate new projects? Will they tell me what sort of a budget I have for the house? I didn't learn any of that in my Seminars for Spouses.

Bill came home at six thirty, just as I was coming back from a walk around the gardens.

"What kind of a day did you have?" I asked him, as he unloaded an enormous stack of reading material onto the desk.

"So busy meeting everyone that I didn't have time to 'do' anything. Tomorrow, perhaps, I'll begin. What did you do?"

"Plan," I answered. "Lots of plans."

"Save tomorrow afternoon," he said. "There will be a reception at the chancery with all the staff to welcome us."

I wonder if they are curious to see me. I'm *very* curious to meet them and see what they are like. The short reception at the airport just became a haze of faces unattached to names.

David woke a little while ago, crying for us, something he hasn't done in years. I stumbled in the darkness of the unfamiliar hall, twisted my ankle, cursed, and finally found a light switch. I held him, sobbing and shaking and pleading: "Don't leave me." I finally carried him to our room, his long legs drooping nearly to the floor, and put him into bed with us, usually a "no-no" in our house. It took him a long time to go back to sleep, and between his sobs, it all came out: "I miss Mark and Bart. I miss Little Nell and our house, and Gramercy Street. I miss my room and my Big Wheel." Poor little fellow. I do, too. And just to keep him company, I let a few tears mingle with his on the pillow. Don't tell me we're having our sinking spell already! That's not supposed to come for another month, and we've only been here over the weekend.

July 19

I had my first good look at the chancery today, before we joined the staff in the rotunda for the party. It's a sand-colored, round building, the only round American chancery in the world. The building is very controversial in Dublin, but I think it's handsome and interesting. The architects took their inspiration from the Irish round towers of the sixth and seventh centuries, and its oddly shaped rectangular windows are based on Celtic designs. Michael Scott, one of Ireland's leading architects, and an American, John M. Johansen (who also designed a stunning new library building at Bill's alma mater, Clark University, in Worcester), were the codesigners of the building.

Inside, there is a large rotunda, with the offices circling it on five floors, two below ground, three above, in keeping with the local zoning laws regulating the height of buildings in the neighborhood.

The staff was already gathered in the rotunda when we came in. Bill made a short, humorous speech, saying that President Carter had sent them two ambassadors for the price of one, and then introduced me. They clapped, and we circulated, trying to meet and chat with everyone. Was I shy or were they? Somehow, I felt a holding back, a certain aloofness, or perhaps a wariness, particularly on the part of the American staff. Is there a barrier between them and us that can't be crossed? Do they resent a political appointee coming into their camp? For some reason, I found the Irish staff, though shyer and quieter, easier to talk with, and warmer in their reception. Obviously, we all need a lot of getting to know each other. I remembered some of the chilling stories of ambassadors' wives that my foreign service friends in Washington had told me; perhaps some of the Dublin staff had fallen under the baleful eye or wicked tongue of a diplomatic villainess in days gone by. Anyway, although I had been looking forward to this reception, I was relieved when it was over.

Tomorrow is a momentous day for Bill, the last step in the long passage from private citizen to ambassador. He will go to "Áras an Uachtaráin," the President's House, to present his credentials to President Patrick Hillery. Until he actually hands over those credentials, Bill's predecessor here, Walter Curley, is still officially the United States ambassador to Ireland.

We had so much been looking forward to witnessing this ceremony, and then I was told just today that wives and children are excluded. Damn! I was *so* mad when I heard that. The boys and I had been dying to see Himself review the troops, which is part of the ceremony. Liam said this morning: "Dad, I bet you go up to every soldier in the line and say, 'Did you brush your teeth this morning?' the way you review the troops at home." I'm determined that I will figure out a way to get us in there to see it.

July 20

Bill dressed in his morning suit. He wore the gray top hat his *New York Times* colleagues had given him as a farewell present, and he carried his new gray suede gloves. He looked like he was born to be an ambassador. We watched him dress, like royalty preparing for a levee, giving him encouraging advice like, "Don't hand the president your top hat and put your credentials on the chair," and "Don't trip over the rug going in." And David, just to even up the score, said: "Go to the bathroom *before* you leave the embassy, Daddy," then roared with laughter at his clever joke. When Bill was dressed, I stuck a carnation in his buttonhole.

The tradition here is for ambassadors to leave their chancery, escorted by an army motorcycle corps, and ride to Áras an Uachtaráin in the Phoenix Park. Since we live in the Park, it was a quick return trip from our residence to the chancery and back to the Park.

The boys and I stood outside the chancery in Ballsbridge, with a small crowd that had gathered to watch. The motorcycle corps, twenty strong, arrived in a flourish of revving motors, gleaming bikes and flashy white gloves. They looked very smart, and even Christopher was impressed. Then a big black Daimler from the Department of Foreign Affairs purred to a stop in front of the chancery and the chief of protocol and his assistant got out.

Bill came down the chancery steps with Jack Rendahl and Colonel John Berres, his military attaché, close behind. The chief of the motorcycle corps came up to him and saluted smartly, then turned on his heel and returned to his motorcycle. Bill got into the Daimler, the motorcycles roared, and off they sped toward the Park. Happily, the sun was shining.

By prearrangement, the boys and I dashed into our waiting car and followed the procession through town. We were stopped at the presidential gates as the official party sped through, and, at this point, I put My Plan into action. I will leave my methods to your imagination, dear journal, because I don't want to implicate anyone else in my less-than-diplomatic gate-crashing (and who knows? I might want to use the system again). Suffice it to say that the boys and I watched the entire proceedings, at least that part of it which was held outside, discreetly stationed behind a large clump of rhododendron bushes, close enough to take good pictures, hidden enough to please the Protocol Office. Unorthodox, but effective. And just for the record, I did not bribe, beg or cajole anyone, but I wasn't a Girl Scout for nothing.

After it was over, we came back to the residence, where we had invited all the American embassy staff and their spouses to have lunch with us and celebrate the occasion.

When the party was over and the house was quiet this afternoon, a couple named Matthews from Nebraska arrived at our gates and asked if they could come in and see the house. Ordinarily we have to turn away the hordes of American tourists who arrive in the Park eager to see the residence, but the Matthewses were different. His father had been ambassador to Ireland in 1951–52 and had died while in office here. The present Mr. Matthews hadn't been back to Ireland since, and was taking his wife on a sentimental journey. I was delighted to show them all through the house. I discovered that I love being a guide, although it is obvious that in the future I will have to enlarge my recitation with a few more facts. Today I'm afraid I glossed over facts with fancy.

Bill came back in time to meet them, and they promised that when they get home they would look in their attic to see if they still have the black top hat from Mr. Matthews' father's ambassadorial days. "He had a big head, too," Mr. Matthews said, looking at Bill's dome. "I'm sure it would fit you. We don't have much use for it in Nebraska, except for school plays."

I wonder if my sons will return here in thirty years' time and have nostalgic memories of this house? And happy memories? I hope they will always receive a warm welcome. I think anyone who has ever lived here is a part of this house and leaves something of himself behind.

July 21

Ginnie Kennealy of the *Irish Press* came out to the house today to do an interview with Bill. She wanted him to talk about his views on Northern Ireland, but he didn't want to commit himself, nor did he want to stray into controversial subjects. But he said later that he was too sympathetic to the press point of view and remembered all the interviews he had done when he was a young reporter, trying to pry information out of wary officials.

The first signature appeared in our brand-new guest book today: "Alistair Cooke." He's here in Dublin to give a speech at the Royal Dublin Society. He and Bill knew each other covering national political conventions years ago, but it was the first time I had met him. He is just as charming in real life as he is on radio and television, and seems to know everyone in this world and quite a few in the next.

July 22

We paid our first "call" together today. It's a tradition for new ambassadors to pay formal calls on their colleagues, and wives do the same thing with each other. After a few weeks go by, each of them repays the call. It seems time consuming, but in fact it is a simple, straightforward way of meeting one's colleagues and establishing the beginnings of a personal rapport.

The Austrian ambassador here is a single woman, so we paid our call on her together. She is a short, plump little Viennese lady with a tart tongue and a great love for Ireland. "This is the last Victorian society," she said, as she poured us each a glass of sherry in her office. She's right, of course. There is a great respect for authority here, inculcated partly by the Catholic Church, which one doesn't find anymore in the rest of Europe or America. There is also a greater emphasis on family life here than one finds at home. I doubt that Ireland has more happy or unhappy marriages than any other country, but divorce is not legal here and so the institutions of marriage and family are still supported and bolstered by society and the law. Whatever people may do in private, they keep up the facade of public morality, which is the essence of Victorian mores.

I had my first group of embassy wives out to the house for tea this afternoon. Remembering the warnings in Washington to be friendly, open and not to slight any of the wives, even inadvertently, I'm having them all out for the afternoon in small groups, to try to chat and get to know each one. A friend in Washington told me that she and her husband had been posted for a year and a half in a large European embassy when, one day, the ambassador's wife approached her at a reception, put out her hand, and said: "Hello, I'm ———. Do you live here?" Since that occasion had happened twenty years before, my friend's memory of it was not only galling but lasting.

July 25

The papal nuncio in Dublin lives just across the Main Park Road from us in a lovely old eighteenth-century house surrounded by enormous trees and a walled garden filled with vegetables. (The day we arrived in Dublin, the nuns who care for the nuncio sent us an overflowing basket filled with a dozen varieties of vegetables from the garden, just to say "Welcome.")

We went to a reception at the nuncio's this evening to say good-by to the departing French ambassador and his wife. I haven't even said hello to them, but departure ceremonies are de rigueur for ambassadors and their wives.

We assembled in the spacious drawing room and were served drinks and hors d'oeuvres (they were *delicious*, definitely not your wilted-cracker variety. The silver trays were filled with tiny puff pastries, miniature pizzas, smoked salmon on brown bread). The farewells in Dublin are always held at the nuncio's because he is dean of the corps. In most countries, the ambassador who has served in the post the longest is dean, but in Catholic countries, it is usually the nuncio. Bishop Alibrandi, the nuncio, would be dean here under either system because he has served longer than any other ambassador.

After thirty minutes of chitchat, we were hushed up and the nuncio and the French ambassador and his wife stood in front of the room while the nuncio read out a little speech of farewell. The ambassador replied, and was then presented with a silver tray engraved with all the ambassadors' names. Champagne was passed around by the nuncio's white-gloved butler, and we toasted the departing ambassador and wished him and his wife bon voyage.

When our turn comes to stand up front and say good-by, I don't want another silver tray to polish. I wonder if one can substitute a nice piece of eighteenth-century furniture instead? Would they be scandalized? I need a sideboard more than I need a silver tray.

This was my first glimpse of the diplomatic corps. There are twenty-three countries represented. For such a formal, traditional reception, it was a warm and friendly occasion. I think I'm going to enjoy the diplomatic life.

July 26

I interviewed three candidates for a job as live-in baby-sitter for David. None seemed just right. I'm looking for a university student who will be in school when David is but who will be here to look after him in the late afternoons and evenings.

In the middle of the interviews, I had a most peculiar and rather disturbing phone call. The caller told Maeve, who had answered the phone, that she was phoning in response to the ad in the newspaper for the baby-sitter's job, but when I came on the line she said:

"I want to welcome you to Ireland, but you should know that, although the Irish people will always pretend to like you and to admire America, they don't. It's just a sham. There is a lot of anti-Americanism here and you should be prepared for that." Then she hung up, before I could say a word.

Well, if I came to Ireland expecting everyone to love me, I might as well have stayed at home. Still, it was an odd call and it echoed in my mind all day.

We gave our first big reception here this evening, for an international convention of trade unionists who are meeting in Dublin. Since the planning had been done in advance of our arrival, we were almost like guests ourselves, except for shaking 350 hands.

I was enjoying myself in my first receiving line, meeting everyone and chatting away, and didn't realize at all that disaster had struck in the kitchen. The catering firm had not arrived with the food; Dennis was dashing from the bar in the ballroom, where he was serving drinks, to the pantry to make yet another frantic phone call to the firm, asking what was going on and when were they coming? But Bill and I just went on blithely shaking hands, oblivious to the crisis. By the time we were finished receiving, everyone was enjoying himself and the food finally arrived. I don't think it had even been missed. When it did come, we pressed it on our guests with persistent enthusiasm. I think people come to an embassy reception to see what it's like, to meet the ambassador, to see the house and to have a drink, and not really to eat. Anyway, if a hostess is worried about the arrangements and shows it, the guests will know it and won't enjoy themselves. The best way to give them a good time is to have one yourself. I am glad that for my first reception I was spared the Crisis of the Caterer. I hope it isn't an omen of things to come!

July 27

Two more names appeared in our guest book tonight. Kevin Mallen, an old friend from California, came out to the Park for dinner with Terence de Vere White, the literary editor of the *Irish Times*. We have read several of Terence's books and much of his literary criticism, and were eager to meet him.

It was one of those evenings that sparkle and glitter from the beginning. Terence lived up to an Irishman's reputation for talk; wit, erudition and eloquence flowed from him as naturally as rain from an Irish sky. He must have inspired the rest of us (he is a good listener as well) because we all shone. No subject was left to languish; books and plays, art and architecture, Ireland in general and Dublin in particular, people we should get to know and people we should avoid. Terence is a sensitive, discerning and somewhat incorrigible "Who's Who in Dublin," and I would relish having him as my cicerone to lead me through the maze of Dublin society, where everyone seems to be everyone's cousin or in-law, where family feuds of long ago still simmer on the back burner, and where a stranger must tread carefully to avoid ancient wounds, real or imagined.

July 28

Can we have been here only two weeks? I feel like I am awakened in the mornings by a demanding tempest that swirls me through the day and slings me back down at night, breathless, exhausted and spent. We did not have a quiet, peaceful period to "settle in" as we had hoped. I am always being asked by people I meet if I have "settled in," and I resolutely say yes, hoping that by affirming it, it will be accomplished. I'm so grateful for the competent, caring staff we have at the residence. The house and all its activities purr along; tempting, delicious food appears on the table; the house is shining and spotless; the laundry is done, the linens cared for, the grates and brasses polished, the fires cleared and rebuilt, the floors polished, the walks swept. The house is filled with flowers, and the gardens are majestic. The telephone is answered, the invitations lists made, the table seating arranged, the receiving lines kept straight. What wonderful luck. So many of the other ambassadors' wives complain about their lack of staff and their inability to find anyone to work for them. I couldn't begin to manage without the help and support I'm given here. I seem to be dashing in and out of the house all day and all night, running in through the back door to greet guests coming in through the front, dashing out the front door to pay a call or go to a reception, checking up on the boys or changing clothes. I didn't know that life was going to be so busy, but surely after I find a school for the boys, finish paying my calls, find a baby-sitter for David and (the blessed panacea of all mothers) when school starts! my life will be less hectic.

We visited St. Michael's College today (secondary schools in Ireland are often called colleges). It's an elementary/high school for boys, run by the Holy Ghost Fathers. Although a long way from Phoenix Park, it's near the chancery, so Bill could drive the boys in with him in the mornings. And they take children as young as David, which many of the schools do not. The classrooms are very small, and the classes large, thirty to thirty-five boys to a class. But there are beautiful, spacious playing fields in back.

We liked Father Flood, the headmaster, and St. Michael's has a reputation in town of being a "happy" school, so if they are willing to take

David and Christopher, we shall enroll them. Liam is holding out for a coed school.

The curriculum at St. Michael's sounds more demanding than that of the boys' public school in Washington, but one can't really tell until classes begin what the quality of work will be. Our boys will be exempt from studying Irish because they are foreign students, but Irish children must take Irish, taught as a second language, from the first grade through the end of high school. It's amazing how few of the people we have met speak Irish, considering the emphasis on it in the schools. We decided that David will take it because he is just beginning "prep," the kindergarten class at St. Michael's, and all of his classmates will also be beginners.

July 29

Our own car hasn't arrived yet, nor has our shipment of clothes and personal effects, so we feel rather like we are still camping out here. Gerry has to drive me everywhere, and although he is a marvelous guide to Dublin, I hate being dependent on him. I'm trying to memorize streets (which isn't easy since street signs are placed in a rather whimsical fashion here), so that I'll know my way when I take the wheel.

The boys are running out of steam, too, with no bikes, balls, tennis racquets and, worst of all, no friends. They are going to start riding lessons next week. I'm more enthusiastic about the lessons than they are, however.

I visited a Christian Brothers School today with Liam, but we weren't seriously interested in it. It's too far away, and it isn't coed. I said to the very friendly brother who showed us around: "The Christian Brothers in America have a reputation for having a heavy hand with a cane."

He laughed merrily and said: "Oh, we're not nearly as bad as we used to be." Rather a chilling reassurance, I thought.

I've interviewed about fifteen boys and girls for the baby-sitting job, and today I hit the jackpot. A freckle-faced girl arrived on her bicycle, in jeans and with curly hair blowing wild in the wind. Her bike fell over as she tried to park it at the front door, and she spilled her tea in her lap and laughed, then told me some hilarious Irish stories, and I hired her on the spot. Her name is Siobhán O'Tierney and she has four brothers and seems to me a girl who could handle anything that David—or Christopher or Liam—put in her way. She's a first-year student at University College in Dublin, and she said she would ride her bike into school each day.

"It's about eight miles each way," I warned her.
"That's not far," she replied cheerfully.

August 2

Horse Show Week. We went to a preshow party a few days ago at the home of Lilian Fay, whose husband was a very popular ambassador to the United States in the 1960s. I'm sure I met half of Dublin in her drawing room, but faces and names are still a fuzzy blur to me. Everyone I met was friendly and welcoming; I don't think I've ever gazed into so many smiling blue eyes in one room.

We were in Dublin for the Horse Show last year, and I remember sitting with friends at the Royal Dublin Society grounds, looking over at the diplomatic boxes, with the Stars and Stripes draped over one of them, wondering who was in it and thinking how much fun it must be to be the host and hostess there.

The Dublin Horse Show is a colorful mosaic of past and present, elegant remnants of Anglo-Irish mingling with country squireens, young farmers and city folk in the tie that binds the Irish together surer than families and funerals; a love of good horseflesh.

Besides being an impressive and exciting competition of international show jumping, it is also a week of balls and receptions, band concerts and craft displays, horse shoeing contests and donkey shows; strolls around the RDS gardens under a summer sun (perhaps!) to meet friends for tea and cakes; blue ribbons for pony and hunter classes, flowered hats and derbies, lost children, and hopeless bottlenecks that bring traffic in Ballsbridge to a standstill. Top hats and tailcoats are brought out of mothballs and worn proudly by the RDS stewards, those stalwarts who keep everyone and everything in order. Ireland's top show jumpers enjoy the adulation of pop-star status for a week, and the talk is horses, horses, horses.

The show jumping events take place each afternoon in the big ring of the RDS grounds. The flag-draped diplomatic boxes along one end are festooned with geraniums and ivy and the ring itself is banked with yellow marigolds. The jumps, freshly painted, stand like formidable barriers along the thick, clipped grass. The scene is brilliant with color, glamour and impending drama. The atmosphere is a curious combination of unhurried languor and electrically charged anticipation.

At 3 P.M. sharp each afternoon, a crisp, authoritative voice announces over a loudspeaker the arrival in the ring of the first rider and horse. There is a different competition each day, but it is always a jumping event, judged either by time or faults, or both. A rider having a clear round in one event competes with another clear round for better time. At the end of each event, a jump-off may be required to narrow the field down to a winner. Six countries participate, with competitors vying for the individual as well as team points. I was disappointed that the United States had not sent a team. Someone told me they don't come anymore because it is too expensive to fly the horses over. Someone else said they worry about security problems because of the troubles in the North.

The jumps look frighteningly high and wide to me, ranging from four and a half feet to seven feet high, with a four-foot spread. It is an intensely competitive, skilled show, and only the top European riders participate. Eddie Macken is Ireland's darling of the show jumping circuit this year, his blue eyes and handsome smile backed up by formidable skill. Since the United States isn't represented, I'm ready to cheer Eddie and the Irish team to victory.

We invited six guests to share the box with us today. At four thirty, a waiter brought us high tea, trays laden with sandwiches, fruit cake and pastries. By 6 P.M. the show was over, I was hoarse from cheering, and Ireland's riders had won the day's events. Without our even noticing it, the sun had gone down over the grandstand and the late afternoon air had become chilled.

"Grand show today, miss," the elderly white-coated attendant who takes tickets for the boxes said, and I agreed.

August 3

I pay calls in the mornings and slip off to the Horse Show in the afternoons. There is always a reception at one of the embassies following the show. This evening we went out to the beautiful Italian embassy in Lucan to meet the Italian riding team. They have been coming to the show in Dublin for years and are very well-known and popular here. One of the women riders shook my hand with a grip of iron; she's obviously been reining in horses for a long time. The men were much smaller than they seem out in the field on those big horses, but in their army uniforms and riding boots, they looked handsome and romantic to me. Alas, they don't speak English, and my Italian begins and ends with *"Arrivederci."*

August 5

It's our wedding anniversary. Is it sixteen years or seventeen since we rode around Central Park in a buggy on our wedding night? I never know. I can't even remember the years the boys were born, and I have to think back to where we were living at the time to arrive at the right dates.

Today I called on Mrs. Haydon, the wife of the British ambassador. They live in a house called Glencairn, built by, of all people, "Boss" Croker, the notorious head of Tammany Hall in the 1890s, when he retired to Ireland. Ambassador Haydon replaced Christopher Ewart-Biggs last year after Ewart-Biggs was assassinated by the IRA. Although the Haydons are heavily guarded and their house and grounds seemed filled with security men, it must be a terrible strain to live here and try to go about your day-to-day business knowing that you are an obvious target for the masked gunmen who pose as Ireland's liberators.

Mrs. Haydon is a pretty, vivacious strawberry blonde who lived for many years in New York while her husband was posted there. We were very soon engrossed in talk of dogs, flowers, children and gardens, topics safe for ambassadors' wives to begin their friendship when paying calls. Outside the French windows, security guards walked up and down by the flower beds, carrying submachine guns.

August 6

Today is the big day at the Horse Show when six country teams compete for the "Nations' Cup," the Aga Khan Challenge Trophy. Our invitation said: "Please assemble in the President's box at 2:45 P.M." I thought that meant the president of Ireland, but it turned out to be the president of the Royal Dublin Society. Dress for ambassadors was spelled out on the invitation: "Morning coat and top hat." The women were left to use their own imaginations. I wore a white silk suit I had bought in Washington specially for the occasion, with a navy blue straw hat. I wore woolen underwear, and even then, I was happy for the blanket the stewards thoughtfully provided.

The president of Ireland and Mrs. Hillery, the taoiseach (the Irish word for "prime minister") and Mrs. Jack Lynch, and various government officials joined us in the box. It was a cool, gray and misty day, but the show was spectacular. Ireland won the cup in a wildly exciting jump-off overtime, narrowly beating the German team. I found myself on my feet, pounding on the back of an ambassador sitting in front of me, shouting myself hoarse for Ireland. (I rather conspicuously made up for a lack of enthusiasm otherwise displayed in my box.) When the day was won for Ireland, the ambassadorial back I had pounded upon turned round to give me a frosty smile and ask if I was happy that Ireland had won. He turned out to be the German ambassador. "Oh well," I said gamely, "someone has to win. *Jawohl?*"

August 7

I'm weary of making calls. I've run out of small talk and I'm overflowing with coffee and cakes. My stop today was with an extravagant hypochondriac, who took me on a tour of her liver, her pancreas and her upper intestinal tract. I was spared her bowels, thanks be to God, but we left her bladder reluctantly as time was running out, and we still had to cover her allergies. At least I wasn't forced to contribute to the conversation.

August 9

I made my grand tour of the gardens today with Michael O'Donohoe, the head gardener here for many years. His interest in every blade of grass, every blossom on the property, is all-consuming, and I share his interest, but with a certain aloofness that I reserve for gardens that aren't really mine. At home, I'm the weed puller, the earth turner, and I watch my garden grow with the possessive, critical eye of its creator. I show off my delphiniums, my clematis, my tomatoes like a proud parent. And although I like the new image of myself here, basket in hand, daintily clipping an endless supply of snapdragons, gladioli, roses and petunias to arrange for the house, I know I won't invest emotion in a garden I haven't planned and planted.

Most of the sixty-nine acres here are in woodland and meadow, circumscribed by a path that goes right around the outer edge of the property. The outside edge of the path drops sharply down about four feet, forming a sort of half-moat, called a ha-ha. It's a sixteenth-century French landscaping innovation designed to keep out deer and livestock without diminishing the view with a fence. Why a "ha-ha"? No one seems to know.

The path is lined with stately ancient beech, oak, elm and lime trees, even a few aspen, rare in Ireland. They bend and groan and creak in the wind in a slightly sinister manner, as if they have stories to tell but don't speak the language. Bill jogs along this path under the trees and does two laps a day, one and a quarter miles in each lap. I watch him flash by each morning from my bedroom window. Well, pass by.

There are two walled gardens; one, called the Pretty Garden, is just for looking at, walking through and admiring. The other is our working garden, filled with vegetables, fruit trees, berry bushes and cutting flowers. And then there is a rather mysterious, unkempt, overgrown hill where David disappears to play for hours each day with the other residence children. When I ask him where he's been, he simply says: "On the Fairy Hill."

I finally queried Michael about it today: "Why is it so wild and unkempt?" I asked.

"It's the Fairy Hill," says he, explaining all.

MICHAEL CRICHTON

Filming The Great Train Robbery *in Dublin: 1978*

"EACH NIGHT I DRAG MYSELF HOME TO MY DUBLIN
HOTEL ROOM. IT LOOKS LIKE THE ANTEROOM TO A
TUBERCULOSIS SANATORIUM. THE FLOORS ARE
UNEVEN, THE WALLPAPER STODGY VICTORIAN. I'D
LIKE TO CALL HOME, BUT THERE IS A TELEPHONE
STRIKE. THEN A MAIL STRIKE."

*Michael Crichton, a Harvard-trained doctor, went on to become a best-selling
author and the director of such films as* Westworld *and* Coma. *He had already
written* The Andromeda Strain *and* The Terminal Man *when his 1975 novel,*
The Great Train Robbery, *won him even more readers. Since then, his novels
have included* Congo, Sphere, Jurassic Park, *and* The Lost World.

In 1978 he went to England and Ireland to direct the film version of The
Great Train Robbery.

I AM THE DIRECTOR OF A FILM CALLED *THE GREAT TRAIN ROBBERY*,
loosely based on an actual train robbery that occurred in Victorian
England. We are shooting in England and Ireland. The cast includes Sean
Connery, Donald Sutherland, and Lesley-Anne Down.

A secret, lifelong desire is fulfilled. I am an international film director,
shooting in foreign locations with big movie stars! What a thrill! Put on
the safari jacket and hang the director's finder around your neck!

But I am also secretly terrified. This is only my third movie, and I'm
not really an experienced director. I've never shot in a foreign location. I've

never made a period picture. I've never worked with a foreign crew. And although I've worked with good actors, I've never directed such big stars.

To direct a movie you must be authoritative, and I don't feel authoritative at all. On the contrary, I feel isolated and under intense pressure. I am alone in Dublin; Loren is back in America finishing law school. There are only three Americans on the show: myself; the producer, John Foreman; and the stunt coordinator, Dick Ziker. John is experienced in foreign filming and I rely on his judgment, but in the end I am the director and I must do the job myself. And I'm afraid.

I've never known what to do with these fears of new undertakings. There doesn't seem to be anything to do but live through them, get past them. At least some of the terror of new undertakings is justified; at least some degree of anxiety will actually improve performance. But here in Dublin, I am not exerting my authority well. It just isn't working. John Foreman has told me the English film crews call the director "governor" or "guv." Nobody calls me "guv." Nobody calls me "sir." They don't call me anything.

Even though I am thirty-five years old, the crew thinks I am too young to know what I am doing. The company tries to second-guess me, to do things behind my back. I ask for something to be done a certain way, and they go off and do something else. We have lots of arguments.

Then, too, there are many differences between British and American filming procedures. In America, the director plans shots with the cameraman; in England, with the camera operator. Scenes are numbered differently. Technical terminology is different. English crews take four food breaks in a day, but Americans break only for lunch. If you want to work overtime, the British crew has to meet and vote.

Even the most basic signals seem to get crossed. In America, I am considered a laconic director, but the English find my energy level bizarrely high. My assistant director, who is openly critical of me to the point of insolence, finally asks if I am taking something. He means drugs, speed. I am astonished and ask him why he should think so. He says the whole crew thinks so, because I do everything so fast. I assure him I am not on drugs.

The first few days of shooting go badly. We have a split crew, half English and half Irish, and the two halves dislike one another, reflecting an ancient antagonism. Whenever something goes wrong, each side blames the other. Our progress is slow. Nobody listens to me. I set up the camera in a certain place and the crew moves it. They always move it, even if it's just six inches. I move it back to where I want it. The weather is terrible. It seems we are always on a food break. We fall behind schedule.

Each night I drag myself home to my Dublin hotel room. It looks like the anteroom to a tuberculosis sanatorium. The floors are uneven, the wallpaper stodgy Victorian. I'd like to call home, but there is a telephone strike. Then a mail strike. I am entirely isolated.

I ask John Foreman what to do. He says, "Talk with Geoff. Geoff likes you."

Geoffrey Unsworth is the lighting cameraman. He's very courtly and distinguished. Everyone adores him. Each day Geoff and I drive to the location together, so there's plenty of time to talk. Geoff seems to understand my difficulties, but it's not easy to discuss the matter frankly. He has his British reserve, and I feel awkward. How can I ask him why I'm not getting any respect? That's a Rodney Dangerfield line. So we talk about technical things: why we're not making more setups, how to get things to run more smoothly.

Geoff keeps saying, "I'd like to see one of your films." I think he's just being polite. My last film, *Coma,* is still in release in America, and it will be difficult to have a print shipped to Ireland.

Meanwhile, the problems continue. After a week or so, Geoff says, "You know, I think the crew would enjoy seeing one of your films." I tell him again of the difficulties of getting a print. But I manage to telex MGM in Los Angeles and order one.

Our problems get worse. The situation is deteriorating. Sometimes there are shouting arguments between the Irish and English crew members. As a group we have no cohesion, and I know it is because we have no leader. We are painfully slow. The work is good, but it is taking far too much time. The film is a negative pickup deal, which means that when the money runs out we will have to shut down production, whether we have completed the film or not. The pressures on me are enormous. Get more setups. Finish more scenes. Pick up the pace.

But the pace never picks up.

Geoff says, "I wish we could see one of your films."

Finally the print comes, and we run it for the crew on Friday night after work. Most of the crew attends.

On Monday morning, I come to work, ready to fight my usual uphill battle. I come onto the set, picking my way among the cables and light stands. One of the electricians smiles at me.

"Morning, guv," he says.

What happened was that the crew decided *Coma* was a pretty good movie, and I must know what I am doing after all. Thanks to Geoff, from then on the atmosphere is entirely different, and our progress much better.

The crew stretches a white bed sheet in the middle of a field so the helicopter will know where to land. A crowd of local people line the fences around the field. They stare at the sheet, waiting for something to happen. Their attention turns the sheet into a work of art, a Christo. *Wrapped Irish Farm Field, 1978.* I would find it funny if we weren't behind schedule.

It is eight in the morning and bitterly cold. We are in a provincial train station outside Mullingar, Ireland, about to start a week of filming on top of a speeding train. Sean Connery has agreed to do his own stunts on top of the train. The little 1863 locomotive is hissing steam in front of the station, with our specially constructed coaches trailing behind. It's time to start filming, but the camera helicopter has not arrived yet from England. I suggest a test ride on the train. We climb up a ladder onto the roof of the cars, and set off.

Within minutes Connery is grinning like a kid on a carnival ride. He's a superb athlete who could have been a professional footballer. Now he hops lightly from car to car, thoroughly enjoying himself. We approach a bridge, and must lie flat on the deck. The bridge whips over us, inches from our faces. Connery laughs uproariously. "Bloody fantastic!"

We return to the station and begin shooting. The exhilaration fades, and the work becomes work. Constant vigilance is required. The Irish Railways have permitted us to use twenty miles of track in the most beautiful part of the country, but since this is Ireland, the twenty bridges that span the rails are all of different heights. Some are very low. We have previously mapped and measured each bridge, but no one is willing to trust a map. Before each shot, we creep slowly beneath the bridge, to check our clearance.

Even more dangerous are the telephone and electrical wires that sometimes span the track; these are unmarked and difficult to see until the last moment.

Then, too, our authentic period locomotive spews a stream of glowing cinders and ash back at us. We literally set the countryside on fire wherever we go. Each night, when we return home, I take a shower and wash my hair. The water hits the tub inky black.

Connery throws himself into his work with abandon. He is one of the most remarkable people I have ever met, lighthearted and serious at the same moment. I have learned a great deal from being around him. He is at ease with himself, and is direct and frank. "I like to eat with my fingers," he says, eating with his fingers in a fancy restaurant, not giving a damn. You cannot embarrass him with trivialities. Eating is what's important. People come over for an autograph and he glowers at them. "I'm *eating*," he says sternly. "Come back later." They come back later, and he politely signs their menus. He doesn't hold grudges unless he intends to. "I spent a lot of my life being miserable," he says. "Then one day I thought, I'm here for the day, I can enjoy the day or not. I decided I might as well enjoy it." There is that quality about him, that sense of choice and control over himself and his moods. It makes him integrated, self-assured. The most common remark about him is "That's a *real man*."

Once, on an airplane, a woman sighs, "Oh, you're so *masculine*." Connery laughs. "But I'm very feminine," he insists. And he means it; he delights in that side of himself. A gifted mimic, he likes to rehearse alone, playing all the parts himself. He does startlingly accurate imitations of everyone in the cast, including Donald and Lesley-Anne, his leading lady. He always seems to enjoy himself. He takes pleasure in all his aspects, all his appetites.

I am not equally open, and he teases me. Once, after a shot, I feel his hand gestures were a little effeminate. I call for a retake, but I'm not sure how to tell Sean what needs to be changed. How do you tell 007 that he's effeminate?

"Sean, on that last shot, you had a hand gesture . . ."

"Yes, what about it? I thought it was good."

"Well, uh, it was a little, uh, loose. Limp."

His eyes narrow. "What are you trying to say?"

"Well, it could be a bit crisper. Stronger, you know."

"Stronger . . ."

"Yes. Stronger."

"You're saying I look like a poof?" Now he's grinning, amused at my discomfort.

"Yes. A little."

"Well, just say so, ducky!" he roars. "Just say what you want! We haven't got all day!" And he shoots the scene again, with a different gesture.

Later he takes me aside. "You know," he says, "you don't do any favors beating about the bush. Making us try and deduce what you mean. You think you're being polite, but you're actually just difficult. Say what you mean and get on with it."

I promise to try. And I do better, but I never manage to be as direct as he is. He says, "You should always tell the truth, because if you tell the truth you make it the other person's problem."

He follows his own dictum; he always tells the truth. Sean seems to live in a kind of present moment, responding to events with an unaffected immediacy that disregards the past and future. He is always genuine. Sometimes he compliments people I know he doesn't like. Sometimes he blows up angrily at his close friends. He always tells the truth as he sees it at the moment, and if somebody doesn't like it, it's their problem.

The days of shooting on the train continue. The crew is extremely careful; no one is hurt. By now we have shot the most hazardous sequences, the ones that require Sean to not see the bridges as they rush up behind him, and to duck down at the last moment, his head missing the bridges by inches. Those shots were carefully arranged and timed, but we are all relieved they are behind us.

Finally we are shooting a long take where Sean comes running up the length of the train, jumping from car to car. Because we are shooting in all directions, the camera operator and I are hanging out on a side platform, and everyone else is inside the train. I am trying to watch the scene and also to remember to duck down at the right time so the camera lens can swing over my head.

Filming begins. Sean runs up the length of the train. I smell a harsh, acrid odor. I feel a sharp pain on top of my scalp. I realize that my hair has been set on fire by the cinders from the locomotive. I am frantically brushing at my hair, trying to put the fire out, because I don't want smoke coming from my head when the camera swings over me.

While I am doing that, Sean jumps to the nearest car, stumbles, and falls. I think, Jeez, Sean, don't overdo making it look dangerous. He is carrying a bundle of clothes, a story point. He drops the clothes as he falls and I realize Sean would never do that, that he must have really fallen. Meanwhile, I am still trying to put the fire out on my head. Sean scrambles to his feet, retrieves the clothes, and moves on, wincing in genuine pain. I get the cinders out of my head as the camera swings over. We make the shot.

Afterward we stop the train; everybody gets off. He has a bad cut on his shin that is being attended to.

"Are you all right, Sean?"

He looks at me. "Did you know," he says, "that your hair was on fire? You ought to be more careful up there."

And he laughs.

His fresh view allows him to reach some surprising conclusions. On the fourth day of filming, we put everybody inside the train except Sean, because we are filming with the helicopter, and the camera will see the entire length of the train. So I am inside, wearing a top hat, with a walkie-talkie in my lap. As the train starts, I hear the engineer call out the speed, "Twenty-five miles an hour . . . thirty . . . thirty-five miles an hour . . ."

We have previously arranged for this speed. The helicopter radios that it is in position. I call for action on the radio, and the shot begins. I sit there, listening to the thump of the helicopter as it moves overhead, trying to imagine the shot, trying to figure out by the sound how it is going.

The pilot announces the shot is good. We stop the train, and Sean comes down from the top. He is furious, stamping and complaining. "It's bloody dangerous up there! This bloody train is not going bloody thirty-five miles an hour!"

"Sean," I say, "it is."

After so many days of shooting, the control of speed has been well worked out. This is essential, because in making a film you must travel at different speeds depending on which way the camera is pointing. If you are shooting sideways to the direction of travel, your apparent speed is faster, and so you must make the train go slower. If you are shooting in the direction of travel, you must go faster than usual. If you do not vary the speed in this way, in the final film the train will appear to go faster in some shots than in others.

So we have long since worked this out. One of the assistant directors is in the open cab of our locomotive, with a walkie-talkie. As we start each shot, he calls out the speeds. When we hit the prearranged speed, we begin filming. This is the procedure we have used throughout.

I click the walkie-talkie. "Chris, how fast was the train going on that last shot?"

From the locomotive, the voice says, "Thirty-five miles an hour."

I look at Sean, shrug.

Sean grabs the walkie-talkie and says, *"How do you know it was thirty-five miles per hour?"*

There is a long pause.

"We count telegraph poles," the voice says.

Sean hands the walkie-talkie back to me.

Slowly the pertinent facts emerge. The engine is an actual 1863 locomotive, and it has no speed instrumentation at all. To estimate speed, the men in the cab time telegraph poles as they go by. But this is obviously a terribly inaccurate method. Suddenly we wonder: how fast was the train really going?

The helicopter was flying parallel to the train for most of the shot. We radio the pilot. "How fast was the train going on the last shot?"

"Fifty-five miles an hour," comes the reply. "We thought Mr. Connery was bloody crazy to be up there!"

Vindicated, Sean folds his arms across his chest. "You see?" he says.

In the end, that episode represented to me all the power of a fresh perspective. We had been filming for days, we had fallen into a comfortable routine, and not one of us had bothered to look at what the cab of the locomotive was like. For days no one had thought to ask, How do you know the speed? The question was always there to be asked. It was just that no one had asked it, until Sean did.

One day, after lunch, Sean says, "I'm through at the end of the day."

"What?"

"I'm through on the train," he says evenly. "Finished. Going back to Dublin, have a kip."

We have three more days of filming scheduled. I don't think we'll need all three days, but I feel there is at least one more full day of work. Why is he quitting?

"I've had it with this bloody train," he says.

It has been such fun, such exhilarating fun, I can't understand why his mood has changed so suddenly. Of course, he has seen all the dailies, and he knows how much good footage we already have. I have already shot about six hours of film to make what will eventually be a fifteen-minute sequence. So I am just being overcautious, as directors tend to be. Is he calling my bluff?

"I'm done," he says. "I'm done." And that is all he will say. He leaves at the end of the day, driving back to Dublin.

The next morning we shoot some final bits and pieces, points of view, establishing shots, and so on. I am on top of the train, with a stunt man and a camera operator. We are going very fast. At high speeds, the train rocks and jerks erratically; it is nerve-racking.

And suddenly, in an instant, I am done with the train, too. The tunnels aren't fun any more, the overhanging wires aren't a challenge any more, the jolts from the track and the freezing wind aren't bracing any more. It is just dangerous and exhausting and I want to stop at once and get off the train. And I realize that is what happened to Sean the day before. He'd had enough, and he knew when to stop. The sequence is finished. It is time to go back to the studio, and do something else.

JOHN COYNE

Taking Dad back to Connemara: 1980

"WE DROVE THERE ON A BRIGHT BLUE AUGUST
AFTERNOON FOR A PICNIC ON THE SITE OF MY
FATHER'S PLACE. THE FARMHOUSE AND BARNS HAVE
WITH YEARS OF NEGLECT GONE TO WASTE, AND
ONLY A FEW STONE WALLS REMAIN."

*John Coyne won a reputation as one of the finest modern writers of horror
fiction with such novels as* Hobgoblin *and* The Hunting Season, *among
others published in the 1980s. His more recent novels include* Brothers and
Sisters. *In 1962–64, Coyne served with the Peace Corps in Ethiopia and has
worked in support of the organization ever since. In 1994 he edited a collection
of memoirs by former Peace Corps volunteers called* Going Up Country, *published by Scribner's. Coyne is now regional manager of the New York office
of the Peace Corps.*

In the following article, first published in Travel & Leisure *magazine,
he tells of the time he brought his father back to Ireland after fifty years'
absence. It's an experience known well by many children of Irish emigrants.*

*In a touching coda to that story, written more than a dozen years later,
Coyne passes on a legacy to his own son, who never knew his grandfather.*

A HALF-MILE FROM HIS BIRTHPLACE IN THE TOWN OF
Cornamona, County Galway, Ireland, my father leaned forward in
the car exclaiming, "Stop, there's the Protestant!"

Ahead I could see a tall, stoop-shouldered old man crossing the narrow mountain road. He was wearing a gray cap, suit coat and tie, knee-high black boots, looking as well dressed as the other farmers I had seen so far in Ireland. The Irish, I had decided, must be the only people in the world who dress up to work in the hayfields.

I halted the car in front of the barn gate, wondering how my father would know this man 60 years after he left Ireland, 60 years since he had lived in Connemara. But when the farmer crossed the tarmac, carrying his wooden rake, my father lowered the window and asked, "Would you be knowing Tommy né Lynch Coyne?"

The old man nodded and quickly replied in thick Connemara brogue, "And wouldn't I be lookin' at him now?"

My father was home, back in Connemara, a district deep in the mountains of Galway on the eastern shore of Lough Corrib, one of the wildest and most beautiful spots in all Ireland.

The Protestant's name was William Crawford. A bachelor, he is the last son of the only such family in that far corner of western Galway. He and my father had been boys together before the 1916 Uprising, the Irish rebellion against England, which led to my father's immigration to America.

He had left Connemara in 1923, arriving in Boston with five English pounds and the addresses of relatives in Ohio. From Boston, he moved on to Illinois to work for 30 years in the steel mills and raise a family of six. Now he had returned with my mother (herself from Castlebar, County Mayo) and me. He wanted to show his youngest son the ancestral home in Cornamona.

The village of Cornamona is only a crossroads on the neck of land between Loughs Corrib and Mask. It consists entirely of a general store and guest house, a garage and gas station, and two pubs. One of them, O'Malley's, was used in the filming of *The Quiet Man*. John Wayne began his famous brawl here for the love of Maureen O'Hara.

First cousins of ours, named Malloy, own the garage and gas station, but the Coynes themselves are from the hills three miles beyond the town—a place called Cremlin, nestled at the curve of a salmon river and at the foot of a natural mountain amphitheater.

We drove there on a bright blue August afternoon for a picnic on the site of my father's place. The farmhouse and barns have with years of neglect gone to waste, and only a few stone walls remain, built into the side of the hill.

All nine children raised in the three-room house emigrated to America. "In those days," my father explained, "there was no work in this part of Ireland, and the land besides was poor." What little land they owned was abandoned or left to distant cousins.

From the slight rise of my father's land I could see into the horseshoe valley. It stretched several miles before sweeping up the steep slopes. Dotting the covering hayfields were several white cottages, and that afternoon farmers moved slowly through the fields swinging long scythes, the steel blades flashing in the bright sun.

Beyond, and surrounding the patchwork farmland, grass grew up the mountainside. The steep hills are used for grazing sheep, and several hundred in a single flock made a tight white mark on the far slope. "Many's the time," my father said, "we'd climb those hills to gather sedge," the long grass used for thatching roofs.

It was also into those hills that they went to take target practice at the time of the 1916 Uprising. "We had only one rifle among us," my father went on, "so we all took turns practicing together, and I was the best shot of the lads."

He continued, pointing now to a single-lane stone bridge that crossed the river below his family's fields. "It was a wooden bridge in my day," he said, "and we'd have dances there at night in the moonlight. The boys and girls would come from miles around when they heard about the dances. Everyone walked over the hills, for there were no cars here in them days."

When my father was 17 he led "the lads" on a midnight bombing of another bridge of the Cornamona River. It was the only guerrilla activity in the village against the Black and Tans, British army irregulars so named because of their uniforms.

My grandfather had a small supply of dynamite—for road repair— and Dad stole it, wired up the 100-foot wooden bridge, and blew a chunk from its center, stopping for a while the movement of troops through the village.

He went on to become a corporal in the Uprising, running secret messages from town to town, and once, after he was believed killed, received a hero's welcome in Cornamona, carried through the tiny village on the shoulders of relatives and neighbors.

There followed gentler stories of rural Ireland. Of walking barefoot to the village grammar school, and of spending the first shilling he ever earned on an English dictionary. My father spoke Irish until he went to school, and speaks it still today—or does to the few people at home who still know the language. For the Irish language, like the thatched roofs, the wooden bridges and the pony and trap carts, is disappearing from Ireland as the outside world closes in on this rocky mountain country.

Back in the village we checked into the small and homey St. Joseph's Guest House, which we used as our base, and drove out daily to visit relatives and the surrounding area. Here in Connemara the signs are all in Irish, and my father had to direct us through the tight, winding roads that crisscross the hills.

We took picnic lunches with us, parked wherever we wished in the mountains or on the shores of Lough Corrib and Lough Mask, or visited with cousins, sitting in the small kitchens, drinking tea and Irish whisky and eating buttered soda bread hot from the oven.

We went from one small white cottage to the next, seeing the McNallys, the Joyces, the Jennings and still more Coynes. We arrived unannounced but expected, as the word had spread through the hills that Tommy Coyne was home, though few of the people from my father's time are left alive in the hills.

"They're all dead now," one relative put it, qualifying the condition, as if they were dead at just this moment but he expected them back in Connemara soon.

We drove on to Clonbur where my grandfather was buried in a grave-yard five miles from his home in Cremlin. "They had to carry him over the mountains," my father explained, "for this was the closest graveyard in them days." It was at the end of the country lane and appeared abandoned, though someone shortly before our visit had cut the hay from among the tombstones and piled it high in yellow stacks. We had to search the un-marked rows for my grandfather's tombstone, but found it finally among the hundreds of other Coynes. Years ago my father and his brothers and sisters in America had paid for a stone at the grave site, and it still stood straight and tall. I took a picture of my dad beside his father's grave, and then we went on to the town of Cong and stopped at Ashford Castle.

It was built in the 19th century, incorporating in its castellated facade the remains of the 13th-century De Burgo Castle and the original Ashford House built in the style of a French chateau. Today the castle is owned and operated as a hotel by an American.

We moved slowly through the castle's 230 wooded acres, pausing in our car to let golfers play ahead, then parked and wandered among the formal gardens and the azalea, rhododendron and heather bushes that flank the castle and run down to the edge of the River Cong.

It is one of the loveliest sites in Ireland, but seems tame and stately compared with the wild hills of Connemara, and I could see my father was anxious to go back to the car and drive home. "This place is only for swells," he commented as we drove away.

We went to church the next morning in Cornamona, to a mass said in Irish, for Connemara is one of the last spots where the language is still spoken extensively. The church was crowded with students from the cities, Dublin and elsewhere, who had come into the mountains for the summer to live with families and learn the language. The announcements, however, were in English, and the priest welcomed the American visitors to Cornamona. In the small church he had easily spotted the strangers, the Yanks back home.

After mass a crowd of old men gathered in the vestibule to meet my father. They were all in their late seventies and early eighties, small, thin, wiry men, several bent and crippled from lifetimes of hard work in the cold, damp Irish weather, but their faces were bright and ruddy with pleasure. They talked excitedly to my father in Irish.

My father called me over to meet the men. "We took the I.R.A. oath together on the same night," he said, pointing out one old man, and then my father went on to tell more stories, his memory of this time still vivid and accurate, full of dates and names from the year of 1916. "Well, God willing, I'll see you again next year," my father reassured them, waving goodbye as we left. It was time to go. The grandchildren led the old men to waiting cars, newspapers had to be picked up at Lowry's store, and then it was off to the farms, isolated in the deep valleys and hillsides.

My father would not be back again, and the old men all knew it. But for a few minutes there, standing in the back of church, it was 1916 and they were all boys again. The best shot in Cremlin. The I.R.A. guerrillas. The lads who blew a hole in the Cornamona Bridge and stopped the Black and Tans.

Later that night I crossed the Cornamona Bridge under the moonlight and stopped in at O'Malley's Pub. The same cars for morning mass were parked beside the road and the small bar was crowded with people, young and old, women and men. A young man back from Australia was playing his accordion. It was a night for singing.

Before I reached the bar itself someone handed me a pint. I had been quickly spotted by relatives lined against the wall. They tipped their glasses to me and smiled under their black caps; I couldn't buy a single beer that night. The pints kept coming, from the McNallys, the Joyces and the

Coynes. At one point, late in the evening, holding a pint in each fist, I looked around the smoky room and realized I was the only Yank in the bar, but nevertheless in Cornamona, in my father's place, I belonged. I had come home.

&

MY SON, JOHN KERWIN, NEVER KNEW HIS GRAND-father; John was conceived on the cold, rainy Easter weekend when we buried my dad in Michigan. I like to think that my son has my father's soul, or at the very least, his heart.

My son does not look like my father. Dad was a short block of a man, with strong, thick muscles, built from a lifetime of work. John is thin and rangy, and has no map of Ireland stamped on his face, but instead, in a heartbreaking way, his mother's cute buttony looks.

Watching my son grow, however, I am pleased to see that he has some of his grandfather's playfulness and certainly his gift of gab. I'm comforted by this, since he will grow up in a world so unlike my father's that I'm worried there will be no link between the two of them, between their generations.

I grew up on a farm south of Chicago, where my family relocated just after World War II began. It wasn't much of a farm; my father fed his six children by working for 30 years in the steel mills of Gary, Indiana. I never knew a time when he wasn't working. He would go from the mills to the fields and back again.

If my father were alive today, he'd be amused by such ideas as orga-nized play for children and "quality time" with parents. "Let the boy out," he'd say, "to run wild in the fields." But there are no fields to run wild in now, not for a boy born in New York City.

My father was an Irish immigrant, what they used to call a greenhorn, from the remote and beautiful hills of Connemara, in northern Galway. He spoke Gaelic until he was 12, flew in his first airplane when he was 50 and never got the hang of using a telephone.

My son dials our cordless phone to call his friends for play dates, has freed the Princess in Super Mario Bros. and flew to California twice before he was 6. Now in fourth grade, he has had more formal education than his grandfather had in 84 years of life.

In Ireland, my father's world was limited by the distance he could walk in a single day. My son is limited only by the speed with which he can flip through the television channels. John Kerwin lives in a global village, and he calls it cable.

Because I work at home, I have been able to spend much more time with John than most fathers do with their children. I do the everyday chores, from getting him breakfast and giving him a bath to buying him sneakers. I wonder whether all the time John and I spend together will make him a better person, or at least better adjusted.

While my father was a presence in my childhood, he didn't raise me. That was my mother's job. I don't remember a time when he put me to bed, stayed up with me when I was sick, or even had time to play ball out back of the barn.

But I don't feel cheated by my father. If I had told Dad that he didn't understand me, he would have handled it by giving me more chores to do. Or he would have told me some dreadful story of how hard his life had been when he was a boy in Ireland.

Those stories are what I remember best of my father. They told us who he was, and in turn, who we were, his children. These were family treasures—not material wealth, but funny and sad tales of distant relatives and quaint folks who filled a valley and a narrow strip of land between Lough Mask and Lough Corrib in a small village called Cornamona.

My father was a vivid storyteller and made a wonderful magical world of those green hillsides, stone-walled farm fields, cold salmon rivers and thatched white-washed cottages, all at the foot of a natural mountain amphitheater in the wildest spot of Connemara.

We keep a photograph of my father on the dresser in my son's room. It is our way of reminding John of his past, of showing that he exists on a continuum of Coynes. It is a photo I shot when I traveled with my father back to Ireland shortly before his death.

In the photo, Dad is standing at the one remaining wall of the three-room, thatch-roofed stone cottage where he was born and raised, the sixth child in a family of nine. He is reaching up to loosen a stone. When he first saw the photo, John asked what his grandfather was doing.

He was searching for the family riches, I tell him, remembering that moment on a sunny day in Galway. All through his childhood, Dad had told me, the Coynes had kept a few pounds behind a loose brick, a make-shift hiding place above the hearth.

Those few pounds had been long since spent, Dad knew, but it was a nice story and a nice photo. I watch my son smile at the possibility of lost treasure tucked away in an old stone wall, grown over with wild ivy and summer heather. John appreciates that possibility, versed as he is in his favorite Broadway show, *The Secret Garden*.

Remembering my father, watching my son smile at the notion of hidden fortune, I see how I am the custodian, curator of family lore and fact that must be passed along to give John a footing in his fluid world, a world in which he seems to live at perpetual fast-forward.

I hope these stories of my father, who lived before my son was born, will stretch his imagination of his own life. They will become his own secret garden of memories and recollections, like lost wealth in an old Irish wall, waiting to be retold someday and shared with strangers, shared with people he grows up to love, shared, in time, with his children, shared with my own grandchildren.

ANTHONY BAILEY

Along the Boyne to Tara with Seamus Heaney: ca. 1980

" 'AH, IT'S A WONDERFUL FIT, SIR,' HE SAID. THE
PRICE FOR THIS PIECE OF OLD WORLD
CRAFTSMANSHIP, AN ANTIQUE THAT HAD NEVER
BEEN USED, WAS, HE ADDED, MERELY A FIVER.
'YOU'LL TAKE FOUR POUNDS FIFTY,' SAID HEANEY."

Although Anthony Bailey's name appears on many books, much of his career as a staff writer at the New Yorker *was made by walking and writing about his walks. Among his well-known pieces are accounts of walks around the edge of the Isle of Wight, along the eighteen miles of the New Hampshire coast, and on the Promenade des Anglais, perhaps the single most famous stretch of the Côte d'Azur. And the following account of a walk in Ireland, along the River Boyne to the ancient site of Tara in the company of poet Seamus Heaney.*

After the death of William Butler Yeats, few poets in this land of poetry won international attention on a large scale, with the exception of Thomas Kinsella and Patrick Kavanagh, until the full flowering of Seamus Heaney's talent in the early 1980s. His reputation was quickly and permanently established with Poems: 1965–1975 *(1980),* Sweeney Astray *(1983), and* Station Island *(1984), and he went on to win the Nobel Prize in Literature.*

From its source in the Bog of Allen in Co. Kildare, the River Boyne flows seventy miles northeastward to where it empties into the Irish Sea at Drogheda. The Battle of the Boyne was fought along its banks in 1690. In a single day, July 12, the thirty-five thousand men of William of Orange, who had been proclaimed king of England in the preceding year, fought and defeated the twenty-one thousand followers of James II, the exiled former king of England.

*Tara, a hill that rises about five hundred feet above sea level in Co.
Meath, was, until the sixth century, the stronghold of the kings of Ireland,
but its history as a defensive and religious site stretches back into the mists of
the pre-Christian era. Archeologists have discovered evidence of burials in the
Bronze Age.*

NOW TARA WAS OUR OBJECTIVE. WE HAD BACON AND eggs, the pleasure of no bill to pay, and lighter loads, for we left most of our gear at the Russell Arms reception desk. We walked up to the main square, a junction of four roads in the center of Navan, where we intended to catch the 9:20 Dublin bus as far as Tara, six miles south. Since we also intended to carry on walking after lunch along the next section of the Boyne, from Navan to Slane, we had decided that auxiliary transportation was permissible on this side jaunt. A number of people were already at the bus stop, but we had fifteen minutes in hand to try to find Heaney something easier on his back than his present bag; he was impressed by the lightweight, unstiffened nylon backpack I had bought for $4.95 in a Mystic, Connecticut, sporting goods store some years ago. Navan still had a saddler's shop, a hundred yards from the bus stop, whose dusty front window disclosed rugged brown suitcases, harnesses, and khaki knapsacks, none looking less than ten years old.

The venerable saddler took one of the knapsacks out of the window, shook the cobwebs off it, and strapped it on Heaney's back. "Ah, it's a wonderful fit, sir," he said. The price for this piece of Old World craftsmanship, an antique that had never been used, was, he added, merely a fiver. "You'll take four pounds fifty," said Heaney, astutely keeping any interrogative note out of his voice, and staring intently at the knapsack's rusty metal grommets. "Oh, it'll do you well. Just right for tramping," said the saddler, as if he hadn't heard Heaney's remark. But he gave Heaney fifty pence change for the five-pound note.

The saddler's wife appeared in the back door to witness what might have been their first sale of the year—or perhaps it was just the historic sight in Navan of two tramping men.

At the bus stop, we joined the would-be passengers—elderly men, middle-aged women, and a pair of girls with most beautiful complexions. For entertainment while waiting, we had the spectacle of three demolition men at work on the Malocca Café across the square. It was a strangely two-dimensional sight. The three workers, wearing woollen caps rather than hard hats, were standing on the façade wall, all of nine inches thick, above the second-story windows. There was no scaffolding. The roof was already gone, and the men, carefully wielding their pickaxes, were demolishing the wall half a dozen bricks at a time beneath their own feet. We waited for one of them to miss or lose his balance, but none of them had done so by the time the bus came in.

The Dublin road first follows the Boyne south, upstream. Then, the river bending away westward toward Bective, the road climbs the slopes of Tara. The driver stopped the bus for us to get out at a junction with a side lane, and we walked up this, still climbing. The lane was narrow and heavy with hedges. The air was moist: not quite raining, not even drizzling; simply wet. One could see how things grew so well in Ireland, but one wondered how they ever ripened. From a nearby field came the sweet smell of new-cut hay. Heaney said that his friend David Hammond had told him the Vikings used to coast along the land until they smelled hay, and then, knowing that there must be habitations, would buckle on their swords and come ashore. I said I thought the east wind was the Vikings' wind, which filled their square sails on the voyage westward from Scandinavia—though no doubt they then coasted with the southwesterlies, which carried the hay smells, first raiding in Ireland and then settling to found such cities (trading posts at first) as Dublin, Wexford, Waterford, Cork, and Limerick.

Tara is a long hilltop; a windbreak of trees around an old church and attached graveyard; and an extensive meadow full of ridges, barrows, mounds, and earthworks. "Tara" means a place with a wide view, and the hill, rising three hundred feet or so above the general level of the rich countryside, allows one to see over much of the center of Ireland—yellow fields, green hedges, black copses, and blue distant hills. Gray processions of rain were marching along the Boyne Valley. Some parts of the horizon were lost in mist or cloud, while others were sunlit. Crows were strutting and cawing in an adjacent field, while farther down the slope a man was driving sheep across a pasture. The mist, reaching us, turned to rain for a few minutes and then became mist again, through which the sun tried to break. The grass was long and wet, my boots not as waterproof as they had once been. Heaney had the collar of his navy-blue raincoat turned up, his tweed cap flat on his head, the empty Navan knapsack on his back. We prowled around separately but occasionally converged on the same site: the so-called Mound of the Hostages; the two long ridges believed by some to be walls of a great Dark Ages banqueting hall; and the mound encircled by twin ditches which is known as the rath—or fort with earthen walls—of the Forradh. On top of this are three pieces of stonework within an iron-railed enclosure. One is a five-foot-high upright pillar called the Lia Fáil—a stone on which the early kings of Ireland were allegedly crowned, but known to local Irish speakers in the nineteenth century as the phallus of Fergus. Another is a Celtic-style cross, with an inscription in Irish, put up to honor thirty-seven insurgents who died in 1798 during a skirmish with government forces in the Tara vicinity. The third is a mawkish statue of St. Patrick, bearded, with a bishop's miter on his head, right hand raised in unctuous blessing and his gaze firmly averted from the erect Lia Fáil. "The triple deities," said Heaney. "Though I suspect that in some ways the good saint here is a hybrid of the other two."

He sat down on a patch of dry gravel in the lee of St. Pat, with his back to the plinth on which the saint stood. St. Patrick was a Romano-Briton who is believed to have been carried off as a slave by Irish raiders at the age of sixteen, to have escaped after several years, to have studied in Gaul and been consecrated a bishop, and then to have returned as one of the first Christian missionaries to Ireland in the mid-fifth century. Like many other invaders, he made his way up the Boyne. At a hill overlooking Slane, Patrick (according to the earliest accounts, written roughly two hundred years after his mission) lit a great Paschal bonfire on Easter Eve. At Tara, King Laoghaire saw the fire ten miles to the north and took it as a challenge to his authority; it is said that he drove over to Slane in his chariot to give the intruder a dressing down, but he was himself let down by his followers, who received the saint's blessing and became believers. Patrick went on to appoint three hundred bishops, attached to ruling families, to carry out the peaceful conversion of Ireland; as far as one knows, there were no martyrs. Almost all the churches in these parts are named after him.

And what about these kings? The Gaels from Gaul who conquered Ireland in the first centuries after Christ became an ascendant class, providing perhaps several hundred ruling families. Ulster, behind its mountains and lakes, held out longest against the Gaels, the Ulstermen being led by Connor MacNessa, the Red Branch knights, and Cuchulain, the heroic Hound of Ulster. The Gaels provided perhaps a hundred and fifty "kings" in a total population of less than half a million. Professor James Beckett, the Irish historian, believes that by the fifth century there were seven provincial kings lording it over the petty kings, and that by this time, too, the king of Tara, one of the provinces, had put in his claim to be *árd rí*, or high king. But the high king's authority was nominal, despite his making a circuit of the island and exacting hostages from the smaller kings. One can see why so many children with Irish parents are told (as I was by my mother, a Molony) that they are descended from an Irish king; in my case, it was from Brian Boru, who fell at Clontarf, outside Dublin, in 1014, successfully defeating a Norse army. And the likelihood that these kings practiced polygamy increases one's chances of being of royal Gaelic descent.

Tara was abandoned as a royal site in the mid-sixth century. The collection of legends that provide the names for the mounds and monuments dates from written sources set down some four hundred years later; in fact, there are more names than monuments. Some archaeological work has been done, however, and excavation of the rath of the Synods (so called because of ecclesiastical meetings St. Patrick and other missionaries are thought to have held there) has shown that dwellers on the site had contact with the far-spread Roman world—a Roman seal, lock, and glass fragments have been found. Yet Ireland was never a part of that world (which is one reason the Dark Ages are so murky in Ireland); Irish ways were never tempered with Roman imperium or Roman law. And that there were kings on this spot seems supported by such finds as two gold torcs, now in the National Museum, Dublin. The kings apparently favored neolithic burial mounds for their habitations; at Tara, a Bronze Age passage grave (ca. 2000 B.C.) has been found with pottery, bone pins, jet buttons, and a bronze awl of that period. Candy wrappers now decorate the ground at the grave's threshold.

When I returned to the rath of the Forradh after my reconnaissance, Heaney was still sheltering behind St. Patrick, jotting words in a notebook. A small military observation plane swooped low and circled twice, apparently observing *us*. "They must think we're an SAS detachment," said Heaney, who looked like a character from *Odd Man Out*, while I, in safari jacket and green jungle hat, was clearly dressed for counter-insurgency operations. Tara remains a commanding height. But we were, in any event, overwhelmed at this point by a busload of children, who came surging noisily over the site, dashing up the mounds and down into the ditches, the places of palisades and homes and graves. They ran to the enclosure where Heaney sat, and thronged round him. Suddenly among schoolchildren, he found himself answering their questions, telling them about the place, as if he were the genius loci. Indeed, the children seemed affected by the spot, as were we. Heaney had used in his lecture the previous morning the term "chthonic forces," which I later got him to define for me as the energies welling up from a place. The forces were strong here, at least in this weather of mist, showers, and watery sun: Cormac and Laoghaire, Fergus and Queen Maeve; the old peoples who lived and died here; kings on hills.

Before leaving, we looked in the little graveyard, where, among the Christian headstones, is a *sile* (or "sheila," as the word is pronounced): a gray rock face on which we could just discern in relief a female figure, knees spread wide as if making water on the ground—an image to avert evil or bring about fertility. In the Banqueting Hall Café, on the road where the school buses parked, we had a twenty-pence pot of tea, nicely timed, as the heavens opened and rain tumbled down. Then, with long slices of blue sky overhead, we went back down the rain-fragrant lane to the main road. It was eleven-thirty, and the next bus came by after one. So we walked along with our thumbs out and, after a while, got a lift into Navan from a heating-appliance salesman, who had what Heaney later called "a touch of the volubilities." In the car, he told us—learning that he was in the company of writing men—that he "used to read books."

After lunch at the Russell Arms, I donned my backpack again. Heaney now had his fully loaded. The sun was mostly out still, and we went looking in Navan for the way to Slane along the river. We were misdirected at first by a local to the banks of the Blackwater, the river which joins the Boyne here, but we soon found some old stone steps beside a bridge spanning the Boyne, and these took us down to a path that ran between the south bank of the river and a long-derelict canal alongside it, which in most places was full of reeds, rushes, and nettles, and looked even less navigable than the river it had been designed to supplant as an efficient waterway. Over it stood small stone bridges with low arches, giving just room for barges to get through. At intervals were old locks, their gates and paddles collapsed and fallen in. The canal was built between 1749 and 1800 to carry coal, grain, and other mill products between Navan and Drogheda, and most of its bridges and locks have inscribed on them the name of their designer, the engineer Richard Evans.

Our path between river and canal was at first graveled, then grassed, then overgrown. Heaney said, putting a travel writer's tone of authority in-to his voice, "At Navan, the character of the river changes." This stretch of the Boyne gives the impression of having been worked over by an eighteenth-century landscape architect. The river is wider, with the Blackwater added to it. Great stands of trees are growing in effective places, funneling the eye up green fields that roll away from the river. There are appropriate ruins and occasional crags. We met one man, hastening toward Navan, his breeches and jerkin giving him the look of a gamekeeper, and after him no one at all. The undergrowth, sometimes growing over the path, became forbiddingly luxuriant. Convolvulus grew larger, dock leaves were giant. We saw a kingfisher as it zipped between the reeds—"like blue voltage," said Heaney. The milestones that we passed, giving the distance to Slane (ten miles by my reckoning), appeared to be measuring the old Irish miles. The wind was from the north, but the sun produced a hint of summer heat. I kept a long stalk of grass in my mouth; it was sweet at first, bitter if one chewed it. Heaney moved with a sort of shuffle—tweed jacket, khaki knapsack, bamboo staff. I walked at a faster pace, and stopped now and then till he caught up, when he remarked about the advantages I had had of national service with a light-infantry regiment of the British Army. Heaney, a Catholic from Ulster, has had experiences of the British Army there, of being frisked and interrogated, that have left him not wholly sympathetic to Her Majesty's Forces, though he sees the difficulties of their peacekeeping role. In fact, many Irishmen, before and after Arthur Wellesley, have made a career in those forces. In 1914, the recruiting teams did good business in the South, and it wasn't just the men of Ulster who died at the Somme; the Irish Nationalist MPs William Redmond and Tom Kettle were among two hundred thousand Catholic and possibly Republican Irish who fought for the British in the First World War. My grandfather Frederick Molony served in the Royal Engineers. His sister Bessie was a nurse on the Western Front in the Queen Alexandra's Royal Nursing Corps. And his brother Tom died during the war in France from (his wife, Great-aunt Kitty, would always say) damp blankets.

Our histories are intertwined. The Boyne has relics of numerous ascendancies. Along here were more legacies of the French-speaking nobility who settled in the twelfth and thirteenth centuries in an area called the Pale. Beyond the Pale were what Shakespeare's Richard II called the "rough rug-headed kerns," and even within it each lord built his house as a castle, fortified against the peasantry, rival lords, and the king. In this landscape, the ruined castles had the air of follies, designed or deliberately ruined to fulfill an idea of the picturesque. Dunmoe Castle, which we passed near Milestone 4, was such a place. Said to have been built by a de Lacy, it last withstood siege during the Roundheads-vs.-Cavaliers civil war, was restored during the reign of James II, and burned more or less down in

1799. When Sir William Wilde, Oscar's father and a well-known Dublin eye surgeon and antiquary, came past here in the 1840s, on a journey of research for a book about the Boyne and the Blackwater, he was told by the peasantry that an underground passage led from the castle under the Boyne to the opposite bank. As we went by, the wind passing over the two castellated towers or through the high empty windows sounded as if someone were blowing over the top of a huge bottle. Between us and the castle, on the north bank, the river fell over a small cascade; the water slithered sideways as it went down. A little farther on, we passed, on our bank, a ruined church, high on a slope over the river, and then a more contemporary structure—a small corrugated-steel shed, possibly for fishermen, on the river's edge. It was nicely provided with no lock on the door and straight-backed chairs, on which we sat outside for a while and watched the Boyne glide, like a smooth moving carpet, over a weir. For such a calm and purposeful operation, the resulting falling-water noise was surprisingly loud.

The temperature went up and down five degrees as the sun went in and out; the path moved away from the river through fields: cowpats, a pheasant, a herd of Jersey cattle, half a dozen handsome horses. The next landmark, halfway to Slane, was Stackallan Bridge, which like most Boyne river crossings has nearby points of interest: here a wayside monumental cross and a holy well dedicated to St. Patrick. We rashly assumed from the map that the path now shifted, as the canal did, to the north bank; apparently, the towing horses would be loaded aboard the barges, and then barges, cargo, and horses would be poled across the river and into the lock on the other bank. We therefore crossed the bridge. Heaney, parched, went to get a drink of water at a nearby house, and brought back the information that it should be possible to reach Slane on this bank, but no promise of how easy it would be.

In fact, the path was soon densely overgrown. An unknown plant, a cross between a mammoth dock and giant rhubarb, had settled here in thick colonies, rising to five or six feet and spreading out huge, salad-bowl leaves. It had to be beaten aside. Over these plants we glimpsed a fine ruined mill on the south bank, next to a splendid horseshoe-shaped weir. Then we were within a few feet of the river itself but couldn't see it. A short clearing gave us hope, but we were at once in jungle again. My boots were soaking from the wet grass. Heaney and I took turns in the van, bashing away at the plant life—not just the Triffid-like things but briars, thorns, and saplings. I broke off one of the last to use as a device for parting the way ahead. We needed machetes. We needed more energy than we had. We were being turned green by the Irish jungle. No one had been this way for years, or several seasons.* We were wet from below and getting wet from above as rain fell and haphazardly penetrated the forest. It was too thick for my umbrella to be of use unless we stood still. When we halted for this purpose for a few minutes, Heaney sat down to rest on an ivy-covered log, which—rotten—crumbled under him, leaving him on the ground; he stayed there.

"You look like Sweeney," I said. He took it as a compliment. Sweeney was an Irish petty king or warlord, the subject of an early-medieval Irish poem called *The Frenzy of Sweeney*, which Heaney is slowly making a version of, called *Sweeney Astray*. Sweeney's problems begin when he is cursed by a local saint and finds himself flying round Ireland, nesting in hedges, treetops, and ditches—in the process speaking, as what Heaney has called "a tongue of the land," some of the most beautiful lines that have been written in description of the Irish landscape. We needed some of the bewitched king's powers now to get up into the tops of the trees and zoom out of this. And, indeed, when the last remaining suggestions of a path came to an end and the vegetation ahead looked impenetrable, we decided that it was time to be flexible about our intention of walking along the Boyne to Slane. We fought our way up into the woods, dragged ourselves up the steep ascent, and found—blessed relief!—open fields. Heaney was suffering not only from the previous day's blister but from an old thigh injury, acquired on the school football field, and, unable to get over barbed-wire fences, had to work his way under them. But we made it into the fields and along their southern edge, and reached the parkland of old trees and rolling ground which is the demesne of Slane Castle, seat of the Earl of Mount Charles. "Demesne" is a fine word, from the French *domain*, and evocative of medieval estates. The present earl had worked briefly for Faber and Faber, Heaney's London publishers, and we hoped that this (and the fact that Heaney had phoned from Navan to reserve dinner for us at the Slane Castle restaurant) would give us entrée if we encountered the earl's gamekeepers before we reached the Navan–Slane road. Luck was

*Or possibly since Sir William Wilde journeyed here in the 1840s, and in the fashion of the time eulogized the landscape, particularly the bank we were on, "where groves of noble beech trees and aged chestnuts fringe the heights, and an underwood of laurels, thorns and sweet-briars mantle upon the undulating surface of the shores beneath . . . Here the river forms a number of sudden curves, each winding presenting us with a new picture more beautiful than its predecessor. The banks spring high and abrupt from the water's edge, so that in some places the massive trees, rising in piles of the most gorgeous foliage, appear toppling over us from their summits, and darken the deep smooth pools they overhang."

with us here, however, and also on the road, where a fine fellow stopped and gave us a lift the last mile into Slane.

Slane had 896 people in 1837 and 526 in 1861, after the famine years; at the last count, in 1971, the population was 483. It is a well-planned eighteenth-century village, with the unusual feature of four nearly identical Georgian houses built aslant the corners of the crossroads, where the Navan-Drogheda and Dublin-Derry roads intersect. It has two churches named after St. Patrick, and a hotel, the Conyngham Arms, which deserves more than the one Automobile Association star it displays. The rooms were clean and well furnished; all light bulbs and bath plugs were in place; the water was hot and the beer cellar-cool. Despite the fact that we looked, if anything, more shattered than the day before, Heaney and I were not asked to pay in advance for our rooms.

Slane was the home of the Irish poet Francis Ledwidge, who was killed in Flanders in 1917. Ledwidge was a gentle, nature-observant writer, in tone and spirit close to the English poet Edward Thomas, who also died in the First World War. In Slane, Ledwidge is commemorated by a plaque on the bridge across the Boyne, which bears four lines from his "Lament for Thomas MacDonagh," a poet and friend of his, who was executed after the Easter Rising of 1916:

> He shall not hear the bittern cry
> In the wild sky, where he is lain,
> Nor voices of the sweeter birds
> Above the wailing of the rain.

And when Heaney and I were being driven to Slane Castle for dinner by Louis Cassidy, who is the local handyman and ferryman-by-car of local people, he told us that Francis Ledwidge's brother Joe, now in his eighties, still lived in the village. Some people in Slane, said Mr. Cassidy, were still offended because a London publishing firm had given a party here some years earlier to celebrate the publication of a biography of Francis Ledwidge and failed to invite a number of people (including Mr. Cassidy, we gathered) who felt they should have been invited. The long Irish memory strikes again.

In the twilight, we drove a short way back up the Navan road and in through the arch of a gatehouse, along a drive past stables, and down a slope to a cellar doorway of Slane Castle. The castle restaurant is one of the activities by which the present Earl of Mount Charles makes the place pay its way; other activities include renting the place to film companies for locations, and throwing balls, to which some guests come by helicopter. We were met at the door by Juliet, Countess of Mount Charles, who is in her twenties, petite and pretty; she nobly disguised her disappointment on finding out that when Heaney had said on the phone "Around nine" he had been talking about dinnertime, not the number of people who would be with him. We did our best to eat for those who hadn't come. Heaney had asparagus crêpes and I rainbow trout Provençal. There were bountiful dishes of *al dente* vegetables. The house red was a fine-bred claret, and Henry, the seventh Earl of Mount Charles, who is twenty-nine years old, having seen his twenty or so other customers properly fed, joined us for the second bottle. He is a graduate of Harvard University, where he was known as Henry Slane; after working for Faber's, he was the Irish representative of Sotheby's. Then his father, Marquess Conyngham, who owns land in England and had potential problems with the Irish wealth tax, asked Henry—as everyone in Slane calls him—if he would like to take over the castle and its thousand acres and make a go of it. This Henry and Juliet were now doing. They employ thirty men and women in the castle and on the farm. Slane has its own dairy cattle, its own fishing rights, and its own game birds. The independence of its present owners is enhanced by its power plant—a private turbine producing electricity from the ceaseless Boyne. (This was installed by Henry's grandfather, who also made much money from a carpet works in Navan; the turbine has been stopped only once in forty years, for an overhaul in 1959.) Henry would have a seat in the British House of Lords when he succeeded his father, and he didn't disguise the fact that in running this sort of establishment for profit (which depends partly on the successful manipulation of the past, of associations, nostalgia, deference, and need for the unusual), a title—a "handle," as he called it—was very useful, though possibly the EEC's Common Agricultural Policy's effect on farm prices counted for more.

After dinner, Henry gave us a tour of the interior. Slane Castle is mostly a product of the late eighteenth century. Henry's ancestors, the Conynghams, were a Scottish family who came to Donegal in 1611. Sir Albert Conyngham fought for King William at the Boyne in 1690. On James II's side fought Christopher Fleming, the twenty-second Lord Baron of Slane, whose family had held the estates from 1175 until 1641, when they were confiscated and sold to the Conynghams. Bits of the old Fleming castle are believed to have been incorporated in the Gothic Revival house that James Wyatt, the architect, designed here, with mock battlements and corner towers, and set on a rocky bastion overlooking a bend of the Boyne. Francis Johnston oversaw its completion. Capability Brown did the stables. Henry has a telephone switchboard and a telex machine in his offices. Of the many elegant rooms, that which serves as both library and ballroom is perhaps the finest—a round room, with crimson walls and white plaster Gothic tracery on the domed ceiling. It was built especially for a visit by King George IV in 1821, and would undoubtedly have appealed to the patron of the Brighton Pavilion. However, the main appeal for George IV at Slane, it is said, was Lady Conyngham. One of the reasons that are traditionally given for the straightening of the Dublin–Slane road—it is one of the straightest roads in Ireland—was George's desire to get to Slane and Lady C. as fast as possible. In reality, though well acquainted with her by 1815, George is thought to have stayed at Slane Castle only twice—once before and once after he was crowned king. It was while he was dining at Slane that George, in fine spirits, suggested sending Lord Talbot, the Lord Lieutenant of Ireland, to look after England while he himself stayed where he was.

In the castle now are various prized mementos of these associations, and statues and pictures of the nobility England and Ireland shared, for better and worse. There is a portrait of the first Marquess Conyngham by Gilbert Stuart (George when he was Prince Regent not only got Lady C.'s husband this title but had him made Constable of Windsor Castle and Lord Steward of the Royal Household). And there is a full-length, life-size portrait of a handsome officer, the Marquess of Anglesey, who was also one of Henry's ancestors. It was at the Battle of Waterloo in 1815, as Henry reminded us, that the Duke of Wellington is supposed to have said to Anglesey, just after a cannonball whizzed by, "By Gad, Harry, you've lost your leg!" and Anglesey is said to have replied, "By Gad, sir, so I have."

Day three: a fine morning. Heaney had to be back in Dublin that afternoon for a meeting and was catching the Dublin bus at ten. He was, I suspected, pleased not to have to put his Dr. Marten's to the test for another day. After an excellent breakfast at the Conyngham Arms, we said goodbye. My boots had been put to dry on the kitchen range at the hotel, and though I went down to Slane Bridge for a glimpse of the distant castle standing on "its swelling bank of greensward" (as Wilde described it), and of the woods overhanging the river that had thwarted Heaney and myself the evening before, I decided to keep my boots dry for the moment by forgoing any excursions into the thick undergrowth between bridge and castle. I took on trust that somewhere in the wet, tangled shrubbery, under yews and beeches, was the ancient ruin known as the Hermitage of St. Erc. St. Erc, one of St. Patrick's right-hand men and the first Bishop of Slane, is said to have often stood for hours at a time in the chill Boyne waters in order to cool his concupiscent desires. From the bridge, alleged to have been a favorite haunt of Mick Collier, the last of the Irish high-waymen, there is also a spacious view downstream past Slane Mill toward the big bend of the river at Rosnaree. I returned to the village crossroads and marched forth on the Drogheda Road, spurning the temptations prompted by the Live and Let Live public house, and leaving over my left shoulder the hill on which St. Patrick lit his Paschal fire.

It was just gone eleven as I walked from Slane. It was fox-and-geese weather—the promise of the early morning already compromised by loose gray clouds scudding behind me, threatening showers. I was going to have to walk faster than Heaney and I had done to fit into this day all that I wanted, and I kept up a light-infantry pace for the first few miles, exercising the freedom of the road to whistle and sing, and swinging my umbrella at the trail, parallel with the ground. I turned right on the first minor road, which led toward the Boyne again and the great neolithic burial mounds of Knowth, Newgrange, and Dowth. A vole ran across the road; at a farm gate stood a pair of milk churns, awaiting collection. But, despite the rural signs, there were also short stretches of ribbon development, as there seem to be on many country roads in the east of Ireland—development, admit-tedly, that often appeared to be proceeding by well-spaced fits and starts. A few new houses here stood empty in plots alongside unfinished houses or old, completed cottages that had for some reason been long abandoned. To whom do these derelict or unoccupied dwellings belong? Will the new houses ever be lived in? Are there sons and daughters in Liverpool or Boston who will one day come to glaze the boarded-up windows and paint the pebble dash? To keep a cow or a goat in one of these small hedged fields?

Heaney had given me the name of the archaeologist, Professor George Eogan, who is in charge of the excavations at Knowth. At the top of a rise, opposite a farmhouse, I came to a high wire fence, through which I could see the huge tumulus, with parts of the covering turf peeled back, and black Polythene protecting some of the excavated ground. I let myself in through a gate and, walking past a pile of spades and picks next to a fork-lift truck, found the prefabricated hut which was site headquarters. There I introduced myself to Dr. Eogan, a sharp-eyed but genial man in his fifties, who has been working on Knowth since 1962, digging during the summers with his students from University College, Dublin, and, during term time, sorting out the results back in the city. A postgraduate student, Aideen Ireland, gave me a tour of the excavations, starting at one side of the central mound, where we walked cautiously on thin ridges of earth left between four-meter-square excavation pits, in which the diggers were working with tiny trowels and toothbrushes, finding, if they were lucky, minute pieces of bone or bead.

The mound itself is a megalithic tomb containing two passage graves. Some three hundred such graves are known in Ireland, and those in the three mounds that form a great cemetery on the Boyne are preeminent. They date, my guide told me, from between 3000 and 2500 B.C. They are the works of a people about whom not much is known except on the basis of these tombs, but who could clearly gather their energies in a project that consumed much time and labor, and who honored their dead, installing the cremated ashes in shallow stone basins set in niches deep in the passage graves. The graves themselves were formed of huge stones. The mound covering those at Knowth extends over one and a half acres; it is some ninety meters in diameter and more than ten meters high. It is surrounded by a circle of large edgestones, decorated with incised motifs— circles, U shapes, diamond shapes, spirals, zigzags, and herringbones. The mound was carefully built in layers, thicker in the middle and sloping slightly downward toward the edges, presumably for better drainage.

We stood on top of the mound in the warm sun and cool breeze and looked out over the valley—to the flat-topped sister mound of Newgrange, a mile away; to the curving river and, beyond, to Tara; and to the Wicklow hills, visible beyond Dublin twenty-five miles south. It was obviously a good site—first time lucky, in a way, since these recently nomadic and hunting people were on the point of becoming farmers and herders, their animals becoming domestic. And settling down seemed to involve giving a permanent dwelling place first of all to their dead—levering tons of stone, slowly chipping away the magical designs with hammers of flint. The early Irish were diggers and navvies and artists. And, after the cremations and burials, the place itself was good for the living, then and thereafter, overlooking and controlling the fertile valley and the river, with its fish. In the Iron Age, people inhabited the mound itself, digging deep ditches round it and building stone walls on top. The Celtic invaders made this cemetery their Olympus, the home of their gods. The Vikings looted it and the Normans built a fort on it. In 1699, the Welsh antiquary Edward Lhuyd came to the Boyne cemetery, the first of a line of inquisitive scientists and excavators. In the eighteenth century, the locals dug here for handy road-building materials.

After thanking Miss Ireland and Dr. Eogan, I walked on down the lane to Newgrange. At a junction, I spurned the advice of the road sign—deciding, after a look at my map, that the sign proposed a route better for cars and longer for me—and, after a few minutes' doubt on the single-track road I'd chosen, had the pleasure of seeing Newgrange appear again over the high hedges, several fields distant. All along here, the elder trees were in flower and blackbirds were singing, as they have in all likelihood since neolithic times to movers of stone, monks, farmers, warriors, and people walking down lanes.

I reached Newgrange at one o'clock. Newgrange has been excavated and restored, and sits dramatically in the middle of a wide field, with green grass all round, an immense wall of small white stones banked up on either side of the grave entrance, and half a dozen standing stones in front and one reclining, heavily incised stone as the grave threshold. Visitors are allowed to walk round and enter the passage grave. A party had just left, but one of the guides—girl students—kindly led me in. The huge stones forming the tunnel of the grave lean inward, the roof stones press down. We squeezed along the passage and into the chamber, where the space expands out into alcoves or niches and up into the corbeled dome. My guide, who was about twenty, leaned back against a stone and gave me a short speech: ". . . passage-grave makers, perhaps from Brittany . . . shellfish eaters . . . some four thousand years ago . . . burials . . . cremations . . . we don't know much about them . . ." How pretty she is, I thought. Was this the age-old conjunction of instincts—sex and death? She told me that at Newgrange on about December 21, the day of the winter solstice, the sun comes up over the eastern horizon and shoots a long shaft of light through a slit in the roof over the grave entrance and down the passage, lighting up the chamber for precisely seventeen minutes. This and the arrangement of standing stones outside suggested that the builders had astronomical knowledge and made calendar observations. She also pointed out the incisions in some stones; the triple-spiral motif, to be seen on several, was a subject of conjecture. I hazarded the idea that it might symbolize Knowth/ Newgrange/Dowth. That, she said, was one of the conjectures.

Outside again: the breeze shaking the full-leafed trees along the lane, sun gleaming off the white stone embankment of the giant mound. I had neglected to bring any lunch. I lay on the grass and read some notes I had made from Dr. Michael Herity's treatise, *Irish Passage Graves*, in which, after much detailed scholarship, he lets loose:

> The whole impression in the Boyne is of a township like medieval Florence, sure of its economy, confidently undertaking the erection of a great cathedral to ensure spiritual sustenance, at its head a ruler of wisdom, strength and leadership.

Dr. Herity believes that three hard-working communities lived in this area, compact enough to have a common purpose, each depending on the labors of some five hundred able workers to build its tombs, over roughly twenty years. He writes:

> When death came, a great mausoleum was ready to house the dead, the spirit of the supernatural watching from its walls, its elevated site and the mass of its tumulus designed to awe the living. After the cremation ceremonies the ashes of the dead, borne in pottery vessels ornamented with the same symbols as those on the tomb walls and accompanied only by the ornamental miniatures they had worn in life, were laid to rest in the house they had planned and built.

There is a line in Lewis Mumford's *The City in History*: "The Egyptians loved life so much they even embraced death." I thought also of a poem Heaney has written, called "Funeral Rites," in which he imagines an immense funeral procession moving from Ulster to the Boyne, to—as he has said in a radio broadcast—"the megalithic burial chambers which were fabulous even in early Irish times. Then people thought of them as the burial places of heroes and semi-gods, but I think of them here as the solemn resting places for casualties, the innocent dead of the past few years."

I walked on, two miles to Dowth. This burial mound is unrestored, unexcavated since the nineteenth century, after which it became a grassed-over crater. No one was about. I stood on the mound and watched the wind move like a demonstration of energy through the long grass. As at Knowth and Newgrange, there was a fine view of the river half a mile away. Newgrange was in sight to the west. Just to the east, next to a ruined mansion, stood the shell of a church, and in the surrounding churchyard, just scythed, a man out of Brueghel was carrying hay on a pitchfork. As I walked back to the road, an elderly, well-groomed lady came by, walking her dog, looking as if she did this every day.

I had found a roadside pump just before Dowth. At it I had filled my grumbling stomach with well water, and this kept me going through the next few miles of warm sun and winding road toward Oldbridge. In the course of the next forty-five minutes, I was passed by two cars. I saw one man, a roadworker, pruning a hedge with a billhook beside a bridge where the little River Mattock runs beneath the road to join the Boyne.

"Keeping fine," I said.

"Yes, not so bad today," said he.

When the Boyne came in sight again, at the junction of the lane I was on and the Slane–Drogheda road, it was spread out and slow-moving. Fishermen were angling from the far bank. More ruined houses loomed through the trees. A midafternoon torpor overhung everything, but I kept going and at ten to three found myself at Oldbridge, where a narrow stone-and-iron bridge spans the river, and another era of Irish history is immanent. And there, too, on a wide grass verge, a piece of ground over which hundreds of troops charged toward the river one July day in 1690, sat a gypsy caravan. It was prairie-schooner-shaped but small. The panels on each side of the back door were painted red, yellow, gold, and green, like illuminations in the Book of Kells. A subsidiary dwelling had been set up on the grass nearby, a sort of nomadic hut made of canvas stretched over wooden hoops—indeed, it looked like an upside-down coracle. The canvas was partly rolled back to reveal bedding inside: mattress, several plump pillows, and an eider-down embroidered or patchworked with a magnificence to match the painting of the caravan. There was something Oriental about these sparse but luxurious belongings. A goat tethered to a stake a few yards away was champing grass. Several horses, seemingly the steeds of the caravan's owner, were in an adjacent field. An iron pot hung from a tripod over a campfire. And in the grass a man lay on his back, holding aloft a baby. The baby was giggling; the man was uttering fond parental noises to make it laugh. I gave them a wave and a hail in greeting, and the man—after a solemn look, presumably to see that I wasn't an agent of council authority or the farmer who owned the field—nodded and smiled in return.

The tide reaches up the Boyne from the sea to this point. Walking onto the bridge, I concluded that the tide was out; this accounted for the present shallowness of the river. It would have been easy to ford, which was the reason William III chose it for one of his four river crossings on the morning of

July 1, 1690, and the reason James II (who was with his staff on the slopes of Donore Hill, to the south) had many of his troops on the other bank, guarding the crossing. (July 1 was the date of the Battle of the Boyne in the old-style, Julian calendar. In the new-style, Gregorian calendar, adopted in the British Isles in 1752, the date is July 12.) In any event, when William realized that the ford at Oldbridge was well covered by the Jacobite forces, he smartly sent a large detachment from his ample army (35,000; James had 25,000) off westward to cross the river at Rosnaree, between Knowth and Newgrange. James thought this feint to his flank was the real thing, and diverted much of his Oldbridge force to meet them. William's deception plan succeeded. The diverting and diverted parties sat and faced each other across a bog all morning while William's main army came across the river at Oldbridge and met the rest of James's.

It was a European battle. William, Prince of Orange, Stadtholder of the United Provinces, had been offered the British throne by those who wished to preserve the Protestant succession and constitutional monarchy. Catholic James, deposed in England, was making his penultimate stand in Ireland with French support. He had fighting for him Englishmen, Scotsmen, Irishmen, Dutchmen, and Frenchmen. William had Dutch, Germans, Danes, Scots, English, Huguenot French, and even some Catholic Irish. To tell each other apart, the Williamites wore green sprigs in their headgear, the Jacobites wore white cockades; but this didn't prevent allies from now and then fighting one another.

Across the bridge there is thick undergrowth on either side—a tough place for a skirmish. It was, one participant recalled, "an excessive hot day." When William's Blue Dutch Guards forded the river, they held their muskets and powder above their heads; as they came up the bank on this side, the fifes and drums were playing "Lilliburlero." I sat down by a desolate gatehouse at the first bend in the road and changed my socks—an old soldier's trick for the restoration of tired feet—rubbing my bare toes in the grass and airing them for five minutes before donning Mr. Bean's boots again. Road signs directed me toward the Jacobite camp, but after a mile or so of uphill plodding along tortuous lanes, I struck out across the fields to Donore Hill, whose summit was crowned by a clump of trees and a small walled cemetery. Among the obstacles were barbed-wire fences, deep ditches full of mud and nettles, thorn hedges, and fields full of cows and possibly one or two bulls; but eventually I was there, seated on the stone wall surrounding the graveyard. 3:50 P.M.

I had my jacket off for the first time on this walk. It was hot, but not excessive. I looked north, down the long slope of hillside on which the last stages of battle had taken place. To the right, three miles or so away, I could see the buildings of Drogheda and, beyond, for the first time, the sea; to the northeast, the mountains of Mourne. It was twenty miles from where I sat to the North-South border, along which there are still ambushes, booby traps, sudden murders, and the working out of old horrors. What is always impressive about battlefields is the fertility of the fields, the felicity of the countryside. But here, without much effort, I could imagine men in the ditches and hedgerows, pikemen holding off cavalry, the confusion of charges, retreats, and orders not getting through. Smoke—bayonets—musketballs—and a good deal of dying and injury less stoically received than Lord Anglesey's. The Jacobites lost nearly a thousand men and William some five hundred. (Even so, seven thousand of William's men had died from disease the previous winter.)

At Aughrim a year later, the Catholic army met its final defeat in Ireland, but this battle at the Boyne has always been considered the real defeat. James retreated that night to Dublin and took ship for France. And in the war of words that has been so much of Irish history, the Boyne is immortal. Most Irish schoolchildren were brought up to identify with one side or the other; the account of the Boyne battle in most Irish history books, until very recently, discloses the cultural, religious, and political bias of the author. Few Irish Catholic children are named William. The Protestant king spent only a fortnight in Ireland, but he became for Northern Protestants the symbol of the Irish-British Union. King Billy is the affectionate title they've given him, though at the time many of his supporters thought him cold and standoffish. He didn't speak English very well. And who knows if—as Ulster iconography insists—he actually rode a white horse on that day of battle? Many in the North, despite the ubiquitous slogan "Remember 1690" painted on walls and gables, have no clear idea of when the battle took place. Some believe it occurred in Biblical times. There is the famous story of the visitor to the North who is puzzled by all the references to King Billy and the Boyne, and asks an old Ulsterman what it's all about. He is told, "Away with ye, man, and read yer Bible!"

Celebrations of the anniversary of the Boyne battle were first held in the North in 1797, as liberal Presbyterianism began to be supplanted by the Orange Order and by a "No Surrender" attitude regarding the maintenance of a Protestant ascendancy. In 1914, that attitude was so entrenched that Protestant Ulster nearly revolted at the prospect of home rule for all of Ireland—a situation in which they feared they would be swamped by the Catholic majority. When it looked as if there might be a Unionist rising in March that year, British generals considered moving the Fifth Army Division from its camps in central Ireland to a line along the Boyne, facing north. But world war provided for the death of home rule—and in turn for the frustrations that helped produce the Easter Rising, in 1916. It was on July 1 (the old-style date of the Battle of the Boyne), 1916, that the Battle of the Somme began, and men of the Thirty-sixth Ulster Division went over the top wearing orange ribbons, shouting "No Surrender" and "Remember 1690" as they plunged into the German machine-gun fire.

That year, after the Somme debacle, there was no Orange parade in the North. But, except for that single omission, each July has seen an anniversary celebration of the Boyne victory. In Belfast, the parade takes two and a half hours to pass a particular spot, with drums throbbing and the fifes playing their shrill tunes. On this day of sashes and banners, the ministers preach and the politicians pronounce as to God's own, a chosen people. A notable example was the speech made on July 12, 1934, by Sir Basil Brooke, then Minister of Agriculture in Northern Ireland and later Prime Minister of Northern Ireland, which illustrates what Catholics in the North were up against for so many years. Sir Basil said, "Many in this audience employ Catholics, but I have not one about my place. Catholics are out to destroy Ulster . . . If we in Ulster allow Roman Catholics to work on our farms we are traitors to Ulster . . . I would appeal to loyalists, therefore, wherever possible, to employ good Protestant lads and lassies."

Possibly it is a sign of progress that, despite the last ten years of Troubles, that sort of statement, reflecting fairly widespread feeling at the time, could be made by probably only one Ulster MP today. And the Twelfth parade itself is no longer quite so fraught with religious or tribal hostility. Some young Protestants are forbidden to take part in it by parents who regard it as a manifestation of bigotry; some young Catholics begin to think of it as a sort of carnival. An increasing number of people are perhaps coming to share Conor Cruise O'Brien's feeling that the Irish have often in the past behaved "like sleepwalkers, locked in some eternal ritual reen-actment, muttering senselessly as we collided with one another." (For that reason, O'Brien chose not to attend a ceremony commemorating the land-ing of arms from Erskine Childers's yacht *Asgard*—a ceremony, he thought, that merely underlined the ancient rivalries and passions.)

On the grassy slopes of the Boyne on a warm afternoon, topography is more impressive than history. This land is unlike so much of Ireland—

a country broken up into areas of poor soil, barren mountains, and bog. The geographical fragmentation of the country has in the past been intensified by the use of the land and by a system of inheritance, in the words of the geographer E. Estyn Evans, that entailed "re-allocating land periodically among close kinsmen, and subdividing already scattered plots among co-heirs." Evans and others believe that such practices, over the centuries, have contributed to the violent feeling that lies just below the surface and has brought about so much internecine bloodshed in Ireland.

In the late afternoon, I abandoned my hilltop perch, my petty kingdom, and made my way across the fields to the lane again. It was two miles of country roadwork into Drogheda, a sizable market and manufacturing town built on both steep banks of the river. Drogheda is famous for its fortified walls, which the English Commonwealth troops of Oliver Cromwell stormed during the civil war in 1649, proceeding to slaughter the Drogheda garrison. Cromwell said, "Our men getting up to them were ordered by me to put them all to the sword." Cromwell saw himself not only as attacking royalists but as the instrument of divine vengeance against those Irish who had rebelled in Ulster in 1641. He wrote from Drogheda, "This is a righteous judgement of God upon these barbarous wretches, who have imbrued their hands in so much innocent blood." The effect of the death of the three thousand Drogheda men was to emblazon his own name in Irish memory as a butcher, and to associate his country with the act.

Drogheda is also noted for disputes about the pronunciation of its name, the English—including the Earl of Drogheda—going for "Drowda," which to me sounds Irish, and most of the locals calling it "Drockeda," which is direct enough. Until recently, communication from one side of town to the other was via a pair of narrow bridges, which had to carry not only local vehicles but much of the coastal road traffic between North and South. Four years ago, a new, wide road bridge was built, and was named by the Drogheda town council Peace Bridge. In December 1976, shortly after it opened, a rally was held on the bridge by the Northern Ireland Peace Movement, whose founders, Mrs. Betty Williams and Miss Mairead Corrigan, won the Nobel Peace Prize the following year. Ten thousand people turned up from North and South and in two columns—almost two armies—surged across the bridge from each side of the Boyne to meet in the middle, embrace, shake hands, or otherwise greet one another. The Peace Movement's leadership has recently been in disarray, and it has been criticized for failing to get support from the city ghetto-dwellers or for dealing in cosmetic solutions. But it seems to me that its dramatization of the possibilities of friendship has been important in a country where the last years have seen rather the reiteration of terror and animosity. Added to which, the Peace Movement has put some of its funds to very good use, by, for example, lending money to small companies that have been unable to qualify for loans from the government or banks. And it may be that one of the "solutions" for divided Ireland is the willingness to try all sorts of proposals, and to analyze and question all deeply ingrained attitudes and beliefs.

I walked across Peace Bridge and along the main shopping street of Drogheda. The fortifications, the cathedral, and the Boyne salmon curraghs (the last basketwork-and-skin boats in Ireland, I'd been told) would have to wait for another day. I was all tramped out. I inquired the whereabouts of the railway station, and, on learning that it was half a mile out of town, asked about buses to Dublin; they, it appeared, were not far down the hill, by the river. There, indeed, a bus was loading up. I had just time to buy some chocolate and apples from a nearby shop and to take a last look, as the queue of passengers moved forward into the bus, over the footpath railing at the Boyne.

ERIC NEWBY

The west, by bicycle: 1980s

**"NO RESORT LOOKS ITS BEST IN THE DEPTHS OF
WINTER . . . AND LISDOONVARNA, WITH THE EAST
WIND HURRYING CLOUDS OF FREEZING VAPOUR
THROUGH ITS STREETS, WAS NO EXCEPTION."**

Among Eric Newby's many books of travel, several—including A Short Walk
in the Hindu Kush, Slowly Down the Ganges, *and* The Big Red Train
Ride—*are well on their way to becoming classics. His colorful life includes
service in the Black Watch during World War II, three years as a prisoner of
war, a career in the garment and fashion business, and the position of travel
editor for the* Observer.

*In the mid-1980s, Newby and his wife, Wanda, decided to undertake a
bike tour of Ireland, citing all the usual reasons for bicycle touring: moving
relatively slowly, the opportunity to see the land and to meet people. For
reasons that remain unclear, however, they chose to begin their tour in December, not—meteorologically—the ideal time of year for outdoor activities
in Ireland.*

ROUND THE BURREN

THE FOLLOWING MORNING WE WOKE AROUND SEVEN-
thirty to find brilliant sunshine pouring in through the bedroom windows. Anxious to make the most of the day, we got dressed and went
downstairs to find no one about, except Gary, the grandson of the house,

a fount of energy and of information about everything connected with the property and its occupants.

"It'll be a good bit yet before you get a sniff of your breakfast," he put it, picturesquely; and indeed it was ten o'clock before it finally appeared, or indeed there were any signs of life at all. It had certainly been a working farm when we had stayed on it last, but now showed signs, in spite of a tractor parked outside, of being an erstwhile one.

Inside, the house was still much as we remembered it, almost twenty years previously, enlarged but still homely and welcoming. The most recent acquisition appeared to be a set of large armchairs, upholstered in delicate green velvet, which would make a happy stamping ground for dogs whose owners had forgotten to bring their dog baskets and for children equipped with bubble gum and muddy rubber boots. Mrs Griffey now appeared, after her late night out with Pan Am, and gave us a warm welcome. Her husband, whom we remembered well, had been dead for some years.

How did we come to stay in this remote, pleasant spot in the first place? Back in 1964 the Irish Tourist Board began to compile a list of farmhouses and other houses in rural situations whose owners were prepared to take in visitors, and at the same time provide a certain modicum of comfort for them, which might or might not be forthcoming if anyone knocked on a door at random and unannounced.

To encourage the farmers' wives and others on whom the brunt of the work would fall, and to give them confidence in their abilities and the opportunity to exchange ideas, courses were arranged in a large country house near Drogheda in County Louth, with the cooperation of the Irish Countrywomen's Association. The courses lasted a week, which was reckoned to be about as long as the average Irish farmer could survive with his family but without his wife. They were a great success: among other subjects they dealt with cookery, interior decoration and household management. The culmination was the answering of an impossibly difficult letter from an apprehensive potential guest. As a result of all this a tremendous esprit de corps was built up among the ladies who had been on what they proudly referred to as "The Course."

As a result, the number of recommended farmhouses rose rapidly. The only trouble was that the guests failed to materialize. Understandably, after the expenditure of so much effort and money by all concerned, depression reigned. Alarmed at their lack of success the Irish Tourist Board asked me, in my then capacity as Travel Editor of the *Observer,* if I would like to visit some of these houses and see for myself what I thought of them. They produced a complete list, helped me to whittle it down to about thirty, and then left Wanda and myself to get on with it in our own way.

It was an extraordinarily interesting experience. Some were working farms with eighteenth-or nineteenth-century buildings, such as the one we were now staying in. Some were not farms at all but quite large country houses, standing in their own parklands, and with or without farms and rambling outbuildings. Some were neat and modern bungalows, rather early prototypes of those we had passed the previous day on the way from Sixmilebridge to Quin, some with plastic gnomes in their front gardens, which were fashionable then. Indistinguishable from ordinary B and Bs, we gave them a miss.

All had one thing in common: they were very clean. Many had washbasins in the bedrooms; others had vast bathrooms with washbasins like fonts, and baths commodious enough to hold a baby whale. In one of them the lavatory was on a dais in a long, narrow chamber so far from the door that, installed on it, I was in a perpetual state of uncertainty as to whether or not I had locked myself in. Students of early plumbing, I noted, would find a visit to such houses worthwhile for these features alone.

Some of the most modest-looking houses concealed within them beautiful fireplaces and remarkable furniture, some of it very fine, some very eccentric, such as bog oak bookcases and extraordinary what-nots. The interior decorations were unpredictable. Some of the ladies, after being visited by a representative of the Tourist Board, panicked and replaced their nice old floral wallpaper with contemporary stuff covered with designs of Dubonnet bottles and skyscrapers, and coated the slender glazing bars of their eighteenth-century windows with a thick coating of bilious yellow paint.

In the course of our journey we played croquet and tennis, got stung by bees, struck up friendships with various donkeys, one of which was called Noël, and innumerable tame rabbits, puppies and dogs. Often there was riding, which we were no good at, and fishing, at which we were not much better but which we enjoyed.

And there was the food, which was always abundant, too abundant. I was anxious to do my best by the ladies but it was not always possible to be kind and at the same time truthful. When it came to bacon, ham, eggs and sausages, soda bread and butter, home-made cakes, jam and cream, everything was fine. Let them loose on a steak, a piece of meat to roast, or even on a cut of freshly landed salmon, and they would turn it into something that resembled an old tobacco pouch, which is, I am sorry to say, in my own judgment, the story of Irish cooking. In spite of this they did me the honour of referring to me very kindly in their brochure, by which time the scheme had become a resounding success.

What followed was what lawyers call a *dies non,* a day on which no legal business may be transacted (a prohibition which has the effect of making them bad-tempered), and what I call a no-day. In some mysterious way, although some parts of it were pleasant, altogether it added up to a day with something wrong with it, and it made us bad-tempered too.

After breakfast that almost qualified as lunch we set off in the brilliant sunshine on a circular tour of the middle part of the nameless plain which extends from the Shannon to the Bay of Galway, or as much of it as we could manage. No sooner had we got to the "soign" at the cross-roads than a downpour of tropical intensity began to fall on us, but by the time we had both struggled into our rainproof suits (the trousers, although made ample on purpose, are particularly difficult to get into when wearing climbing boots) it had stopped and Wanda insisted on taking her trousers off. Within a couple of minutes it began to rain all over again, so she put them back on. The trouble was it was unseasonably warm with it, and in the sort of conifer woods which should only be allowed in Scandinavia, Russia, Siberia, the Yukon and Canada the insects were beginning to tune up for what they apparently thought was the onset of summer. At this point I took my waterproof trousers off. All this effort to see Dromore, a castle of the O'Briens, in a region where castles, except as appendages to the land-scape, or notably eccentric, can easily become a bit of a drug on the market.

We pedalled on through these endless woods and past Ballyteige Lough and fissured beds of grey, karstic limestone, duplicates of similar beds in the Kras, in Wanda's native Slovenia, to which so many times in the course of our life together she had threatened to return, leaving me for ever. Then on past a couple more castles and across a snipe bog on a narrow causeway, with Ballylogan Lough beyond it, golden in the sun, and ahead the mountains of the Burren, stretching across the horizon as far as the eye could see like a fossilized tidal wave. Overhead, clouds with liver-covered undersides, pink on the upper parts where the sun caught them, drifted majestically eastwards. Here it was colder. I put on my trousers again.

In the middle of this bog, we met three young men gathered round a tractor who stopped talking when we passed them and didn't reply when we said it was a lovely day, something so unusual in our admittedly still limited experience of talking to the natives that it gave us both the creeps—another nail in the coffin of the no-day. Dogs to match them emerged from a farm on the far side of the bog and tried to take chunks out of our costly Gore-Tex trousers.

Beyond the bog was Coolbaun, a hamlet in which most of the houses were in ruins. In it the minute Coolbaun National School, built in 1895 and abandoned probably some time in the 1950s, still had a roof, and its front door was ajar. Inside there was a bedstead, a table with two unopened tins of soup on it, a raincoat hanging on a nail and a pair of rubber boots. It was like finding a footprint on a desert island. Hastily, we beat a retreat.

The first real village we came to was Tubber, a place a mile long with a pub at either end (neither of which had any food on offer), in fact so long that on my already battered half-inch map one part of it appeared to be in Clare, the other in Galway. The pub nearest to Galway was terribly dark, as if the proprietor catered only for spiritualists; the other had three customers all glued to the telly watching a steeplechase, none of whom spoke to us even between races. Meanwhile we drank, and ate soda bread and butter and Spam bought in the village shop. "Is this what they call 'Ireland of the Welcomes'?" Wanda asked with her mouth full. Another coffin nail.

The nicest looking places in Tubber were the post office and Derry-vowen Cottage, which was painted pink and which we passed on the way to look for something marked on the map as O'Donohue's Chair. What is or was O'Donohue's Chair? No guide book that I have ever subsequently been able to lay my hands on refers to it. Is it, or was it, some kind of mediaeval hot seat stoked with peat? Or a throne over an oubliette that precipitates anyone who sits on it into the bottomless rivers of the lime-stone karst? Whatever it is, if it isn't the product of some Irish Ordnance Surveyor's imagination, further inflamed by a Spam lunch in Tubber, it is situated in a thicket impenetrable to persons wearing Gore-Tex suits, and hemmed in by an equally impenetrable hedge reinforced with old cast iron bedsteads, worth a bomb to any tinker with a pair of hedging gloves.

After this, misled by two of the innocent-looking children in which Ireland abounds—leprechauns in disguise—we made an equally futile at-tempt to see at close quarters Fiddaun Castle, another spectacular tower house more or less in the same class as the unfindable Danganbrack. "Sure and you can't miss it. It's up there and away down," one of these little dumplings said, while the other sucked her thumb, directing us along a track that eventually became so deep in mire that it almost engulfed us. From the top of the hill they indicated, however, we did have a momentary view of the Castle and of Lough Fiddaun to the north, with three swans floating on it, before the whole scene was obliterated by a hellish hailstorm.

The next part of our tour was supposed to take in the monastic ruins of Kilmacduagh, over the frontier from Clare in Galway. However, one more December day was beginning to show signs of drawing to a close, and so we set off back in the direction of Crusheen. It really had been a no-day. Not only had we not seen the Kilmacduagh Monastery, but we had not seen, as we had planned to do, the early nineteenth-century castle built by John Nash for the first Viscount Gort on the shores of Lough Cutra, similar to the one he built at East Cowes on the Isle of Wight, now scandalously demolished; or the Punchbowl, a series of green, cup-shaped depressions in a wood of chestnut and beech trees where the River Beagh runs through a gorge 80 feet deep and disappears underground, perhaps to flow beneath O'Donohue's Chair; or Coole Park, the site of the great house which was the home of Augusta, Lady Gregory, whose distinguished guests, among them Shaw, O'Casey, W. B. and J. B. Yeats, AE (George) Russell and Katherine Tynan—a bit much to have all of them together, one would have thought—used a giant copper beech in the grounds as a visitors' book. To see all these would have taken days at the speed we were travelling. Well, we would never see them now.

So home to dinner, after which Tom took us to Saturday evening Mass in Crusheen. His mother was going the following morning, but if you attended Mass on Saturday evening you didn't have to do so again on Sunday. If asked, he said, we were to say that he too had been present. Meanwhile, he headed for Clark's, to which most of my own impulses were, I admit, to accompany him.

The church was almost full; and the subject of the sermon was Temperance, an obligatory one in Ireland for the First Sunday in Advent. This being Saturday, perhaps the priest was giving it a trial run. He certainly had a large enough audience for it. He was a formidable figure, this priest. Was he, I wondered, the same one we encountered in O'Hagerty's taking a dim view of the contents of a collection box? To me priests in mufti look entirely different when robed. Ireland, he said, was as boozy as Russia—a bit much, I thought, to accuse any country of being, with the possible exception of Finland. He then went on to castigate the licensed trade as spreaders of evil, something I have always fervently believed myself. If any

Guinnesses had been present they would have been writhing with embarrassment. "Just too awful," I could imagine them saying, but then one imagines that any Catholic Guinnesses, if such there be, give the First Sunday in Advent and the Saturday preceding it a miss. And there were prayers for the wives of drunks, but none for the drunks themselves, or the husbands of drunks, all of whom I would have thought were equally in need of them.

We were in bed by nine-thirty, slept nine hours and woke to another brilliant day, this time completely cloudless. After another good breakfast, we set off on what, for Wanda, proved to be a really awful four-mile uphill climb to Ballinruan, a lonely hamlet high on the slopes of the Slieve Aughty Mountains, where a Sunday meet of the County Clare Foxhounds was to take place. Its cottages were rendered in bright, primary colours, or finished in grey pebbledash—one house was the ghostly silver-grey of an old photographic plate. The church sparkled like icing sugar in the sunshine, and across the road from it, in Walsh's Lounge Bar and Food Store, four old men, all wearing caps, were drinking whiskey and stout and sharing a newspaper between them.

The view from the village was an amazing one. Behind it gentle slopes led up to a long, treeless ridge; immediately below it, and on either side, the ground was rougher, with outcrops of rock—a wilderness of gorse and heather interspersed with stunted, windswept trees. Out beyond this a vast landscape opened up: the level plain, part of which we had travelled through with so many setbacks the previous day. Its innumerable loughs, now a brilliant Mediterranean blue, blazed among green fields of irregular shape, bogs, woodlands and tracts of limestone, with here and there a white cottage or the tower of a castle rising among them.

And beyond all this, the far more immense bare limestone expanses of the Burren rose golden in the morning sunlight; Galway Bay could just be seen to the north-west; while to the south, beyond the Shannon, were the hills and mountains of County Limerick, their feet shrouded in a mist which gave an impression of almost tropical heat.

At twelve-thirty the hounds arrived in a big van, very well behaved, and soon more vans and horse boxes trundled up the hill, some drawn by Mercedes. Here, the hunt was more or less on the extreme limits of its territory. It normally hunted over stone walls on the west side of the County, and over banks and fly fences on the east and south. The rough country round us, on the other hand, might give shelter to hordes of hill foxes. Anyway, they were safe today. This was a drag hunt in which the hounds would follow an artificial scent.

By one o'clock those horses still in their boxes were becoming impatient, kicking the sides of them, and catching the air of excitement that was gradually gathering in the street outside. People were beginning to saddle up and mount now, especially the children, of whom there were quite a number. A big van with four horses in it arrived and one of their owners said to the driver, "It's a lovely day! Let's go and have a jar now in Walsh's." By now the bar was splitting at the seams.

This was not a smart hunt such as the County Galway, otherwise known as the Blazers, the County Limerick, the Kildare, or the Scarteen, otherwise the Black and Tans. It was not the sort of hunt that Empress Elizabeth of Austria, who loved hunting in Ireland more than anything else on earth and was so proud of her figure that she had herself sewn into her habit every hunting day, would have patronized. Most were in black jackets and velvet caps, some were in tweeds, others wore crash helmets, and one man with a craggy, early nineteenth-century face wore a bowler. One man in a tweed coat sounded suspiciously like a Frenchman, there was an elegant American girl in a tweed coat, and what looked like several members of the scrap metal business. A cosmopolitan lot.

The hounds were released; there were eight and a half couple of them, which is a hunter's way of saying seventeen. After a brief period in which they were allowed to savour delicious smells, one of the Joint Masters, who was wearing a green coat with red facings and black boots with brown tops, took them up the road to cries of what sounded like, "Ged in! Ged in!" and "Ollin! Ollin!" Then they were suddenly turned, and ran back down the street through a press of people and out through the village, down and over the flanks of Derryvoagh Hill and into the eye of the now declining sun. Soon they were lost to view to us and other followers, watching their progress from one of the rocks below the village.

"By God," someone said, "the next thing we'll be hearing of them they'll be in America."

I left Wanda to take the long downhill back to Crusheen and the farm, where Tom was very kindly waiting to take her to Ballyvaughan, on the shores of Galway Bay, where we were going to stay for a few days. Then I, too, zoomed downhill bound for the Monastery of Kilmacduagh, which we had failed to see the previous day. I was so exhilarated by the fast cooling air that I almost felt I was flying.

Six miles out as the crow flies from Ballinruan, I zoomed past the site of a ruined castle on the shores of Lough Bunny, then right, past a field in which a small boy was trying to catch a wild-looking horse and bridle it, the Burren blue-black against the setting sun, the plain close under it already in shadow, and on, having missed the road to Kilmacduagh, through the bare, limestone karst from which black and white cattle were somehow scratching a living, spotting an occasional small white farmhouse in what was effectively a limestone desert. Suddenly, there was the monastery, far off to the right across a wide expanse of limestone pavement riven with deep, parallel crevices that looked like an ice floe breaking up: a collection of silver-grey buildings with the last of the sunlight illuminating the conical cap of its enormously tall round tower—112 feet high and two feet out of the perpendicular. This was the monastery founded in the sixth century by Guaire Aidhneach, King of Connacht (I was now just in Galway and therefore in the old County of Connacht) for his kinsman St Colman Mac-duagh, on the very spot where the saint's girdle fell to the ground. The girdle was preserved in the monastery until the seventeenth century.

I pedalled on for another four or five miles through the bare limestone plain, the only visible living things in it now blackbirds and rooks. The last of the sun on this beautiful day was shining on the high, treeless tops of the Burren mountains, so convincingly sculpted by nature into the forms of prehistoric camps and forts that it was difficult to know whether I was looking at the work of nature or of man.

At the intersection of this loneliest of lonely roads with the main road, I nearly ran into the car in which Tom was taking Wanda and her bicycle to Ballyvaughan, together with Gary, the infant prodigy. A signpost still showed thirteen miles to Ballyvaughan and I cycled on, a bit tired, through a landscape by now an improbable shade of purple. I passed a wild-looking girl on a bicycle, and saw two young men in an enclosure full of rocks pushing them to one side with a bulldozer, the only way in the Burren, which is Ireland's largest rockery, in which you can ever create a field. Until the invention of the bulldozer the inhabitants of the Burren removed all the rocks by hand, either using them for building walls or forming great mounds with them, which are still to be seen. In those days it would have required the help of many people, possibly an entire community, to make a field; now most of those people are either dead or emigrated or both.

The road ran close under the Burren mountains now and along the side of Abbey Hill, which conceals within its folds the beautiful, pale, lichen-encrusted ruins of Corcomroe, a Cistercian abbey built by a king of Munster. High above it, on a saddle, are the three ruined twelfth-century churches of Oughtmama, all that remain of yet another monastery of St Colman Macduagh. To the right, fields of an almost impossible greenness ran down to the shores of Aughinish and Corranroo Bays, long, beautiful, secretive inlets from Galway Bay. Then a delicious descent to a little hamlet called Burren, beside a reedy pond. Then up and down again to Bell Harbour on Poulnaclough Bay, the water in it like steel, with the mountains black above it and above that cobalt clouds against an otherwise pale sky in which Venus was suspended. When it comes to thoroughly unnatural effects it is possible to equal Ireland, difficult to surpass it.* By the time I got to Ballyvaughan I had covered forty-five miles and it was dark.

LAND OF SAINTS AND HERMITS

THE WHITEWASHED COTTAGE WE WERE TO STAY IN (looking at it no one would have guessed that it was built with breeze blocks), at which Wanda had already arrived in Tom's car, with her bike strapped precariously on top, had a thatched roof and a green front door with a top and bottom part that could be opened separately so that if you opened the bottom and kept the top closed, or vice versa, you looked from the outside as if you had been sawn in half.

The ceiling of the principal living room went right up to the roof and was lined with pine. The floor was of big, olive-coloured grit flagstones from the Cliffs of Moher, and there was an open fireplace with a merry fire burning in it, fuelled by blocks of compressed peat. There was a large table which would have been ideal if I had actually been going to write a book instead of thinking about doing so, which I could do better in bed, and traditional chairs with corded backs and seats. To be authentic they should have been upholstered with plaited straw, but straw had apparently played hell with the guests' nylons.

The rugs on the floor, all made locally in County Cork, were of plaited

---

*I wondered what Evelyn Waugh would have thought of it. He had a nasty experience of an aesthetic sort, watching a sunset over Mount Etna. "Nothing I have ever seen in Art or Nature was quite so revolting," he wrote.

cotton which produced a patchwork effect, and there were oil lamps on the walls with metal reflectors behind the glass shades, but wired for electricity. A wooden staircase led to a room above with two beds in it, the equivalent of a mediaeval solar. Leading off the living room was a very well-fitted kitchen, and there were two more bedrooms on the ground floor: altogether, counting a sofa bed and a secret bed that emerged from a cupboard, there were eight, a lot of beds for the two of us. The rooms, primarily intended for the visiting Americans, could be made fantastically hot: they had under-floor heating, convectors, a portable fan heater upstairs, infra-red heating in the bathroom, plus the open fire. Gary was bowled over by all this. He was even more pleased with it than we were. "Never," he said, "in all my born days" had he seen anything like it.

"When I get married," he confided, "I'm going to bring my wife here for our honeymoon."

"How old did you say you are?"

"Eight."

"Tell me," I said, "is there any girl you really like?"

"There's one in First Grade. I like her."

"How old is she?"

"About six."

"But would you marry her?"

"I would not."

"Why wouldn't you?"

"Because she's an O'Hanrahan. You can't marry an O'Hanrahan in the parts we come from."

Later, after he had eaten three apples, a banana and a large plate of salted nuts and drunk three large bottles of Coke, left as a welcoming present by the proprietors (together with a bottle of gin for us), Wanda asked him if he spoke Gaelic.

"No way!" he said firmly.

"But I thought they taught you Gaelic in school."

"No, they only teach us Irish," he said.

After this we went to a pub where he ate all the nuts on sale there and drank three large orange juices.

Ballyvaughan is a small village and one-time fishing port. Until well into the twentieth century it imported Galway turf for fuel in sailing vessels called hookers—something which makes Americans when they read about them or see a rare survivor go off into peals of laughter—exporting in return grain, bacon and vegetables. Until the First World War and for some time after it there was a regular steamship service to and from Galway in the summer months.

There was not much of Ballyvaughan but what there was we liked: two streets of cottages and shops, one of them running along the shore with a pub restaurant at the western end, open most of the year, which served fish. In the other street there was the post office, Claire's Place, a restaurant now closed for the winter, a couple of miniature supermarkets and two of the four pubs. Of the pubs, O'Lochlan's was of the sort that in Ireland was already a rarity: dark in the daytime behind the engraved glass panel in its front door; at night still dark but glittering with light reflected off a hundred bottles and off the glasses and the brass handles of the black wooden drawers stacked one above the other like those in an old-fashioned apothecary's shop. Behind the bar was a turf-burning stove which kept whoever was serving warm.

The equivalent of Piccadilly Circus in Ballyvaughan was where the roads from Galway and Ennis met; the equivalent of Eros was a monument-cum-fountain equipped with faucets in the shape of lions' heads erected in 1874 by Colonel the Hon. Charles Wynn, son of the Baron Newborough, who at that time was Lieutenant of Clare. Behind the village the steep, terrace limestone slopes of a mountain called Cappanawalla, which means "the stony tillage lands," rose 1,200 feet above it.

Our cottage stood in a meadow in which cows grazed and overlooked one of the two jetties in the harbour which, apart from one fishing boat, was empty. Beyond it was the expanse of Galway Bay and beyond that again, the best part of forty miles away and barely visible, the Twelve Bens of Connemara, at the feet of which, completely invisible, was the Lough of Ballynahinch. This still held the record for having more rainy days in a year than anywhere else in the United Kingdom and Ireland—309 in 1923—and was somewhere that I felt we should do our best to avoid.

The next morning was cold, cloudless and brilliant with an east wind, and with what looked like a vaporous wig of mist on the mountains above. While we were eating rashers and eggs we received a visit from an elderly man wearing a long black overcoat and cap to match who offered to sell me a walking stick he had made—one of the last things I really needed, travelling on a bicycle. "I'll bring you a pail of mussels this evening, if you like," he said, negotiations having fallen flat on the blackthorn. The whole coast was one vast mussel bed where it wasn't knee-deep in oysters, but as the tide was going to be in for most of the morning and it was also very cold, it seemed sensible to let him gather them for us.

Our destination that day was Lisdoonvarna: " 'Ireland's Premier Spa,' "
I read to Wanda in excerpts from Murray's *Guide* (1912) over breakfast.
" 'Known since the middle of the 18th century . . . situated at a height of
about 600 feet above the sea . . . its climate excellent . . . the rainfall never
rests long upon the limestone surface. The air, heated by contact with the
bare sun-scorched rock of the surrounding district, is tempered by the
moisture-laden breezes from the Atlantic three or four miles distant, and
is singularly bracing and refreshing owing to the elevation.' " It also spoke
of spring water conveyed to the Spa House in glass-lined pipes, thus en-
suring its absolute purity. More modern authorities spoke of a rock which
discharged both sulphurous and chalybeate (iron) waters, rich in iodine
and with radioactive properties, within a few inches of one another, the
former to the accompaniment of disgusting smells.

The town was equally famous as a centre of match-making. Farmers
in search of a wife were in the habit of coming to stay in the hotels in
Lisdoonvarna in September after the harvest; there they found unmarried
girls intent on finding themselves a husband. The arrangements were con-
ducted by professional match-makers, in much the same way as sales of
cattle and horses are still concluded by professional go-betweens at Irish
fairs. This marriage market is still said to thrive, although to a lesser extent
than previously. Professional match-makers, masseurs and masseuses,
sauna baths, sun lounges, springs, bath and pump houses, cafés, dances
and pitch-and-putt competitions, all taking place on a bed of warm limestone—it all sounded a bit like Firbank's *Valmouth*. With the addition of
a black masseuse it could have been.

"Did you know," I said to Wanda, "that according to the *Illustrated
Ireland Guide* 'its sulphur water contains more than *three times as much
hydrogen sulphide gas as the spring at Harrogate*'?" To which she uttered an
exclamation, the equivalent to "Cor!" in Slovene, which I knew from a
lifetime of experience meant that she wasn't in the slightest bit interested.

We set off in the sunshine in the general direction of Lisdoonvarna,
this being the nearest thing attainable in this part of the world to going
from A to B by the shortest route. All was well at first. The road ran through
meadowy country interspersed with hazel thickets, "fairly level but with a
strong upward tendency" as the Cyclists' Touring Club *Irish Road Book* of
1899 rather charmingly put it, en route passing close to the Ailwee Cave,
closed for two million years until its discovery in 1976, and now closed
again because it was winter.

At this point the "strong upward tendency" began in earnest—a succession of steep hairpin bends up Corkscrew Hill. At the same moment the sun vanished and we found ourselves in what seemed another world, enveloped in dense, freezing cloud which whirled across our path borne on the wings of the east wind and reduced visibility to not more than twenty yards. In spite of all this, once she had stopped changing up instead of down, and falling off when her Wild Cat subsequently ground to a halt, Wanda very nearly succeeded in winding her way to the top, and only had to get off and push the last fifty yards or so.

From the top, if it really was the top, there was nothing to be seen of the famous view over the Burren to Galway extolled by every guide book. Indeed it was difficult to imagine that on every side now, enveloped in what resembled cold gruel, were a host of natural wonders, some of them so extraordinary as to be positive freaks of nature: what are known—how uncouth the terms used by geologists sometimes sound—as clints, grykes, glacial erratics, and potholes and turloughs (what Wanda knew in her own country as *doline* and *polje*).* Here, the last glaciation took place only about fifteen thousand years ago, making this one of the most recently created landscapes in the whole of Europe. What we were riding over now was hollow; beneath us rivers ran, quite literally, through caverns measureless to man down to a sunless sea.

It was equally difficult to imagine that hidden among these arid rocks, nurtured by often infinitesimal quantities of soil, something like a thousand different species of flowering plants and ferns were waiting for spring and summer to appear, at this meeting place of the northern (Hibernian) flora, brought here in the form of seeds during the last glaciation, and the southern (Lusitanian) flora, which had previously flourished there and continued to do so. Among them were creamy white mountain avens, spring gentians, hoary rockroses, fairy foxgloves, limestone bugles, various violas, greater butterwort, ladies' bedstraw, bloody cranesbill, seven types of orchid and broomrape.

About the only thing currently visible on the High Burren and able to continue growing there throughout the winter was grass. The limestone retains the heat of the summer sun, turning it into a species of giant storage heater and making the hilltops and the higher valleys much warmer than

---

Clints are the blocks of limestone paving. *Grykes* are the open crevices in the clints. *Glacial erratics* are rounded blocks of limestone, some of them very large, deposited in the wake of an ice-cap. *Turloughs* are grassy hollows, sometimes created by the collapse of the roof of an underground cavern and often filled with water from below (*doline* being the smaller ones and *polje* the larger ones, the biggest of which is the Carran Depression in the eastern Burren).

the low-lying country below. For this reason the cattle are left high up to forage for themselves from November to late April and are then taken down to the lowlands for the summer months, the reverse of what happens in most other places. Herds of wild goats perform an invaluable function in keeping down the hazel scrub which rampages in summer.

At this moment, as if wanting to prove to us that they really were living up there, a herd of Burren cattle came sweeping round a corner towards us in close formation, steaming and smoking and completely filling the road, and looking to me very much as the Sixth Iniskilling Dragoons must have done to the French infantry when they were being charged by them on the afternoon of Waterloo. We did what the French would probably have done had it been available: took refuge in the entrance to the Corkscrew Hill National School, built in 1885 and now abandoned, while they thundered past it and on down the hill, apparently unaccompanied, in the direction of Ballyvaughan. Where did they think they were going? To the seaside for a dip?

For the next seven miles the only living soul we met with was a young Australian girl, sopping wet, padding gamely through the muck in her training shoes with a big, rectangular pack on her back the size of a large suitcase. She was a bit pissed off, she said, having been given a lift from Ballyvaughan post office by this old guy who said he was bound for Lisdoonvarna, but then changed his mind and dumped her at a fork in the road, with a six mile hike to go. Unfortunately, there was nothing we could do to help her. "You should have brought a tandem," Wanda said to me. "Then you could have given people lifts."

Lisdoonvarna, when we reached it after a gratifying downhill run, came as a bit of a shock after all the build-up it had been given by the various guide books I had consulted. In fact I wondered if some of the authors could have been there at all. Admittedly, no resort looks its best in the depths of winter—that is, unless it is a winter resort—and Lisdoonvarna, with the east wind hurrying clouds of freezing vapour through its streets, was no exception. I tried to imagine excited farmers with straw in their hair, accompanied by their match-makers, pursuing unmarried ladies through its streets and down the corridors of the Spa Hotel, which had broken windows and looked as if it would never open again, but failed.

Now, in December, it seemed a decrepit and terribly melancholy place, like the film set of a shanty town. Its hotels, souvenir and fast-food shops had closed down in October and would not re-open until March, some of the hotels not until June. But would what the Irish call the crack—what others call the action—start even then? Rough-looking youths stood on the pavement outside a betting shop, one of the few places open at this hour. The wind struck deep into the marrow of one's bones; in spite of being dressed in almost everything we possessed we were frozen, and took refuge in a pub, the Roadside Tavern, run by two nice ladies, the walls of which were covered with picture postcards. They stoked up the fire for us and we gradually thawed out in front of it while we ate ham and soda bread and I drank the health of the priest at Crusheen in Guinness, while Wanda drank port.

Too fed up with Lisdoonvarna to seek out the various sources of its waters, smelly or otherwise, and the various pleasure domes in which customers were given the treatment, we quitted Ireland's premier spa, and set off westwards up yet another cloud-bound road. Suddenly, as suddenly as we had left it at the foot of Corkscrew Hill, we emerged into dazzling sunshine on the western escarpment of the Burren. Below us it dropped away to a rocky coast on which, in spite of the wind being offshore, heavy seas were breaking, throwing up clouds of glittering spray. Just to look at the shimmering sea after the miseries that had gone before gave us a new lease of life—and we roared down towards it via a series of marvellous bends with the Aztec Super brake blocks on our Shimano Deore XT cantilever brakes screaming (a malfunction) on the Rigida 25/32 rims (for the benefit of those who like a bit of technical detail from time to time), past the ivy-clad tower of Ballynalackan Castle, a fifteenth-century seaside house of the O'Briens perched on a steep-sided rock high above the road, with a magical-looking wood at the foot of it, and on down to the limestone shore.

We were at Poulsallagh, nothing more than a name on the map. Somewhere out to sea to the west, hidden from view in their own mantle of cloud, were the Aran Islands. To the right dense yellow vapour flooded out over the Burren escarpment as if in some First World War gas attack, over a wilderness of stone, interspersed with walled fields and extravagantly painted cottages, their windows ablaze in the light of the declining sun, while high above, squadrons of clouds like pink Zeppelins were moving out over the Atlantic. Here, the haystacks were mound-shaped and covered with nets against the wind, or shaped like upturned boats, hidden behind the drystone walls. To the left, between the road and the sea, were endless expanses of limestone on which the glacial erratics rested, like huge marbles, rolled down from the screes above. Here and there a walled field gave shelter to giant sheep solidly munching the green grass. At Fanore, six miles north of Poulsallagh, we spoke with the first human being we had set eyes on since leaving Lisdoonvarna. He was a small man of about fifty, who was working in a plot beside the road. He had a large head, abundant flaxen hair with a touch of red in it, of the kind that always looks as if it has just been combed, a high forehead and very clear blue eyes like T. E. Lawrence. And he had a voice of indescribable sadness, like the wind keening about a house. After exchanging remarks about the grandness of the day I asked him about the absence of people.

"Ah," he said, "there are more than meet the eye; but most of them are old, and are by their fires, out of the wind. You can see the smoke of them."

"But what about the school? It's quite new. There must be some children," Wanda said.

"There are children," he said, "but when those children leave the school, their parents will leave Fanore, and the school will be closed. They are the last ones."

"But what will happen to their houses? Surely they won't be allowed to fall into ruin?"

"The old ones will be allowed to fall into ruin. The newer ones will be holiday houses. Many of them are already."

"And what will you yourself do when the old people are dead, and the children and the younger people have all gone away?"

"I will give an eye to the holiday houses," he said.

As if to prove his words, a few miles beyond the lighthouse at Black Head we came to a ruined village. Close under the mountain the cottages, or what remained of them, were hidden under trees, moss-grown and covered with ivy, some of it as thick as a man's arm. It was difficult to believe that people had lived in it during our own lifetime. The ruins might have been prehistoric. Down by the water below the road there was a slip, and smooth rocks with numbers and a white cross painted on them. A little further on was a ruined tower with a spiral staircase leading to the upper part, turrets and machicolations. Nearby was an overgrown, roofless church with gravestones in the churchyard that were simply unworked limestone rocks from the Burren; and Tobar Cornan, a holy well with a little Gothic well house, where a human cranium used to serve as a drinking cup until a priest put a stop to the practice.

By the time we got back to Ballyvaughan, having covered a modest thirty-six miles, the wind had dropped completely and in the afterglow the still waters of the bay were the colour of the lees of wine. Thirty thousand feet or so overhead jets bound for the New World drew dead straight orange crayon lines across a sky still blue and filled with sunshine. There was a tremendous silence, broken only by the whistling of the oystercatchers and the gulls foraging in the shallows. The inhabitants of Ballyvaughan were eating their evening meals and watching telly. If we hadn't seen them going about their business we might have thought they were dead. Looking at what they presumably subsisted on lining the shelves of the supermarkets, it was surprising that they weren't. Did they really eat prepacked mashed potato and tins of meat and fish that could easily have doubled as pet food with a change of labels, on which the additives listed by law read like the formula for something nasty?

Famished, we took the edge off our appetites with scones and raspberry jam—the mussels had arrived and stood outside the door in a sack, a huge quantity for £2, enough for two copious meals. Then we went to O'Lochlan's and sat in its magical interior, a bit like an Aladdin's Cave with newspapers on sale. Mr O'Lochlan, it transpired, was a member of one of the historically most powerful septs in this part of the Burren. They had owned the great hazel thickets which still grow at the foot of Cappanawalla, and the great stone fort of Cahermore up among the limestone pavements, and the Ballylaban Ringfort, down near sea level, which contained a single homestead and which, with its earth walls crowned with trees and its moat filled with water, is as romantic as the limestone forts are austere.*

Mr O'Lochlan spoke of the past: Ballyvaughan was not a particularly old village, he said; it really dated from the early nineteenth century when a quay was built for the fishing boats. In 1829 or thereabouts this collapsed and a new one had to be built by the Fishery Board. Gleninagh ("Glen of the Ivy"), the deserted village that looked old enough to be a candidate for carbon dating, apparently still had eighty-five men fishing from it in the mid-1930s, using *currachs*, rowing boats consisting of a light framework of laths covered with tarred canvas. In the summer they fished for mackerel, three men to a boat using long lines; in winter, two men to a boat to fish for lobsters, while others dug for worm bait.

*According to Bord Failte's *Ireland Guide,* 1982, there are between 30,000 and 40,000 of these ringforts in Ireland North and South. No one can be sure who lived in most of them, or when: the hundred or more sites excavated in Ireland shows evidence of occupation as early as the Bronze Age and as late as the Middle Ages, the most populous period being the early Christian one.

I told him what the man at Fanore had said about the school and he had more to add. "From Loop Head," he said (which is the extreme south-westerly point of County Clare at the mouth of the Shannon), "very soon you will be able to draw a line five miles inland from the sea, to the west of which, apart from people involved with holidaymakers, there will be no local inhabitants at all." In the fifteen years from 1963 to 1978 it was thought that two-thirds of the population of marriageable age had emigrated. This tale of woe even extended to the holiday cottage in which we were staying, and its neighbours. They had been built to encourage tourists to visit the area, with money put up by the local inhabitants (who held 60 per cent of the shares), the Irish and regional tourist boards and the local councils; even some local schoolchildren held shares by proxy. But so far none of the locals had had any return on the money they had invested some sixteen years ago, and this had created a great deal of ill-feeling.

After this we went home to a delicious dinner: mussels, very good sausages, runner beans and soda bread, then walked in the rain to the end of the jetty, where the steamers from Galway used to be met by horse cars to convey their passengers to Lisdoonvarna. They had to walk up Cork-screw Hill en route.

That night our dream lives were preoccupied with the Royal Family. I dreamt of King George VI. Both of us were in naval uniform, the King like a brother. As we walked together up Old Bond Street I asked him to have dinner with me, but he said, "Come and eat with us," which turned out to be a group of about a dozen at a table under a sort of *porte-cochère,* rather draughty and with no view. At the same time Wanda was dreaming of walking in a garden with the Queen Mum, who was very friendly. Wanda's father featured too, having trouble with a member of the SS. He hit on the idea of having a Mass said, and that, as Wanda said, speaking of the SS man, "put an end to him!"

It was in fact fortunate that in my dream encounter with King George VI he had not accepted my invitation to lunch. We were now in dire straits for money and I would have looked pretty silly having to borrow from him, especially as English kings and queens never have a bean on them. There was no bank in Ballyvaughan, and my Coutts cheques and various credit cards were treated with extreme suspicion. Finally, Mr O'Lochlan offered to help, provided we could work out what the exchange rate was.

We had intended to seek out together a very esoteric remain known as St Colman Macduagh's Hermitage which was hidden away at the foot of a mountain called Slieve Carron, but by the time we had negotiated this deal and arranged for a local farmer to give us a lift to Ennistymon the following morning, it was nearly midday. The weather was beautiful, so we decided to go to a place called New Quay on the south side of Galway Bay where we could buy oysters.

New Quay was nice. There was a pub, a house or two, the sheds of the oyster company, and a jetty which the tide was doing its best to sweep away as it came ripping into Aughinish Bay at a terrific rate, covering the dark, whale-like rocks and penetrating into other bays within, Corranroo and Cloosh. On the promontory beyond it was a Martello tower, built to discourage Napoleon from landing an army there. The sea and sky were bright blue and everything else bright green, except for the grey stone walls and buildings, and the rocks along the foreshore.

Three men were working outside one of the sheds, selecting oysters and putting them in sacks. At their destination they would sell for £1 a piece, one of them said. "Not for the likes of us," said another. But here Wanda bought a dozen for £3.50 and they threw in two more for luck. Even here, almost at the source, lobsters were £6.50 a pound. Leaving Wanda to ride back to Ballyvaughan, where she had an appointment with a fisherman who might be able to sell her a lobster on more advantageous terms, I set off on my bike for the Hermitage, which was some eight miles off on the east side of the Burren in a wilderness called Keelhilla approached by the first section of a hellish hill, six miles long.

The Hermitage was hidden from view in the hazel thickets at the foot of the cliffs of Slieve Carron, across about three quarters of a mile of limestone pavements full of parallel and apparently bottomless grykes, so I hid my bike in one of the thickets that bordered the road and set off on foot. Some of these grykes had had slender pillars of limestone inserted in them at intervals, as if to mark the way to the Hermitage, but after a bit they came to an abrupt end in the middle of one of the pavements.

I passed a small cairn and came to a drystone wall, beyond which was the wood. Like so many other old walls in the Burren, this one was a work of art. It had been built with an infinite expenditure of effort, using thin flakes of stone set vertically instead of being laid horizontally. I climbed over the wall and went into the hazel wood. It was a magical place. Everything in it—the boles and branches of the trees and the boulders among which they had forced themselves up—was covered in a thick growth of moss, dappled by the last of the sun. The only sounds were those of the wind sighing in the trees and of running water.

By absolute chance I had arrived at the Hermitage. It was in a clearing, among the trees and the boulders. There were the remains of a minute church with a white cross in front of it, and two stone platforms one above the other. The water I had heard came from a spring in the cliff and ran down into a sort of box-shaped stone cistern in a hollow. Above the church in the face of the cliff was a cave, big enough for two people to take shelter in, though in considerable discomfort.

It was in this remote place that St Colman spent seven years of his life with only one companion, sleeping in the cave. Before retiring to his hermitage he founded churches on Inishmore, one of the Aran Islands, and the monastery at Oughtmama. It was for the saint and his companion, slowly dying of starvation in Keelhilla, that angels spirited away the Easter banquet of King Guaire Aidhneach, founder of the Monastery of Kilmacduagh. And it was across the water-eroded beds of karstic limestone known thereafter as Bothar na Mias (the Road of the Dishes) that the King and his followers pursued their banquet, all the way from his castle on the shores of Kinvarra Bay. Here, a *patron*, or parish celebration, is still held on the last Sunday in July.

It was now three-thirty and the sun had left the Hermitage. I retraced my steps across the Road of Dishes, found my bike and continued to climb the awful hill, to a ridge between the Doomore and Gortaclare mountains, where the road, to my horror, began an endless descent into the great, verdant Carran Depression through the whole of which I was pursued by a really savage dog. From it I climbed onto a great, grass-grown plateau that looked like a golden sea in the light of the setting sun, then down again and up again, the map giving no inkling of these awful undulations. On the way I passed a wonder called the Caherconnell Ringfort, but was dissuaded from visiting it by yet more wretched dogs which came streaming out of the neighbouring farmyard to attack me at a time when any reasonable dog would have been watching television. By now the sun had gone from the Burren and its expanses were, apart from the dogs, silent and mysterious. By now I was fed up with hills and was grateful for what followed, a wonderful, five-mile descent from the escarpment all the way to Ballyvaughan in the dusk, to find that Wanda's lobster catch had failed to appear. It didn't matter—we still had half a sack of mussels to get through.

The following morning, with fully laden bikes, we embarked in the farmer's Volkswagen van, bound for the town of Ennistymon. The sky was overcast, the wind now westerly and it looked like rain. In other words it was a grand, Irish day.

There was another passenger—a friend of the farmer's who was, he alleged, "just going up the road a bit to take a look at his sheep." In fact his "up the road a bit" comprehended almost the entire journey. He settled himself firmly in front next to the driver, so that I found myself, having paid for the van hire, crouching in the back holding up the bikes and trying to avoid being stabbed to death by brake levers. As a result, I saw nothing and he got an additional eyeful of the scenery he saw every day of his life.

The driver, who was short on conversation, was in a hurry to return to his fields, so I failed to get him to stop at Cahermacnaghten, yet another ringfort with immensely thick, high walls which stands high up in the Burren, five miles from anywhere. All I saw of it as we roared past was a gateway, a white farmhouse and a grove of windswept trees. Just as with Caherconnel, I had never had any luck with Cahermacnaghten. The last time I had tried to visit it I had been beset by a tribe of tinkers and their flaxen-haired children who were camped with their carts close by, and had literally had to run for it.

It was a pity. Cahermacnaghten was more than just another Irish fort. From mediaeval times until late in the seventeenth century it housed within its walls a law school run by the O'Davorens, known as O'Davoren's Town, as unlikely a situation for a law school as the middle of Dartmoor. It was here that Dubhaltach MacFirbhisigh studied, the distinguished compiler of *Craobha Coibhneasa Agas Geuga Geneluigh Gacha Gabhala dar Ghabh Ere*, otherwise *The Branches of Kindred and Genealogical Boughs of Every Plantation in Ireland*, which he completed in 1650. His family were the hereditary historians of the O'Dubha chieftains in what is now County Sligo; it was they who performed their initiation ceremonies by raising a wand above their heads and pronouncing their names. They were also responsible for an extensive collection of historical, genealogical and ecclesiastical writings in both prose and verse. After the dispossession of the O'Dubha in 1643, soon after the commencement of the Eleven Years War, Duald MacFirbis (as he was known) continued to work in Galway and later in Dublin. At the age of eighty-five he was stabbed to death in Doonflin, County Sligo, by a drunken Englishman who had been attempting to kiss a shop assistant and regarded MacFirbis as a witness to this shameful act who would be better dead.

At Kilfenora, a village about five miles short of Ennistymon, the driver stopped to fill up with petrol and we made a desperate dash for liberty, taking refuge in the Cathedral of St Fachtna, or what was left of it. In the chancel was a pair of tomb effigies: one of a bishop, said to be the saint, who founded a monastery and what became a famous theological school at Rosscarbery in County Cork, in the act of blessing all and sundry; another of a weird figure with an immensely elongated neck and head, apparently wearing a kilt. "You know who the Bishop of Kilfenora is?" the man at the pump said when we got back to the van (the whole visit had taken just over two and a half minutes—see Ireland and die of heart failure). "The Pope." I'm still pondering this gnomic utterance. There was also a Burren Museum which I would have liked to have seen, but it was shut for the winter. All the shops were shut, too, and apart from the pump attendant there was not a living soul in sight.

By the time we got to Ennistymon and had been deposited at the top of its main street by a large Gothic Protestant church with an octagonal tower and a handless clock face, it was eleven o'clock and the first shops up at this end of the town were beginning to show tentative signs of opening, like early daffs. We put up at Mrs Mary MacMahon's B and B which was situated in Church Street above a pub of the same name, of which her husband was the proprietor.

We were given a room next door to the TV Room on one of the upper floors. The TV Room was unlike any other TV Room I had ever seen. It was full of religious images executed in plaster-of-Paris, all balanced on a rather precarious-looking what-not, and on a facing wall was a large oleograph of Jesus with his heart exposed and flames coming out of it, surrounded by a circle of thorns with a cross on top. There was a lot of blood about. Religion was everywhere. Even the lavatory had the Virgin and Child of Kiev balanced on top of a spare roll of paper on top of the cistern, which made use of the arrangements extremely hazardous. In fact as soon as I set eyes on it I began to rehearse how I would break the bad news to Mrs MacMahon, who was religious and nice with it, that her picture of the Virgin and Child of Kiev had just fallen down the hole, and please where could I find the nearest religious picture repository for a replacement.

Fifteen years ago Ennistymon, which at the last count had 1,013 inhabitants, had forty-eight pubs. According to Mr MacMahon, when they were last counted, a few days previously, there were twenty-one—out of a total in Southern Ireland of 10,000 (in 1985 there were 11,000) and numbers were closing every day. The town is also famous for some of the best shop fronts in Ireland. On the left-hand side going down Church Street was C. O'Lochlen, Draper and Outfitter, with what was probably Mr O'Lochlen transferring some of his stock on to the pavement outside, having come to the risky conclusion that it wouldn't rain today. Down from him was Keane's, Saddler and Harnessmaker; a butcher who described himself as a victualler; Nagles, a pub that was also, conveniently, an undertakers; and on down the road, in a little square, Killybegs Fresh Fish Stall was doing a brisk trade.

On the right hand was C. Hayes, with a perfect austere pub façade, bottles of Paddy in the window and a dim interior full of drink, which never opened during our stay and now probably never would; the premises of Twoney Walsh, Outfitter and Draper, in which Wanda brought a two-yard skirt length of expensive-looking tweed for £9. Next to that, more or less in the same line of business, was T. J. Mahoney, who emerged from his premises to present her with a card on which was printed "*Very Special Value—T. J. Mahoney.*" The drapers in Ennistymon carried stocks that would have made department store buyers curl up and die from apprehension. One of them, in a town with a thousand inhabitants, stocked five sixty-yard lengths of identical material all in the same colour. Others had enormous stocks of shoes and clothing in outmoded styles and would, I felt, if asked, produce a pair of 1950s winkle-pickers at the drop of a hat.

And so on, past more pubs, open and shut, for sale and haunted, than I had physique to visit and record, among them E. Burke, with another beautiful façade. Then Considine and Sons, a pub now a gift shop;* Hyne's, mysterious dark façade, closed, use unknown; Vaughan's, black-shuttered and said by an old man with a bike to be haunted, also use unknown; Nagle's Bar, "Traditional Musicians Welcome," closed and for sale; McGrotty's Medical Hall, open; O'Leary's Undertakers with the smallest possible window filled with artificial flowers. Here at the far end of Church Street, perched on a hill, were the remains of a church and a cemetery.

Downstream of the bridge, which spanned the falls of the Cullenagh river, was the old Falls Hotel standing among magnificent trees on the right bank, and on the left bank was a betting shop housed in a black, corrugated iron shed, and an old house with windows painted so that it looked as if people were looking out of them. The Catholic Church, built in 1953, was much more attractive than any other modern Catholic Church we had so far seen in Ireland.

Photographs taken in the 1930s showed Church Street on market day filled with horse-drawn vehicles and people. It was a bit different now.

*A pub in Ireland can sell anything. In Kinvarra, where King Guaire Aidhneach had his Easter Banquet spirited away by angels, there was a dark, cavernous pub that had its windows dressed with cans of weedkiller.

DAVID A. WILSON

Donegal, Sligo, Irish music, and a bicycle: 1990s

" 'MMMM, THIS BLACK THING TASTES GOOD,' I SAID,
SLICING OFF ANOTHER STICKY PIECE OF PUDDING
WITH MY FORK. 'WHAT IS IT?' 'THERE ARE SOME
QUESTIONS THAT ARE BEST LEFT UNASKED,' SHE
REPLIED."

David A. Wilson teaches Celtic studies at St. Michael's College, University of Toronto. He has written on Irish history and made radio documentaries on Ireland for the Canadian Broadcasting Corporation.

He also likes bicycling and playing the Irish tin whistle. Combining his interests, he undertook a bicycle trip around most of the coast of Ireland, including Northern Ireland, searching out pubs where local musicians get together for traditional Irish music and offering to join in. Some of his adventures in pubs turned into misadventures, requiring on short notice a hasty exit via the narrow window in the men's toilet.

Wilson was born in Northern Ireland but left while still a child. His parents were liberal-minded Protestants. During World War II, his father had quickly learned that the Catholic chaplains slipped a few extra cigarettes to Catholic soldiers. Wilson Sr. instantly decided that he was Catholic too and that the ancient Northern Ireland conflict between Catholic and Protestant was not for him.

In the selection that follows, Wilson travels through Donegal, the northernmost county of the Republic of Ireland, and an Irish-speaking Gaeltacht like Connemara, through Glencolumbkille, Killybegs, Donegal town, Ballyshannon, the seaside resort town of Bundoran, and on to Sligo.

I know the Donegal road, and it's provided some of my most vivid images of Ireland. I can still see the old men, in their shapeless black suits, lined up against the white wall of the small church in Glencolumbkille on a rainy Sunday morning. And in Bundoran: pink-cheeked Irish children on holiday, bundled up in their macs and caps against the icy wind from the North Atlantic—and licking ice-cream cones.

THE NEXT DAY, I MOVED FROM THE HILLS OF DONEGAL to the Glenveagh Mountains, where saw-toothed ridges cut into the sky and green fields merge into rust-brown uplands. Travelling through the moors, you can see the flat-topped Muckish Mountain ahead, a pig's back stretched out against the horizon. A bend in the road suddenly brings Errigal Mountain into view, like a giant cockleshell turned on its side. There is a strong wind at my back, sweeping across the grass; the road runs by mountain streams fed by mountain lakes. This is a vast, howling, elemental landscape, which seems to go on forever; there's a turf-cutter in the distance and no one else for miles. It is now twelve o'clock; back in Toronto, it's seven in the morning. The cars are beginning to crowd together on the 401, packing the Don Valley Parkway bumper to bumper, filling the city with a clinging cloud of exhaust fumes, crawling towards a lake where fish cannot live and people cannot swim. But here, the air is pure and the streams are clear; here, there is only the sky, the mountains, and the soft purples and greens of the moorlands.

Driven by the wind, I pass beside the scree-scraped slopes of Errigal, above the long lake that reaches towards Gweedore and the Donegal coast, where Irish is still spoken as a first language. Narrow roads take you from Bunbeg, through the Rosses, to Burtonport and Dungloe, towns that are feeding on tourism. Country-and-western music is everywhere, piped through speaker systems, played on the radio, coming out of pub windows. It's far and away the most popular form of music in Ireland, with disco as a close second; traditional music is much further down on the list, even here in the heart of the *Gaeltacht*, the Irish-speaking area. Sometimes you encounter bizarre musical mutations—country-and-western songs in the Irish language, country-and-Gaelic if you like, complete with all the subtleties of the genre, such as key changes. Most of the music, though, is in English; you get the latest hits from Nashville, alongside home-grown Irish songs performed by home-grown heroes like Big Tom.

The American connection isn't really as surprising as it seems; some of the classic country and cowboy songs simply grafted American words onto Irish tunes. "The Streets of Laredo" originated as a song about the Irish patriot Robert Emmet, and, from the other side of the political divide, "The Old Orange Flute" provided the melody for "Sweet Betsy from Pike." More recently, Bob Dylan extended the process into the world of folk music; songs like "Restless Farewell" and "I Pity the Poor Immigrant" are reworkings of Irish ballads. There are other similarities; in both the Irish singing tradition and American bluegrass music, the emotional range encompasses no more than two degrees, whether the subject of the song is a train wreck, finding Jesus, or strolling down the road and having a smoke. In many ways, the west of Ireland is closer to the United States than it is to Britain; the next parish, as they say in Donegal, is New York.

Still, there are differences as well. American country songs are mainly about hurtin', lyin' and cheatin', with layer upon layer of Pain and Self-Pity, like a wedding cake when the cream has gone sour. In one verse alone your dog can be run over by a pick-up truck and your mother can be called home to heaven, while your chick-babe leaves you for another man, the finance company repossesses your home, and your last whiskey bottle is drained of everything but your own tears. Generally speaking, the songs fall neatly into three categories: Before Divorce, Divorce, and After Divorce. But they don't allow divorces in Ireland, on the assumption that comely lads and lasses live happily ever after, or at least that "till death do us part" really means what it says, for better or for worse. Country-and-Irish music is thick with the syrup of sentimentality, with countless variations on the "we still love each other after all these years" theme. There's also a strong streak of nostalgia, of the kind that can romanticize "Dublin in the rare ould times" while conveniently forgetting that the city used to have the highest death rate in the Western world.

In Bunbeg, Burtonport, and Dungloe, I inquire at local pubs about traditional music sessions, and am told that "it's too early in the season," that "there's not enough demand for it around here," that "the musicians charge too much money nowadays." It's seen as a commodity for tourist consumption, rather than something that people play for its own sake, for their own enjoyment.

The demands of tourism contradict the spirit of sessions. Tourism requires order and regularity—times posted on a pub window: "Traditional Music Tonight, Starts 9.30"—so that people know where and when things are happening. But sessions are by their very nature unpredictable and spontaneous; they seem to spring up out of nothing. When traditional musicians get together for a session, the last thing they think about is the time of the year, or the state of popular demand—although a few free pints would go down well enough. They are there to share a few tunes, a few laughs, and a few drinks; they are there, in short, for the fun of it. And if other people share the enjoyment, well, so much the better.

There's no doubt that tourism has helped the west; it brings in the money, provides hard-up musicians with something approaching an income, and breathes new life into the area each summer. But, in line with the Heisenberg Principle, the act of observing changes the character of that which is being observed. Once a session is performed for an audience, it is no longer a session. You wind up with a commercial version of a communal activity, and you separate the music from the culture that sustained it in the first place. It's part of a wider problem: tourists are attracted to the area largely because of its hospitality, its slower pace of life, its distinct culture; but tourism is subtly altering the culture by turning it into a marketable commodity, by making it self-conscious. At its best, tourism promises to reinvigorate the region, to give it new energy and life. At its worst, it threatens to turn the west of Ireland into the largest Theme Park in Europe.

Leaving Dungloe on a bright, breezy morning, I cycled by bogland and mountain, past the beautiful Gweebarra Bay where the sandbars almost touch each other. At a village shop near Glenties, I met up with an old fellow whose molecules were mixed into an equally old bicycle; he was dressed in a faded brown suit and looked as if he'd stepped out of a sepia photograph. He inspected my bike carefully and closely, with its wide tires and its multiplicity of gears, and marvelled at the technology. I inspected his bike equally closely, with its heavy black frame and its complete absence of gears, and marvelled at his stamina. "You'd need to be in pretty good shape to handle these hills on that bike," I said. "Well now," he replied, "I'm getting on a bit, you know, so I have to walk up a few of them." And off he went, bolt upright on the saddle, cycling steadily up a hill that would break your back, waving goodbye without turning around, and probably smiling to himself as well.

At Ardara, I wandered into Peter Oliver's pub, where the walls were lined with pictures of fiddle and accordion players, a photographic history of traditional music in Donegal. Beside the pictures there were ancient, played-out instruments, leaning on the wall like old bicycles. The session scene was stronger in those days, Peter said, the days when the fiddle and accordion players had packed the pub with music, and the instruments on the wall had been full of life. "All the older players are dying off," he said, "and the younger ones are emigrating."

Still, I wonder if he is right; young people have been leaving the west for generations now, but the tradition lives on. In Ardara, Peter and his daughter kept it going themselves and started a session of their own later in the evening. He played the accordion, guitar, and mandolin (not at the same time, though; he was talented, but not that talented), and his daughter played a sweet-sounding fiddle, while the barman poured some of the smoothest Guinness in the world. It may not have been as lively or as brilliant as the sessions of old, but it was good enough; the fellows looking out from the photographs would have waved and maybe smiled as well.

The next morning began slowly; I sat outside on a park bench, recovering from the revelry, steeling myself for the ride up the Glengesh Pass to Glencolumbkille. It was one of those rare, clear, cloudless days that sharpens the senses and brings everything into focus. Just south of Ardara, I turned west along the mountain road towards Glengesh, tracing the course of a rapid-flowing river that coiled its way back to the coast, past sheep's wool fleeced on barbed-wire fences, the hares running through the fields, and the butterflies dancing lightly over wild flowers. A gentle, rolling slip-jig called "The Butterfly" floats into mind; it could have been composed on a day like this, in a place like this, so well does it fit the feeling. And then, gradually at first, the road begins to steepen, and turns into a heart-pounding haul of increasingly impossible spirals, drawing all the energy out of you, until it finally flattens out. I stop, rest, and play the whistle to the valley below, to the winding road turning in tune with the stream, and to the distant Blue Stack mountains in the east, at one with the music, at peace with the rhythms of the day.

A few miles later, Glencolumbkille comes into view, below the mountains and before the sea, the place where Saint Columbkille once travelled as he sought to graft Christianity onto the culture of the Celts. There are ancient, mysterious pagan monuments here, standing upright like Christianized phalluses beside the Anglican church. And beyond them lies Glen Bay, sheltered by high cliffs splintering into the sea, where the sunset suffuses the sky with a soft-red haze and the waves pulse in like the heartbeat of another world. I walk back to the village, under constellations of stars, points of light from pre-Christian times, and hear drifts of music coming out of distant windows. But this time I do not go in; I want this space, this openness, this place where past meets present, land meets sea, earth meets sky, in the vast silence of the night.

And then, sometime in the darkness, the silence shuddered with the wind, clouds closed in from the north, and the sound of rain began to rap on sleeping houses. It angled in on the streets, black and cold, drenching early risers, driving people back into doorways. As the morning went on, the wind became stronger and the angle became sharper—unrelenting, unremitting rain, looking like it would fall forever. Cycle through Ireland for any length of time and it will eventually catch up with you. Liquid sunshine, they call it, coming down in buckets from the sky. Local weather forecasters will share their wisdom with you: "If you can see Aran Island, it's going to rain," a Donegal man told me in Burtonport; "if you can't see it, it's already raining." "It only rained twice last summer," someone else said; "the first time from May to June, and second time from July to August."

What to do? I'd like to wait until it passes, but then I could be caught in Glencolumbkille for the rest of my life. So, I resigned myself to getting soaked, and set off reluctantly up the ferocious hill that takes you out of town towards Carrick and Kilcar. I try to be philosophical about the situation: You need the rain to appreciate the sun; you need the hills to appreciate the plains; you need the wind against you to appreciate the wind behind you. But I don't mean a word of it. All I want is a dry day, a road that always runs downhill, and a breeze that is permanently at my back.

Away to my left, high on Glen Head, the distant ruin of a grey tower looks out over a grey sea; it is eventually enveloped by black Atlantic clouds and blotted out by the rain. Like the sea mirroring the sky, the moorland changes colours with the weather and becomes as dark and green and heavy as a sponge, while the mountains appear and disappear through a thick wet mist. A few miles out of Glencolumbkille, I turned off the road towards blustery Bunglass, up the steep and narrow track to Slieve League, where cloud-shrouded cliffs sheer down two thousand feet to the sea. A bitter north wind sweeps showers of rain across the hills, saturating everything in its path. A soft day, as they say; a soft day with a fresh breeze; I wouldn't like to experience a hard one.

By the time I reached Killybegs, I was ready for a drink. The pub was full of fishermen, who'd just come back from ten days of hauling cod and whitefish out at Rockall; it was only lunchtime, and they were already three sheets to the wind. "I hate fishing," said one of them. "I'm a trained carpenter, not a bloody fisherman. Is there any work for carpenters in Canada?" Tommy, his mate, hated fishing as well; he was heading out that night on the Galway bus, looking for some other kind of work, any other kind of work, anywhere but here. He put his arm around me, eyes half-closed from alcohol, and smiled blearily: "You're a bollix." And then, for emphasis: "You're a right fuckin' bollix." I'm not entirely sure, but I'd like to think that this was a friendly greeting; generally speaking, it's when people stop insulting you that you have to start worrying. Holding me in a half-embrace, he began to sing "Fiddler's Green," a song about the final resting place of fishermen:

> Now, Fiddler's Green is a place I've heard tell
> Where fishermen go if they don't go to hell
> Where the weather is fair and the dolphins do play
> And the cold coasts of Greenland are far far away.

And then the chorus:

> Wrap me up in my oilskins and jumper
> No more to the docks I'll repair
> Just tell my old shipmates I'm taking a trip mates
> And I'll see you one day in Fiddler's Green.

I try to join in, but have trouble following him through a maze of modulations; he changed key more times than a country-and-western singer on speed. "You're a right fuckin' bollix of a bollix," he said. I began to worry that I would be trapped there for the rest of the day, held in a permanent arm-lock, singing off-key, swopping prolix bollix stories until the Galway bus carried him away. There was only one thing for it—the old Escape through the Men's Toilet trick. Out the side-door, into the yellowing yard where rain and urine and beer swilled together in the gutter, over the wall, down the alley, and back on the bicycle. Hou-fuckin'-dini would have been proud.

I cycled on to Mountcharles and Donegal Town, before turning southwards to Ballyshannon, home of one of Ireland's finest folk festivals. After checking into a bed-and-breakfast on the Bundoran road, proprietor Mary Doherty, I walked back to the town centre and took in the scene. There was a marquee at the bottom of the hill, holding the formal concerts, where the folkies happily listened to the music in a kind of self-created cigarette-free zone. And there were pubs all around, holding the informal sessions, where everyone else in town laughed and drank and happily choked themselves to death on nicotine. A Canadian friend once suggested to me that someone should organize package Smokers' Tours to Ireland, as one of the last places in the Western world where you can inhale with impunity—Guilt-Free Smoking in the *Gaeltacht,* Nicotine Nirvana Holidays Incorporated, Toxic Tours of Tipperary.

I started with the clear air of the concerts and the brilliant music of groups like Donegal's own Altan, with their dazzling array of fast-paced jigs and reels. Some people complain that they are too fast, and that the music gets lost in the rush. But their playing explodes with energy, and they combine speed with subtlety; it's the kind of thing you could listen to all day and all night. There were singer-songwriters as well, people like Kieran Goss with his mischievous smile and deadpan humour, singing Tom Paxton's folk classic "The Last Thing on my Mind," and adding an extra verse for good measure:

> *Well I met this young lass at a folk club*
> *Like you do, like you do.*
> *So I bought her a drink and we chatted*
> *Wouldn't you, wouldn't you.*
> *And then after the show, she invited me home*
> *Said our interests were one of a kind.*
> *Then she played me every record that Tom Paxton ever made*
> *And you know that was the Last Thing on my Mind.*

Dolores Keane and John Faulkner were up next, two of the finest traditional singers around, giving us songs like "The Bonny Light Horseman," about a woman lamenting the death of her lover in the Napoleonic Wars, and "Sliabh Gallion Braes," about emigration from Ireland—death and emigration being compulsory themes in all traditional song sets. Dolores was mildly inebriated, and so were we; the chorus of "Sliabh Gallion Braes" was loud enough to lift the marquee off its moorings.

And then we came down with a bump. The last singer of the night was so bad that I have blocked his name from memory; he was a very large man with a very loud voice, a veteran from the folk boom of the early sixties. When he sang raucous, rambunctious drinking songs, full of the obligatory whack-fol-de-daddio's and too-ra-loo-ra-loo's, he was just about listenable, if you liked that sort of thing. It was when he attempted anything remotely requiring the least shred of sensitivity that he went beyond the boundaries of the bearable. He took the most beautiful songs in the world and pounded them into the ground; the effect was like a pneumatic drill splitting through granite, or dental work without the anaesthetic. After ten minutes, I ran for cover, only to find that there was no escape. "I wish I was in Carrickfergus," he growled. So did I. But his voice was so loud that you could probably hear him there as well. It carried southwards to the moors of Cornwall, northwards to the shores of Scotland, and eastwards to the Accursed Ridge of Leinster. It pierced the hearts of all the people and terrified them, so that men lost their colour and strength, women suffered miscarriages, children lost their senses, and animals and trees and soil and water all became barren. "I heard him play at the Oxford Folk Festival last May Eve," whispered a Welshman next to me, as if afraid of being overheard; "if you want my opinion, he should be locked in a stone chest and buried in the deepest fuckin' pit you can find."

By the time he had stopped singing, I was back at the bed-and-breakfast, dazed and disoriented, tired and emotional, cold and hungry. Mrs Doherty, proprietor, was nothing if not flexible; knowing that sessions and concerts tend to run late, she offered a twenty-four-hour breakfast service to cover all eventualities, from German tourists who insisted on getting up at the ungodly hour of six in the morning, to mad Irish musicians who were straggling in as the Germans were checking out. "Have you eaten tonight?" she inquired as I came in, still trying to scrape the gravel out of my ears. I shook my head; she ordered me to sit down. And fifteen minutes later, a classic Irish breakfast, the Ulster Fry, suddenly appeared on my plate—fried eggs, fried sausages, fried tomatoes, fried bacon, fried soda farls, fried potato bread, fried potatoes, fried white pudding, and fried black pudding, a veritable festival of cholesterol.

I was light-headed from drink and ready to eat a year's supply of food. "Mmmm, this black thing tastes good," I said, slicing off another sticky piece of pudding with my fork. "What is it?" "There are some questions that are best left unasked," she replied, smiling to herself and shovelling another round of hot, well-greased sausages onto my plate. But I knew what it was—black pudding, a euphemistic expression for congealed animal blood served up in layers of lard. In the cold light of sobriety, I wouldn't go within thirty-three miles of the stuff.

That night, I had strange dreams; I was running naked in a field of lettuces, feasting on salads, rolling in alfalfa sprouts and water cress. When I awoke, a thick sediment of sludge lay heavily on my stomach. I heaved myself into the shower and imagined that I could still smell the stuff frying in the pan. Slowly, horribly, it dawned on me that the aroma was all too real; down in the breakfast room, Mrs Doherty was serving up more of the same to unsuspecting guests. And, in true Donegal fashion, she was singing country-and-western songs while she was doing it: "My tears have washed I love you from the blackboard of my heart," "I'm Riding High in the Saddle Again," "Home, Home on the Range." She brought me a plate of Fried Everything, topped off with three extra black puddings. "Since you liked them so much last night," she said happily, "I thought I'd treat you to some more this morning."

Out on the streets, Ballyshannon was blinking back into life. Halfway up the hill, the Old Rope String Band began an open-air show of slapstick session music. They would start their pieces with slightly excessive seriousness, and then break into cheerfully controlled chaos—juggling the instruments with one other, performing acrobatic routines, making human pyramids, and never so much as missing a beat. In one song, "Fire, Fire, Fire," the fiddle player not only imitated the sound of a passing fire engine, but also threw in the Doppler effect for good measure. At the time, he was balancing one leg on the head of the guitarist, who was himself standing on the shoulders on the banjo player. "Now that," said the man next to me, "that is a rare and a wonderful talent."

Down the road, on the rooftop terrace at Sweeny's pub, a bagpiper was tearing through "The Atholl Highlanders," one of the most energetic jigs ever written; pints of lager were accumulating around him in appreciation. At the Thatch pub on top of the hill, three sessions were going on at once. In the back yard, fiddle players and accordionists straddled beer barrels and played themselves into a stupor. Upstairs, in the loft, a dozen people sat around a large table and exchanged songs and stories, from blues to folk. And in the main room, bunged with people, there was a boisterous, irreverent, outrageous Silly Song session, with rock or rap versions of done-to-death Irish songs—the Beachboys singing "The Wild Rover," or Ice-T attacking "Whiskey in the Jar."

At one point, an American in the bar called for silence, asked everyone to be serious for a moment, and began to talk with great earnestness: "I'd feel very proud and privileged if you'd all allow me to sing a song which meant a great deal to me when I was growing up in Chicago, and which still means a great deal to me to this day. It's a song about an island which all of us here know only too well—an island beset by conflict, but an island that is also famous for its sense of humour; an island that is loved by the people who live on it, but an island that cannot hold them, an island that they feel compelled to leave. Please raise your voices with me." And with that, he launched straight into the theme tune of "Gilligan's Island."

By late afternoon, the sessions had spilled out onto the streets. Outside the Thatch, I played a set of polkas on the whistle for dancers who wove around each other like the whorls of a Celtic tapestry. Then it was down the hill, past fried food stands, along a trail of old chip-bags to the marquee for the evening's concert—a night of Celtic-jazz-rock music by Davy Spillane, one of Ireland's best uilleann pipers, and his band. It's a powerful combination; Celtic music and jazz are both characterized by improvisations around set themes, and deep inside many traditional Irish players there's a rock 'n' roll star trying to get out. The effect was electric; the uilleann pipes and the saxophone canoned off each other, and then wheeled and dipped and soared together in flight, while the lead guitarist drilled out deep-purple riffs, and the bass and the drums split the sky, There was a wildness in the air, a wildness that drove us to our feet and carried us through the night. The dancers were silhouetted against the stage, puppets wired to vibrating strings of sound, shaken into life by music that thundered around us like an Atlantic storm blowing into Ballyshannon.

Exhausted and exhilarated, I walked slowly back along the road to Bundoran and the bed-and-breakfast. As I opened the door, Mrs Doherty appeared out of nowhere, wearing her dressing gown, wielding a spatula. "Have you eaten tonight?" she inquired as I came in. "Yes; yes I have thanks," I replied, lying through my teeth. My face turned as green as a plate of fried tomatoes; I made up my mind to be on my way first thing in the morning.

THE TAR ROAD TO SLIGO

IRELAND IS THE ONLY COUNTRY IN THE WORLD WHERE you can experience all four seasons in one day. I left Ballyshannon in a soft rain, cycling by the flowers of spring; by the time I reached Bundoran, it was the first month in summer, a day of sunny banks and green meadows. But later in the afternoon, dark clouds began to gather over autumn woods; and when I rounded Benbulben mountain on the tar road to Sligo, it was the twenty-eighth of January and the hailstones were bouncing off my helmet.

Sligo is the home of Ireland's most precious poet, the remote, the spiritual, the ideal William Butler Yeats; the land of the gaels and the land of the gales. Coldness was cast on me as I passed by the Yeats Grave, just before the Yeats Tavern (Food Served Daily) where the tour buses were pulling in. A few miles down the road, you could arise and go to Inishfree Motor Factors Company Ltd, and drive your car with peace of mind. Fingers were fumbling in the greasy till. Romantic Ireland was dead and gone; commercial Ireland was making a killing.

If you want to understand a people properly, someone once said, you should take their dominant self-image and turn it upside down. Canadians think of themselves as a northern people and identify with the wilderness; the vast majority of them actually live as far south as they can get and enjoy the most centrally heated civilization on Earth. The English think of themselves as a garden people and identify with images of rustic beauty; in fact, they are crowded into cities and live in one of the most industrialized countries in the world. The Irish think of themselves as a nation of romantics and identify with their Great Writers; but cycling through Sligo, you get the sense that they are really one of the most practical people on the planet, ready and willing to milk their cultural heritage for all it's worth, and maybe a bit more besides.

The wind seared across the mountains, sweeping the storms in from the sea; you'd have a hard time finding anything romantic about this weather, at any rate. Somewhere near Drumcliff, I passed a farmgate with a forbidding sign: BEWARE OF BULL. There wasn't a bull or a cow or a pig or a sheep within nine miles. BEWARE OF BULL—the sign should be posted at every airport and seaport in the country, as a Government Health Warning to all unsuspecting visitors, alerting them to the perils awaiting an Innocent in Ireland. "There are two rules for survival here," a Canadian friend told me the day after she'd landed in the country. "First, don't believe anything that anyone tells you. And second, don't take anything or anyone seriously." She knew what she was talking about. The sense of humour consists not so much in the telling of jokes as in the making of stories; the laughter lies not in the punchline, but in the process. And the essential equipment is a very, very long piece of string.

It happened to me shortly after I arrived in Whitehead, when two characters whom I shall call Bernie and Harry (since those are their real names) took me for a ride in the country. We passed a field in the distance where there were buses, cars, flags, and streamers. "What's going on there?" I asked. Mistake number one: you think you are asking a simple question, but you are really setting yourself up. Bernie and Harry turned it into a kind of play:

HARRY: Well now, I wouldn't like to say . . . I'm not sure, really . . . I wouldn't know.

BERNIE: Best say nothing. (To me): Best forget that you ever saw anything. Fine day, now, isn't it?

DUPE: No, no, tell me. What's happening?

[Long silence]

HARRY: Well, all right then. It's a Dog Worry, if you must know.

DUPE: What on earth is a Dog Worry?

BERNIE: (Incredulously) You don't know what a Dog Worry is? D'ye hear that, Harry; this fellow doesn't know what a Dog Worry is?

HARRY: Hmmmmph. Calls himself a student of Irish history, and he's never heard of a Dog Worry. What's the world coming to? Talk about declining standards of education.

BERNIE: Well, now. Have you ever heard of a cock fight?

DUPE: (Nods).

HARRY: Well that's something, I suppose. At least he's heard of a cock fight; there's hope for the world yet.

BERNIE: A Dog Worry is just like a cock fight, except they use dogs. They dig a large pit, and throw in a couple of dogs. After the animals have a good set-to, they pull out the winner and bury the loser.

HARRY: Alsatians, usually, although pit-bulls are becoming more popular these days.

BERNIE: It's an old Irish custom. I'm very surprised you've not heard of it.

Now, I'm an unreconstructed dog lover—as they very well knew—and although I have sometimes been theoretically seduced by notions of cultural relativism, I find that I don't hold with them at all when I actually meet them in practice. "I don't care whether it's an old Irish custom or not," I said; "it's disgusting and it ought to be stopped." Time to slacken the line a little; the more string, the more fun.

HARRY: Ah, well, I'm not saying it's good and I'm not saying it's bad, but still it is illegal nowadays, you know.

BERNIE: It is, it is. But that doesn't stop people from doing it all the same. Just look at all the coaches and cars out there.

HARRY: True enough. It's even rumoured that you'll find the occa-
         sional priest going along as well. Sure it's part of our heri-
         tage, whatever way you look at it.
DUPE: (With excessive moral indignation) Taking two dogs, throw-
         ing them in a pit, making them tear each other to pieces,
         and burying the loser—that's absolutely barbaric.
BERNIE: Not at all, not at all. In a barbaric country they would bury
         the winner as well.

They never did tell me what was actually happening; it was only the next day I learned from a friend that I had really witnessed the crowds gathering for a Gaelic football game. I would like to think that he was telling the truth.

BEWARE OF BULL—on the streets, in a car, in a pub (especially in a pub), in a restaurant, in a house; take nothing on trust, and assume that you are surrounded by congenital liars. I once heard a story about a woman who invited two people who did not know each other for dinner. Beforehand, she told the first guest that the other was a bit deaf, so he'd have to speak loudly and distinctly; then she told the other that the first was a bit odd. And with that, she sat down to enjoy the meal. BEWARE OF BULL—anywhere, everywhere, except in an empty field just outside Drumcliff.

And so to Sligo, to dry out and rest before a weekend of music. I walked along the riverbank and watched the swans resting on the water. Suddenly, there was a sharp sound like wire whipping through the air; turning around, I saw a swan in full flight, with its straight, outstretched neck and its powerful wings, heading for home. Further up the river, I came to the Blue Lagoon Discotheque, where Sharon Shannon and her band would be giving a concert later in the evening. Sharon Shannon has two things going for her: she is an excellent accordionist and she has the nicest smile in Ireland. The combination is unbeatable.

In the bar, before the show, she was sitting with her band around the TV set, watching the opening ceremonies of the Eurovision Song Contest. One of the best things about living in North America is that you don't get this thing inflicted on you every year—a succession of Ever-So-Nice singers from every country in Europe, singing a succession of Instantly Forgettable songs, followed by a succession of Politically Dubious votes to decide the winner. The definition of Europe is expansive enough to include countries as far apart as Iceland and Israel; this makes for a rather long evening. And because a successful song must appeal to all cultures and all languages, the principle of the Lowest Common Denominator kicks in with mathematical certainty. You want to write a song that will appeal equally to people who speak Turkish, Hungarian, and Danish? Cut down on words from your own language—after all, these are necessarily exclusive—and replace them with lively banging noises that everyone can enjoy and understand. Fill your song with lots of bings and bongs and billy-billy bongs, make sure that your singer smiles a lot, and pray that the English judges haven't got it in for you. The total effect can only be described as mind-numbing; you'd be better off trapped in an elevator with the Singing Nun. Ireland has been winning the Eurovision Song Contest a lot recently, almost as a matter of routine—a trend that I, for one, find distinctly disturbing.

But the music in the Blue Lagoon was much more exciting, vibrant, and creative than anything coming out of the contest; there was nothing remotely bland, boring, or banal about the Sharon Shannon band. She sat on a chair in the middle of the stage, moving from light-hearted waltzes to high-speed reels, deep inside her own world, thoroughly immersed in the music, swaying and smiling with the currents that flow beneath it all. Accordion, fiddle, guitar, and bass were rushing and running together, thundering into a breakneck finish with "The Foxhunter's Reel," leaving us shouting and stamping for more. Meanwhile, in the other room, Ireland was busy winning yet another Eurovision Song Contest.

There is never any shortage of traditional music in Sligo. The next day, I made my way down to TD's pub for the regular Sunday afternoon After-Mass Session. At first, I thought I was in the wrong place. The sound system was playing the kind of country-and-Irish music that would make you cringe—"That's the Way the Girls Are from Texas," sung in a fake American accent that actually outstripped the fake Irish accents you hear in America: Sligo's Revenge for those old Bing Crosby movies, with all their begorrah's and top o' the mornin's.

But then the sound system was shut off, and three fellows started up on piano and fiddle and accordion. Before you knew it, the man at the next table moved to the centre of the floor and began a dazzling display of dancing, arms straight, legs flying, feet beating out syncopated rhythms to the reels. And when he'd finished, another man from another table got up and tried to outdance him, amid shouts and cheers of encouragement. For the next half hour or so, just about every able-bodied male in the pub got up to dance, while I hid in the corner behind the Sunday paper, for safety's sake.

An uilleann piper, another accordionist, and a guitarist settled themselves around the musicians' table and took the session into high gear. "What's that tune called?" someone asked after a particularly lively set of reels. Now one thing you can be sure of about session musicians is that they never know the names of the tunes they're playing; it's almost a point of honour with them not to know. But that never stops them from making up answers on the spot, in much the same way that someone who hasn't a clue about the location of the pub you're trying to find won't shrink from giving you directions anyway. "That was 'The Sow's Lament over the Empty Trough,' " said the piper. "Not at all," replied the fiddler; "it was 'My Mother Drowned in the Holy Water at Lourdes.' " B E W A R E   O F   B U L L   flashed in imaginary neon through my mind.

But it's true that the same tune can have a dozen different names, just as the same name can have a dozen different tunes. A jig like "The Black Rogue" has, appropriately enough, an assortment of aliases: "Come under My Plaiddie," " 'Tis a Bit of a Thing," "The Irish Lass," "Nature and Melody," "Johnny McGill," "Michael Malloy," and "Tom Linton," to name but a few. And there are at least six different pieces that go under the name of "The Lark on the Strand." Some of the names are so bizarre that they're in no need of a little bull to help them along: "Johnny with the Queer Thing," "The Gudgeon of Maurice's Car," or "Wallop the Spot," not to mention "Cock Up Your Beaver," about which no questions should be asked.

Traditional music is nothing if not fluid; particular tunes will be popular for a while, fade into obscurity, and re-surface some time in the future. To survive in sessions, you have to be able to learn tunes quickly. You could tape a session, spend the following year learning all the pieces, and find when you returned that the musicians had moved on to a completely different repertoire; it's hard on beginners, but it keeps the music fresh.

On occasions, the music will flow back into itself and form cyclical patterns through the streams. A friend of mine once taped a reel from the fiddle playing of Paddy Glackin during a late-night kitchen hooley. He took the tape home, learnt the tune, and incorporated it into his repertoire. Not knowing its name, in the true traditional manner, he called it "Paddy Glackin's Reel." More than ten years later, he found himself playing once again in a session with the Man Himself; fortified with alcohol, he started into the reel, expecting Paddy to join in. But Paddy just sat there, listening closely, and nodding approvingly. "That's a fine tune," he said when it was over. "Where did you pick that one up?" And by way of thanks, my friend taught it back to Paddy.

After "The Sow's Lament over the Empty Trough," the session at TD's ran towards Holy Hour, when the pubs are supposed to close for an afternoon break. The musicians finished up in an unorthodox way; they broke into a kind of free-form Celtic-Chaos meltdown, full of clashing keys and discords, with each player trying to be more outrageous than the other. "That was called 'A Clatter of Shite,' " said the guitarist when it was over, giving birth to yet another new title. But it's hard to close a pub in the middle of the day, and things weren't quite over yet. An old fellow commandeered the fiddle and began to play The Greatest Hits of Vera Lynn— "We'll Meet Again," "The White Cliffs of Dover," you name it. He was in his element; there was no stopping him. Realizing this, and acting on the principle that if you can't beat them you might as well join them, the guitarist started to accompany him with beautiful, haunting jazz chords. When the fiddler had finally exhausted his repertoire of Vera Lynn tunes, he suddenly broke into a foot-stomping version of "The Irish Washerwoman," and then just as suddenly stopped. "There's nothing more I can do with it," he said, as he handed the fiddle back to its owner. He drained his glass, said goodbye, and wandered out the door.

The streets of Sligo were full of life; there were face painters and clowns and acrobats and magicians, drawing circles of people around them. Half-way up the hill, there was a marvellous man dressed in bright sunshine yellow, top hat over grey hair, sitting behind a bright red row of wooden dancing puppets. He played a cymbal with one foot, and with the other tapped on a board that set the puppets in motion; this was street entertainment straight from the nineteenth century, and it was still pulling in the crowds. It was as if he had stepped out of a song, a song about the Liverpool puppeteer Seth Davey, who had delighted thousands of kids outside Paddy's Market back in the 1890s:

> He sat on the corner of Bevington Bush,
> 'stride of an old packing case,
> And the dolls on the end of the plank
>   went dancing,
>   as he crooned with a smile on
>   his face:

Come day, go day, wish in me
heart for Sunday,
Drinking buttermilk all the
week, whiskey on a Sunday. *

And from time to time, you could catch him taking a surreptitious swig from the mickey of whiskey that was concealed in his coat pocket.

In the evening, I made my way to McLynn's pub, tucked away on a side street, for one more Sligo session, before moving on to Mayo. Donal McLynn, the owner, was in the back room, playing the guitar with a couple of friends and singing a wide range of contemporary folksongs; soft voices filled the room for the chorus of "Caledonia," Dougie McLean's lovesong to Scotland, and for American tunes like "Boulder to Birmingham." Everyone was welcome to join in, or to take the lead for a while. An American with a hammer dulcimer played a delicate, lilting version of "The Butterfly" slipjig, bringing memories into this crowded room of the open spaces and soft air of the Glengesh Pass. And then, a well-dressed man who looked vaguely familiar, someone you might have seen on TV, was invited to sing. He was introduced as Joe Hunt, back in Sligo after making his seventh record, en route from Las Vegas to the Talk of the Town in Palma. He had a voice like a night-club singer, smooth as treacle, an Irish Willie Nelson. Like the other floor singers, he was given the regular two songs; in his case, "You Were Always on my Mind" and "For the Good Times." He certainly would not have looked or sounded out of place in Las Vegas or in Parma. But, as always, BEWARE OF BULL.

*"Whiskey on a Sunday" (Seth Davey) (The Puppet Song). Words and music by Glyn Hughes. © Copyright 1967 (renewed) TRO Essex Music Ltd., London, England. TRO—Essex Music, Inc., New York controls all publication rights for the U.S.A. and Canada. Used by permission.

DAVID W. McFADDEN

Galway and Claddagh, Clifden and Connemara, and Yeats's grave, in Morton's footsteps: 1990s

"ALL THE LITTLE IRISH COTTAGES THAT WOULD HAVE BEEN HERE IN MORTON'S DAY HAD DISAPPEARED, LEAVING ONLY MODERN LITTLE REDBRICK HOUSES, WITH ALUMINUM FRONT DOORS, AMONG THE STRANGELY PATTERNED NETWORKS OF ANCIENT WALLS."

Among Canadian author David W. McFadden's dozen books are A Trip Around Lake Huron, A Trip Around Lake Erie, *and* A Trip Around Lake Ontario. *He's an engaging traveling companion.*

His plan, recounted in An Innocent in Ireland, *was to walk in the footsteps of H. V. Morton. Though not uncritical of Morton, he admits to being a fan; he also admits to having read none of Morton's dozens of books other than* In Search of Ireland.

"My plan," he writes, "was to follow Morton's route through Ireland, to match my perceptions with his, and to try to determine how things had changed since his visit, and how things had remained the same. In retrospect I'm amazed at how many of the traditional values noted by Morton (not necessarily with his approval) were intact—the tradition of tremendous hospitality, the tradition of great seriousness and great levity, the tradition of great conversation, the tradition of the Irish as a race of poets, an oasis of benign lunacy in an ugly world."

McFadden's traveling companion in Ireland is Lourdes Brasil, a Spanish chambermaid working in his Dublin hotel, twenty-five years old, a published poet in a small way in her native Spain, who has a month off that corresponds with his travels, and who insists—insists!—that he let her accompany him.

The selection that follows covers much the same ground as that in the selection by Morton himself.

LOURDES HAD A STRONG SPANISH ACCENT, BUT HAD also been developing an idiomatic Irish way of putting things. "They dress well, the Irish," she observed. "They have very nice suits." She'd been flipping through my heavily marked copy of Morton on the way across the country, and, after reading his rhapsodic descriptions of Galway, she found the place a bit disappointing.

"Galway's not as beautiful as Morton claims," she said.

She said she had read Morton's book on Spain, and it wasn't to her taste. She figured the art of being a tourist was to dress and act in such a way that no one would immediately peg you as a tourist. If you looked like a tourist, she declared, people would shy away from you. Tourists made people nervous. You have to look a bit mysterious and intriguing if you want to meet the natives. Tourists are so boring. They buzz into town and immediately want to see what you've never bothered going to see all the years you've lived there. Tourists are stupid, because they have the effron-tery to make the locals feel stupid. Tourists tend to look as if they're holding their breath all the time. And they tend to have what the Irish call "Saxon smiles" on their faces—the forced smile as deadly weapon.

"Look, everybody hates tourists," she said. "That's the bottom line. They're a nuisance, they have prejudices, they don't do their homework, they don't read up on the place. And they ask stupid questions, and when you start to answer them they don't listen, they fade out."

"Glad we're not like that."

Galway was a mini-version of Cork, vaguely Italian in look, with lots of fine stone walls, iron gates, courtyards, old pubs, bridges, seafood places, hotels, sea air. Mrs. Quilty of the Mullet Bottom Hotel, when we booked in, saw a sympathetic look in my eye or Lourdes's eye and started com-plaining that she wouldn't wish this job on anyone, the hours were too long. She was an attractive woman, pushing forty, with a look of comically ironic acceptance of her own ambivalence. She kept chuckling merrily as she spoke of her misery.

She was interested in Lourdes and me, what we were up to, and a little unsure of her own role in life, halfway between independence and subservience. We didn't notice at first that she was pregnant.

"Long hours, but a lot of fun, right?"

She looked as if she were having fun, at least at that moment.

"Well," she said, "you certainly meet unusual and interesting people from all over the world."

"Nice people?"

"Not necessarily."

She said she liked people, fortunately, since she was stuck in this job, and she particularly liked people who liked people, and she had us slotted in that category. She gave us a large room with a large fireplace and a large bathroom en suite, all very inexpensive. A series of oversized windows all around offered panoramic views of the town and out over Galway Bay to the Aran Islands—delicate light-filled watercolour strokes on the horizon— where the playwright John Millington Synge went, at the turn of the century, to study Irish.

Synge observed in his book *The Aran Islands* that most of the people who came to the islands came to "study Irish, so that the Aran islanders have been led to conclude that linguistic studies, particularly Gaelic studies, are the chief occupation of the outside world." In fact he quotes an islander as saying, "Believe me, there are few rich men now in the world who are not studying the Gaelic."

But since I was following Morton rather than Synge, my desire to get to the Aran Islands was not great. Morton had not gone there, and there was enough rain and rock and mud on the mainland to suit me.

This was a lovely old hotel, with dining rooms, assembly halls, weirdly interconnecting corridors, strangely varied views from every window, surprising pieces of antique furniture here and there, patches of interesting wallpaper, plastering, and shelving, wonderful old prints on the walls. The by-now-long-dead tradesmen who did the plastering and carpentry had been skilled in the old school.

Some nineteenth-century prints showed the Claddagh of Galway, about which I'd been reading—make that misreading, as I was soon to find out—in Morton, but which was apparently no more.

"The Claddagh, now that is where the Tinkers live, is it not?" I asked Mrs. Quilty's husband, Mr. Quilty, who had heard some laughter, popped his head in, then taken over from his wife.

"Oh, no!" He looked stricken. He couldn't believe his ears. He had a serious look on his face—one of those Irish faces not meant to look serious—as if it was a pity that I had been so misled. He'd be telling this story for the rest of his life. Gad, the things tourists say. He wished he knew the name of the villainous blackguard who had so scandalously fed me such vile misinformation.

"No? But it used to be?"

"Oh, no!" He put his hands over his ears, closed his eyes, and held his breath for several agonizing seconds. Then he calmed down and spoke slowly and softly, as if to a child. "They were old Galway, those people of the Claddagh. Real old Galway people. They were fishermen, mostly. They were never—Tinkers. The Tinkers were itinerant. The Claddagh were a poorer class of people but they were never itinerant. They were mainly fishing people but never ever itinerants."

"They're highly regarded though, the Tinkers, right?"

He paused, shot a look at my eye to see if I was mad, then figured I was just misinformed. He seemed to be saying to himself there were two kinds of tourist: the uninformed and the misinformed.

"Well, they're trying to settle them now, they are, settle them down permanent-like. But it'll take years. One girl has qualified as a teacher now. Some of them go to school. Some of them are educated."

"And they speak the Irish?"

"No. Some of them might, who go to school."

"How about the Claddagh people, do they speak the Irish?"

"They did years ago, but not too much now."

He said that a hundred years ago his great-grandfather didn't have the English, and the old guy's son, Mr. Quilty's grandfather, didn't have the Irish. That's how quickly things changed in the history of this country, full as it has been of dramatic turnabouts and tragedies. And yet they somehow understood each other perfectly. This sort of thing was common in Ireland in the nineteenth century.

And he spoke, as many others had, of how the priests beat him as a kid for making mistakes in Irish lessons, and he stopped learning it as soon as he could because of the bad taste the beatings gave him.

"And nobody looks down on the Claddagh people?"

"Oh God, no!"

"And nobody looks down on the Tinkers either?"

"Eh, not really. But they don't like them moving in beside them, either, you see."

"Why not?"

"They break in and they do damage. And they collect rubbish and dirt. And you know, they're untidy."

"Some people have been telling me that the Tinkers are very well thought of because they have a strict pre-Norman moral code and they never steal things, and—"

"Oh, but they do steal things! And at the moment now they're—a lot of them, that is—they're actually attacking old people living on their own and taking their furniture and that."

"No."

"Yes. Some of them are all right, but some of them are drinkers."

"It's poverty that drives them to it, I bet."

"Oh no it's not. Because the government looks after them so well. They all get the dole and they get all free medical aid. It's just the breed."

"Ah. People sort of think of them as if they were Gypsies?"

"Yes. They are really Gypsies. They don't brush their teeth, ever. And they let their animals roam."

"They do? I hadn't heard that."

"Oh yes, they do."

"What kind of animals? Old horses and ponies and donkeys?"

"Yes, some of them. And dogs."

The strain of talking about Tinkers seemed to be getting on Mr. Quilty's nerves, so I changed the subject by asking about an interesting-looking old painted board, sitting behind the front desk, with little numbered squares, one for each room.

He sighed with relief. "It's a relic from years ago," he said. "It doesn't work now. But we keep it there because it looks so nice. Actually you see them in hotels all over the Republic, you do. But they are now only decorative."

"They'd just be thrown out in Canada, because over there we don't have the same strong, instinctive feeling for the past."

"Now that's a pity."

"How would it have worked?"

"Well, you see, you would ring the buzzer in your room, and a little ball would fall into the square with your room number on it—and bingo!"

Mrs. Quilty came back in with a tall young boy and introduced him as their son Desmond. He was fifteen.

"Are you planning on taking up the hotel business, Desmond?"

He stammered shyly.

"No," said his mother. "We're just waiting for a rich American to buy . . . this hotel."

"Oh, I thought you were going to say to buy Desmond."

Desmond looked startled.

"Oh no, we'd never sell him."

"Does he have any career ambitions?"

"He loves . . . art and all that kind of stuff."

"Oh, he's the artistic type!"

"He's very good at still lifes."

"Well, I'll be darned. Are you going to go to art school, Desmond?"

"I hope to."

Galway is one of those cities that take on a different character at night. The narrow streets of Galway become charming and alluring after the sun sinks into the Atlantic behind Galway Bay. There are lots of interesting things to look at by the dim light from a distant streetlamp. The streets are under-illuminated, and the pub life is extraordinarily vibrant. Lourdes came for a walk with me. We stood in the middle of the bridge as the River Corrib in spring runoff roared down to Galway Bay. H. V. Morton was luckier. When he leaned over the same bridge, the salmon were running. I seem to remember him getting smacked in the face with one. And of course he managed to hang on to it, though not without immense difficulty, and he wound up giving it to a poor family to take home for dinner. What a guy, eh?

"The parapet of Galway Bridge is worn smooth as glass by the arms of those who lean over it when the salmon come up from salt water," Morton wrote. He added, oddly, "This is one of the sights of Ireland."

At McDonagh's, where we had fresh salmon, we ordered a pint of Guinness each, and the waitress said we'd have to go across the street to the pub to buy them and bring them back, owing to licensing regulations. The restaurant was only licensed to serve wine, but you could drink anything you brought in.

I went over to a crowded pub, the Quais, and brought two pints back to the restaurant. They were marked on the bottom, so at the end of the night they'd be sorted out and returned to the pub.

When we went back to the hotel, Mrs. Quilty was complaining of an ear blockage. Had she tried washing it out with a syringe?

"No, I have to do something about it soon, that's for sure."

"It's very unpleasant," said Lourdes.

"Oh it is. I've had it three weeks now, and I been coming and going."

"Is it from a cold?"

"No it is not."

"Is it infected?"

"No, it's not. Well, I am pregnant. And I guess the whole system breaks down. I was in hospital for a week with a hiatus hernia and also an ulcer."

"Did they fix you up?"

"No, they did not. They cannot. Not yet anyhow. It'll probably right itself afterwards."

"How far are you?"

"Six months. I have a seventeen-year-old and a fifteen-year-old, a ten and a seven. So this was a big surprise."

"Maybe this will be the one that will be a special comfort to you in your old age."

"By golly, I hope so. There's not much comfort now."

One in four elderly people were living in terror and afraid to open their doors at night, according to the front-page story in the Galway morning paper. Tinker trouble. But this smear campaign was balanced by a two-page photo story inside featuring Tinker women complaining of prejudice.

The elderly residents (non-Tinkers) were living in terror of itinerants (Tinkers, also known as Travellers, or sometimes Lazy Travellers, or Gypsies). A local boy had been savagely attacked by a dog (owned by Tinkers) and had to receive medical attention. Residents in the area of Clogheen had been plagued by an itinerant encampment since October and had demanded the removal of the itinerant families from the side of the road. The five itinerant families had harassed and intimidated the elderly. The children were afraid to pass Cappagh Cross because of the dangerous dogs and horses. Farmers were pestered by roaming goats, horses, and fowl.

This made me want to head back to Cahir and chat some more with Mr. Looney. What was going on here? How could I reconcile Mr. Looney's comments with all these news reports?

Oh yes, and public roads were used as toilets, and these people kept fowl which were used for cockfighting and vicious dogs which were used for dogfighting, both alleged to be an important part of Tinker cultural life.

The first of a series of scandals that would later force well-loved long-time prime minister Charles Haughey to resign hadn't broken yet. Haughey was still very popular. He was always delivering long Churchillian speeches on the radio. He was all set to become the first Irish prime minister to go to Belfast. What did Mrs. Quilty think of Haughey going to Belfast? When she talked politics, all her aches and pains seemed to disappear and she'd start breathing fire. But she was having problems finishing her thoughts. They sort of trailed off as new ones bubbled up to the surface of the simmering stew of her mind.

"Well, it's hard to keep a good man down. They can't stop him from going to the North if he wants to go in his capacity as . . ."

"He's a good man, wouldn't you say?"

"Ah, I like him a lot, I do, I do. But you know what? At the end of the day, honest to God, Haughey is a wealthy man. He doesn't have to give a damn about what's going on in Ireland. The money he's getting, oh it's terrific, but believe you me it's only chicken feed for him, that money. But I tell you, by God, if everyone had the courage that Haughey has . . ."

"A rare commodity, courage."

"These days for sure, and there's another side to it. When they're going around campaigning, he's not a muck-thrower, he never throws the muck if he ever dreams of it. I can't understand it."

"Would he be your favourite politician?"

"Good God, yes! The rest of these guys are university professors, and in the universities they should have stayed, because that's what they are, university professors, they should have stayed there . . ."

"What do you think of this Ian Paisley telling Haughey not to come to Belfast?"

"Oh, Paisley's cracked. He's crazy. Paisley wants nobody there. When you are what you are in a place like that, you want nobody to come in to destroy it . . ."

"He feels a bit insecure?"

"Oh, believe it. But he has a place in Canada, did you know that?"

"I did not know that."

"Well, know it from now."

"Hm!"

"You seek out your own information over there. He has a place in Canada, and if the going ever gets rough here, zip he's gone. He's surrounded night and day by bodyguards, and the police are all around his place morning, noon, and night. That must be why he hasn't been knocked off long ago. There wouldn't be too many sorry, unfortunately, I'm sorry to say."

Lourdes piped up. "He wants to keep the bad old days, with everybody fighting. He doesn't want people to get along."

"That's *right!*" exclaimed Mrs. Quilty as a particularly lengthy flame ejected from her mouth. "And he had to go to America to get his degree. He couldn't get it at home. Doctor Paisley. Phhwt!" She spit on the rug. It sizzled.

"Anybody can get a degree in America," said Lourdes.

"Yes, if you pay for it, you know. In the front door and out the back door or whatever, in the back door and out the front. That's the thing about Paisley. But Paisley is crazy, you see. I think he's a great husband and father, but he roars his head off, you see. The Reverend Doctor Mister, I don't know what."

I mentioned that I'd heard something about the Catholics in the North supporting Ian Paisley and how could that be? Mrs. Quilty's eyes told me she'd heard me, but it took her a while to get back to that.

"In Paisley's collection in church dare you to put a fifty-pence coin in the plate and make noise. Oh, no! A silent collection, if you please. Make it all notes. But I was told it must be five years ago maybe longer that he had a place in Canada and if it ever got too rough, whiz he was gone. A plane out overnight from Belfast. I am sure of that, you know."

"What makes you so sure?" said Lourdes.

"We have our sources."

Lourdes mentioned something about the former European parliamentary president being the first person to put Paisley in his place.

"Right you are," said Mrs. Quilty. "He started shouting and boiling over in Brussels. She had him out. 'Outside, get him out, get him out of here,' she said."

Mrs. Quilty was swinging her arms with extreme vigour and with a constant volley of sparks shooting several inches out from her mouth. A glittering display of pyrotechnics, it was all the more delightful for being so unexpected.

"And out," she wailed. "He was thrown out." Her voice dropped conspiratorially. "Major and all them hate him, Thatcher hated him like the blazes, don't talk about the Queen and all those, they have to put up with him, you know."

"Would you say he has some kind of irrational hatred of . . ."

"Oh Lord, yes," she cried, inflamed with passion. "He takes care of the poor Catholics on the side in his riding and that's how he gets their vote. I'm told this for a *fact* . . ."

"You mean he slips them the odd ten-pound note when they look as if they could use it."

"Yes, or a load of groceries—with his name on it."

"Well, there you go."

Lourdes was a big supporter of close European union.

"I think the way for countries to get along is to trade," she opined.

But Mrs. Quilty didn't respond. She was still swooning over her memories of Haughey's gentlemanly, courageous, even heroic, campaigning in the face of all that mudslinging.

"It's truly a terrible way to be, going around campaigning for an election and all the time mud-throwing at the other guy. But Haughey has never done anything like that, I've watched him. Years ago he was supposed to have been in the business of bringing arms into Ireland, but it was never proved against him."

Was she in favour of the extradition treaty, which was the big issue at the moment? Whether suspected terrorists could be nabbed at home in Ireland and forced to stand trial in Britain.

"I'm neither for nor against it."

"How could that be?"

"The very word IRA." Her voice dropped wistfully. "It meant such a different thing in Ireland at one time. When you think about it now, it makes you weep. All those people who gave their lives for us. Where would we be now? What would we have? We'd have nothing. We'd be downtrodden as we always were. And I think these people who call themselves the Provisional IRA are not an Irish organization. They're based in Ireland, a lot of them, but—"

The thought was snapped off by the sudden appearance of Mr. Quilty, who must have assumed nothing of importance was being said, since it was merely his wife who was doing the talking. Why, she must be boring us silly. He'd fix that. He immediately butted in and started telling us that his grandfather bought the hotel for twelve hundred pounds seventy years ago.

Mrs. Quilty checked to see what I thought of this boorish interruption, and I gave her a look of sympathy and at the same time pretended I was dozing off. Mr. Quilty, noting a certain lack of response to the news of his grandfather's interesting purchase, told us that there was only one other family in all of Ireland named Quilty.

"It's not Irish, is it?"

I had thought it was a name brilliantly invented by Vladimir Nabokov, just taking the g and turning it into a q to represent the lecherous, envious, and loathsomely encroaching quilty-guilty pedophile playwright in *Lolita*.

"Oh, but it is. The other chap, he runs a little school for girls down in County Cork somewhere. Elocution, deportment, shorthand, typing, all that sort of thing. Skibbereen, I think it is. They go for that sort of thing down there."

"More so than up here, would you say?"

"Oh, nothing like that up here."

"Why would that be?"

"There's just not the interest these days. Years ago there was a school like that up here, but interest faded. And that fellow and I, we get each other's bills."

"So in Skibbereen, County Cork, there's a fellow named Quilty running a school for—"

"Yes, it's a little school for girls. He ran one for some time in Galway, but it didn't work out. He couldn't attract the students somehow."

Mr. Quilty took me down a long sloping corridor to show me a grand photo of Galway, an aerial view, circa 1940. I said he must know everybody in town pretty well, his father having bought the hotel seventy years ago and all.

"My grandfather, it was."

"Sorry."

"I know all the old fogies anyway. The old town was very small."

We stopped at the large framed picture, on the landing of a back staircase.

"My old man was the mayor then," he said.

Morton—who did a bit of photography on the side with his early Leica—had raved about the picturesque Claddagh: "Nothing is more picturesque in the British Isles than this astonishing fishing village of neat, whitewashed, thatched cottages planted at haphazard angles with no regular roads running to them."

"Where would the Claddagh be here?" I asked Mr. Quilty.

He pointed it out, but said it had been in a state of ruin and uninhabited by the time the fifties rolled around. Now there's nothing left of it. In the photo—taken a mere decade after Morton's visit—you could see the thatched roofs were falling apart. Now it's all identical brick rowhouses.

The Claddagh had originally been a settlement of Irish families which had sprung up outside the old walls of Galway, at a time when the town of Galway itself was restricted to Anglo-Norman families, fourteen of them to be exact, known as the Tribes. I began to realize how diplomatically Mr.

Quilty had dealt with me last night when it somehow had got into my mind that the Claddagh was where the Tinkers lived.

Lourdes told Mr. Quilty that it was cold and frightening crossing the bridge last night, with the water screaming by so high and rushing in the spring runoff.

"It gets higher," he said. "The eyes get all plugged with water."

Lourdes looked confused. "The eyes get plugged with water?"

"Yes, them, the eyes of the bridge." He pointed to the old photo and showed us where the eyes were.

Young Desmond Quilty slouched by wearing an Australian sweatshirt with "Down Under" (upside down) on it. It was a gift from his grandparents who were world travellers.

"Yes," said Mr. Quilty. "They go everywhere. They belong to the Scholars' Club. It's a tourist organization. They take trips all around the world."

We got talking some more about the Claddagh. In the picture on the landing, in spite of the roofs badly needing thatching, each little house had its own long patch of garden stretching out behind it, and under active cultivation.

"Ach, but not now," said Mr. Quilty. "Everybody's too lazy to have a garden. They just buy what they need."

Good heavens! Those Trappists from Mount Melleray are setting a bad example for the entire country.

"When are you going to run for mayor like your grandfather?"

"Father."

"Sorry. Father."

"I'm not. No bloody way. No politics for me."

The population of Galway was seventy-five thousand and growing. People came in for jobs in the computer factories. But for every five who moved into town only one got a job and the other four stayed and went on the dole. People who came here from other places just didn't want to leave, he said.

"And a lot of tourists in the summer?"

"Yes. It's a nice town. A lovely town, really. No tough police force, no one-way streets, no major crime, really. Best city in the country, really. Not a bad place to live."

He agreed with Morton's figures on the population of Galway: forty thousand in 1910, but by 1930 it was down to fourteen thousand. And during all this time his father was the mayor.

"He was alarmed by the decrease. He ranted and raved about it. He'd be glad to know it's up to seventy-five thousand now."

"Well, goodbye, Mr. Guilty," said Lourdes. It was time to move on. He looked at me and smiled, then looked back at the beauteous Lourdes.

"Not Guilty, dear, it's Quilty. Guilty is something else entirely."

"Mr. Quilty."

"And it's Ken, not Mr. Quilty. Mr. Quilty was my father."

"Okay, Mr. Ken," said Lourdes. "Good luck with the baby!"

"It's not me that's having it, it's the wife. Haw haw haw!"

Mrs. Quilty followed us to the door. "I just wanted you to know not all of us are so prejudiced against the Travellers. I like the Travellers. I think the settled people are jealous of the Travellers. They grumble and complain about the Travellers, and they say things like, 'Those cursed Tinkers have the devil on their side.' But it's just jealousy, you know. Because there's a bit of the Traveller in everyone."

UNDER BEN BULBEN

THERE WERE NO PREHISTORIC MONUMENTS IN H. V. Morton's *In Search of Ireland*. His mind filtered them out. Yet here we were, heading into Connemara, which he adored. We were following his route west from Spiddle along the north shore of Galway Bay, and there were megalithic tombs and little ring forts all over the place, practically in everybody's backyard.

Stone fences Morton does mention. He thinks they were so ubiquitous and enclosed such small patches of land, particularly in this area, because of the high population density. But it makes more sense to think that the enclosures were so tiny simply because there were so many stones in the fields. If the fields had been made larger, the fences would have had to be much higher, requiring much more work, and the stones would have had to be lugged further.

The fence builders weren't trying to keep people out or animals in or make fences per se. They were merely clearing the land for agricultural purposes. They had to do something with the rocks, so they piled them up in straight lines every twenty feet or so: the rockier the area, the closer together the fences, the smaller the enclosures.

And in almost every wall you'll see one boulder many times larger than the others. This would be an erratic—or sometimes, as at King Lear and the Three Daughters, a bonafide dolmen—and rather than try to move it, the builders would incorporate it into the fence, which would explain why the fields are so irregular in size and shape. Any stone that seemed too difficult to move would be incorporated into a fence. In agricultural matters, function traditionally follows form.

Protection from wild animals doesn't seem to have been a factor, because the fences aren't high enough to offer such protection. It doesn't appear that the land was being cleared to provide grazing for animals, for the animals were perfectly capable of grazing among the rocks. Those fields were cleared to provide garden land, pure and simple.

The old stone fences were everywhere along the sea coast here. There were houses sitting every which way, fairly dense population for such a remote part of the country, swarms of children coming home from school. All the little Irish cottages that would have been here in Morton's day had disappeared, leaving only modern little redbrick houses, with aluminum front doors, among the strangely patterned networks of ancient walls, Gulf Stream pink limestone beaches with turquoise water, stubby little palm trees, stubby herds of cattle.

Morton was a brilliant and indefatigable crowd-pleaser as far as the describing of landscapes was concerned. But he needed to be; he was writing for a popular audience that didn't travel much, bourgeois travel being too expensive and time-consuming, and he was writing for a pre-television audience that had not become sated with colour images and documentaries from all ends of the earth. Every technological change seems to alter our psychology profoundly (though certain futurists maintain technological changes take our psychology where it wants to go anyway). Morton was writing for a different crowd. "The talk rattled on as Irish talk does," he writes, "leaping and jumping about like a leprechaun on a hill."

It rained when Morton came charging through these parts, but today in Connemara it was a beautiful sunny day in early spring. We stopped to gaze at the ruins of a fairy-tale castle on an island in the middle of a lake. The lake was a field of diamonds, picking up light from the sky and reflecting it in all directions at a higher intensity for anyone who cared to observe it. The castle was almost as big as the island, and its ramparts were covered with thick green ivy, just as the lake was surrounded by thick green forest. As the sun moved lower in the sky, the diamonds caught fire with a bright gold flame.

We discovered our first North American–style motel in Ireland. It was called the Connemara Inn and it was falling apart and had been closed for fifteen years.

A rumpled Brendan Behan in early middle age was stumbling along the main street of the remote town of Clifden at the western end of the Connemara Peninsula. He had a rumpled newspaper in his pocket, with a number of articles he wanted to read again or show a friend to prove a point. He was wearing a long, rumpled black overcoat, flecked with cat hairs and cigarette ash, had long, rumpled black hair, and he was an awful mess. His coat collar was turned up, yet he had a sweet, innocent look on his face, like Dylan Thomas, and his eyes met mine with an expression that said, simply, I wouldn't mind becoming your best friend, that is if you happen to be in need of such a thing, and really when you think of it who isn't?

He turned into the chemist's shop and I followed him. He was chatting with the young, handsome, well-groomed chemist, who nevertheless had a terrible case of the shakes. These two seemed to be great drinking buddies. They were talking about some concert coming up, some group from Dublin. Brendan smoothed his newspaper out on the counter.

The chemist fixed my glasses, which had fallen apart on my face as we drove into Clifden. I handed him the tiny screw. He got out a razor blade to use as a screwdriver. I was afraid he'd cut himself, his hands were shaking so badly, which was a terrible thing to see in a man so young. The blade broke into pieces, but he kept at it with a little sliver of the original blade and finally got the screw in without bloodshed. He handed me the glasses and said, "You'll be needing these for all the scenery." He laughed when I asked how much that would be, and he wouldn't take a cent.

Lourdes missed all this, having remained in the purple Satori, parked diagonally on the broad main street of Clifden. She was sitting in the passenger seat, leaning up towards the rear-view mirror and grimacing as she plucked the occasional wayward curly hair out of her bushy eyebrows. She was so intent she didn't notice me coming from the left, nor the small group of kids and adults on the sidewalk to the right, watching her with looks of wonder on their faces, standing back a suitable distance so she wouldn't notice them staring.

In just about every Irish hotel there's a sign saying "Residents Only," though its meaning is far from clear, for nobody ever gets kicked out of the bar simply because they don't have a room—at least in my experience.

Perhaps the sign is used as an excuse to get rid of any Tinkers who might come in. But at the Alcock Brown Hotel in Clifden there was a sign saying "Non-Residents Welcome." On the wall over the bar was a framed front page from a 1938 paper, with stories about Hitler, Czechoslovakia's impregnable defences, and a little story about Ireland's pavilion at the World's Fair in Glasgow, with its display of Irish butter, eggs, and bacon.

Excitement was mounting about Ireland's chances in the World Cup. The young bartender was wearing a World Cup T-shirt depicting a large green shamrock and a lot of little acronyms in green too. He explained the complicated procedure and listed the teams the Irish would have to beat before getting into the final.

"How did they qualify for the first round?"

"It was because they played in Europe, they played against four European teams."

"I bet you know the names of every player, right?"

"Oh, you gotta."

"And their age and where they're from and their height and weight and all their individual stats."

"Pretty well for sure."

"On the Irish team, that is."

"Oh, I don't know all that many on the other teams."

When H. V. Morton was in Clifden, he heard a lovely story about an Irishman, who had been in the United States for thirty years, coming back to Ireland to look up his younger brother, with whom he had not been in touch all that time. He got off the ship at Cork and hired a limousine and chauffeur to take him up to County Mayo to pay a surprise visit to his brother, who had supposedly been running the family farm all this time. Now the older brother was a "terrible teetotaller entirely," and severely chastised the chauffeur when he caught him "with his face in a pint of porter." But when he arrived at the farm, he discovered that his brother had sold it long ago and had bought a pub with the proceeds. They proceeded to the pub and found the brother sitting there behind the counter sound asleep and dead drunk. He tried to awaken him, but the fellow just snored all the louder, so finally the older brother commanded the chauffeur to drive him back to Cork, and he caught the next boat to the United States.

Also while in Clifden, Morton failed to impress the locals with his genially ostentatious display of wealth:

In the post office I waited while a young Connemara girl, fresh as a peach, painfully addressed a letter to New York; and then I drew twenty pounds in much-travelled one-pound notes—money that had been wired to me—and not one person in the post office showed any surprise, although this sum must have seemed to them real wealth.

Lourdes was stooping at the shore, cleaning her muddy boots in the clear waters of Lough Gill, a mile or two south and east of Sligo. From the shore could be seen William Butler Yeats's Lake Isle of Innisfree. My grade-10 teacher is whacking his desk with his yardstick, splinters of wood flying in all directions, and screaming that this is the greatest line in all of English poetry. "I thought it was Irish, sir." "Pipe down and listen, McFadden. Just listen to the *l*'s." He beats time by whacking the yardstick on his desk and intones mournfully, in the Dylan Thomas mode: "I hear lake water lapping with low sounds by the shore." I can't remember the teacher's name now. His wife taught gym at the same school. He had a bad back and a Ph.D., his thesis having been a brief-but-scintillating (so he told us) treatise on the works of Alfred North Whitehead, and he was always muttering, when things were going badly, as they always were, that he could triple his salary in advertising.

"Well, why don't you, sir?"

"How could I abandon you kids? My devotion and sense of responsibility to you is too great."

"We wouldn't mind, sir."

"Achh!"

He takes another yardstick and smashes it against his desk.

Lourdes was photographing me standing reverently by Yeats's limestone (he had insisted on limestone) grave marker—Yeats who, in spite of his chilling political ambiguities, had given our hearts so much mysterious pleasure. I had to arrive on this spot to understand his famous inscription, which Hugh Kenner wrongly finds arrogant:

> *Cast a cold Eye*
> *On Life, on Death.*
> *Horseman, pass by!*

In A.D. 575 Saint Columba founded a monastery on the site where Yeats is now buried. And high above, like a cold eye in the clear air, sits the axe-faced Ben Bulben, on the slopes of which Diarmuid, much to Gráinne's dismay, was killed by the wild boar. Earlier in the day, in the shadow of the sacred Croagh Patrick, a perfect volcano-shaped mountain beloved of penitent holy pilgrims painfully trudging their rocky barefoot way to the top, stands an impressive statue of Saint Patrick. It was life-size and of recent vintage, but it looked down from the top of a much-older hundred-foot nineteenth-century imperious neoclassical pillar. The original statue had been taken down and replaced with Patrick, and the original engravings on the side panels of the base, no doubt offensive to true Irish sensibilities, had been chiselled out and new panels placed in: "I am Patrick, a sinner, most unlearned, the least of all the faithful, and utterly despised by man."

Then there was the volcanic Mount Nephra, in the heart of County Mayo, looming to the west of Lough Conn. Its bald head was flecked with dandruff-like snow, at least on one side, and on the other the snow patches were striated in long narrow parallel lines, like lines of cocaine, or like cornrows on the head of an aged Jamaican woman.

From the ruins of the thirteenth-century Errew Abbey, sitting on a tongue-shaped peninsula of deep pathless mud jutting out into Lough Conn, a little puff of grey cloud could be seen floating over Mount Nephra in the darkening blue sky. And through the field glasses from our side, a couple of hundred yards downside from the peak, could be seen the offset puckered shadowy volcanic crater, like a crater on the moon. The red fireball of the sun was setting over the early Victorian hunting lodge we'd passed two miles west of here. It was derelict but with all windows curiously intact, and dusty old curtains still hung in the upper windows.

Purple mountains surrounding us were lying low on the horizon—except for Mount Nephra, looming snowy and craggy in the immediate distance—and surrounding us on three sides were herds of cattle and broad stretches of silvery pink and golden water.

The grim grey cloud above Mount Nephra looked like a puff of smoke coming out of the crater, the crater resembling an old man's puckered navel. It was a kidney-shaped and kidney-coloured mountain, and its name means kidney.

For Lourdes's intellectual pleasure, though not to be taken seriously, I gave her my latest theory: The stones used in building wedge graves were taken from as close as possible to the spot where the dead person had been born and put down at the spot where he died.

Legends indicated that, at least in some cases, such graves were built at the spot where the person therein interred actually did die. Near Cahir, for instance, at the top of a mountain, there was a cairn grave in which lay the body of a poet who had been caught and murdered by enemies of the king. In order to confuse the invaders, the poet had agreed to flee the court in disguise, dressed in the king's gear, but he was caught and killed. The actual king, deeply moved by the poet's sacrifice, built the cairn grave, visible for ten miles in all directions, in a show of sorrow, gratitude, and respect for the great courage of the poet who died rather than admit he was not really the king. This was told to me by Mr. Looney.

"It's a wonderful story," said Lourdes. "I'd like to meet that man."

"I know you would, and you probably will."

"Ignorance is bliss, I believe that," she added.

"You do?"

"I do. For instance, this is a better trip for us than it would be if we knew a lot about archaeology. Archaeologists always look so miserable. They spend their whole lives working on one small problem."

The improvement in her English was taking my breath away.

Cherry blossoms, old abbeys, Fujiyama-style extinct volcanoes, sunsets, glorious lakes, mountains all around us, a great gibbous moon, and Lourdes Brasil had written her first poem in English:

Pale moon flying in the sky
How do you stay up there so high?
I've never seen you look so grand
Flying above old Ireland.

PERMISSIONS
ACKNOWLEDGMENTS

bings. Reprinted by permission of Laurence Pollinger Limited and the Estate of Robert Gibbings.

DEBORAH LOVE   From *Annaghkeen* by Deborah Love, originally published by Random House, 1970. Copyright © 1970 by Deborah Love. Reprinted by permission of Random House, Inc.

DAVID W. MCFADDEN   From *An Innocent in Ireland,* originally published by McClelland & Stewart, Inc., 1995. Copyright © 1995 by David W. McFadden. Used by permission, McClelland & Stewart, Inc., the Canadian Publishers.

JAN MORRIS   From *Travels* by Jan Morris, originally published by Harcourt Brace Jovanovich, 1976. Copyright © 1976 by Jan Morris. Reprinted by permission of IMG Literary. All rights reserved.

H. V. MORTON   From *In Search of Ireland,* originally published by Methuen & Co. Ltd., 1930. Reprinted by permission of Random House UK Limited.

ERIC NEWBY   From *Round Ireland in Low Gear,* originally published by Viking, 1988. Copyright © Eric Newby, 1987. Reprinted by permission of HarperCollins Publishers Ltd.

TIM ROBINSON   From *Stones of Aran: Pilgrimage,* originally published by the Lilliput Press Ltd. in association with Wolfhound Press, 1986. Copyright © Tim Robinson, 1986. Reprinted by permission of the Lilliput Press, Dublin.

ELIZABETH SHANNON   From *Up in the Park,* originally published by Atheneum, 1983. Copyright © 1983 by Elizabeth Shannon. Reprinted by permission of Elizabeth Shannon. Boston University.

HAROLD SPEAKMAN   From *Here's Ireland,* originally published by Dodd Mead and Company, Inc., 1925.

ARTHUR SYMONS   From *Cities and Sea-Coasts and Islands,* originally published by W. Collins Sons & Co. Ltd, 1918.

PAUL THEROUX   From *Sunrise with Seamonsters* by Paul Theroux. Copyright © 1985 by Cope Cod Scriveners Co. Reprinted by permission of Houghton Mifflin Co. All rights reserved.

Other *READER'S COMPANION* volumes
available in Harvest paperback editions
from Harcourt Brace & Company

The Reader's Companion to Alaska
The Reader's Companion to Cuba
The Reader's Companion to Mexico
The Reader's Companion to South Africa